INDEFENSIBLE

Also by Michael Griesbach

The Innocent Killer: A True Story of a Wrongful Conviction and Its Astonishing Aftermath

INDEFENSIBLE

MICHAEL GRIESBACH

KENSINGTON BOOKS
http://www.kensingtonbooks.com

Some names have been changed to protect the privacy of individuals connected to this story.

KENSINGTON BOOKS are published by

Kensington Publishing Corp.
119 West 40th Street
New York, NY 10018

All Kensington titles, imprints and distributed lines are available at special quantity discounts for bulk purchases for sales promotion, premiums, fund-raising, educational or institutional use. Special book excerpts or customized printings can also be created to fit specific needs. For details, write or phone the office of the Kensington Special Sales Manager: Kensington Publishing Corp., 119 West 40th Street, New York, NY 10018. Attn. Special Sales Department. Phone: 1-800-221-2647.

Kensington and the K logo Reg. U.S. Pat. & TM Off.

Library of Congress Card Catalogue Number: 2016946110

ISBN-13: 978-1-4967-1013-0
ISBN-10: 1-4967-1013-4
First Kensington Hardcover Edition: September 2016

eISBN-13: 978-1-4967-1014-7
eISBN-10: 1-4967-1014-2
Kensington Electronic Edition: September 2016

10 9 8 7 6 5 4 3 2 1

Printed in the United States of America

To my wife, Jody, the greatest blessing of my life

"The prosecutor is the representative not of an ordinary party to a controversy, but of a sovereignty whose obligation to govern impartially is as compelling as its obligation to govern at all, and whose interest, therefore in a criminal prosecution is not that it shall win a case, but that justice shall be done. While he may strike hard blows, he is not at liberty to strike foul ones. It is as much his duty to refrain from improper methods calculated to produce a wrongful conviction as it is to use every legitimate means to bring about a just one."

—*Berger* v. *United States,* US Supreme Court (1935)

"Or let's say I die tomorrow. I don't think I will. I think I have a lot more to do. I just want people I love to know that whenever I die . . . that I was happy. That I was happy with what I did with my life."

—Teresa Halbach

CONTENTS

FOREWORD

Indefensible recounts a three-month journey I embarked upon after I watched the Netflix documentary *Making a Murderer*, along with tens of millions of other viewers around the globe in late December 2015. The trip was strange because I thought I'd already taken it—twice. Once, when I watched Steven Avery's murder trial unfold in the county where I work as a prosecutor, and again three years later when I reviewed its high points for the final section of a book I was writing about the Avery case entitled *The Innocent Killer*. That book, published by the American Bar Association in 2014, focused on Avery's wrongful conviction in 1985, not his 2007 trial.

In neither of those trips did I pay close attention to the landscape of the murder trial. It wasn't my trial, after all; I was not directly involved. To my surprise, I began to wonder while watching the series, whether I had taken a wrong turn ten years earlier and reached the wrong conclusion when, like everyone else in my line of work, I had assumed the evidence-planting defense in the Avery trial was nonsense. Avery's accomplice, Brendan Dassey, had confessed and identified his uncle as the main culprit. And there was overwhelming physical evidence linking Avery to the scene of the crime. It was, as some prosecutors like to say, a slam-dunk case for the state. At least that's what I thought at the time.

Was it possible we might all have been wrong? I knew the documentary's producers were biased in favor of Avery. They had interviewed me for the project, and they even tried to get me to come around to their way of thinking. But some of the material in the docu-series was new to me, and none of it was complimentary to the police with regard to how the evidence was found and the interrogation methods used on Brendan Dassey, Avery's sixteen-year-old learning disabled nephew and accomplice in Teresa Halbach's murder.

So I decided to journey through the trial again, but this time more carefully—as if my life depended on it—because it might. Half the country, it seemed, was convinced the police had set up Avery again, that lightning had struck twice and that he had been wrongly convicted a second time. Many people were angry. Some made threats on my life and the lives of others because we were part of Manitowoc County law enforcement and had spoken out publicly of Avery's guilt in the wake of *Making a Murderer.*

Indefensible recounts my independent search for the truth about the Steven Avery case. I thought I knew that truth, but it was to some extent fractured by *Making a Murderer.* As I delved deeper into the circumstances surrounding Teresa Halbach's murder, the truth became whole again.

As in any issue as complicated and as controversial as this one, the truth is elusive in the Avery case. Peruse the Reddit pages on the topic of Steven Avery for an hour and you will see what I mean. I tried to be as careful and unbiased as possible when I conducted my research for this book, but in the end perfect objectivity is only something we can strive for.

I'm still a prosecutor in Manitowoc County, Wisconsin. This is the background I come from. I'm not "pro prosecution" in the usual sense. I have believed for a long time that the criminal justice system is broken to some degree, and needs to be reformed. I have given presentations about wrongful convictions and police and prosecutor misconduct. I have written about these issues as well and about what can go wrong if prosecutors lose sight of their calling and seek convictions instead of justice.

I share with the creators of *Making a Murderer* a desire to draw attention to broken aspects of the criminal justice system so that it can be reformed where needed. I also serve on the advisory board at the Wisconsin Innocence Project, a role that should not be—but is—a rarity among prosecutors. That's not to say my judgment is free from any and all bias. No one's is. So take what you read as you will and decide for yourself.

There are a few things you should know at the outset. First, although I am still a prosecutor in Manitowoc County, I wrote this book in my personal capacity as a private citizen who has made his home in a Wisconsin community that has been bedeviled by the Avery case for thirty years. I played a role in Mr. Avery's exoneration in 2003, but I was not involved in his wrongful conviction in 1985 nor in his murder trial in 2007. Mr. Avery's thirty-six-million-dollar lawsuit against the county, its former sheriff, and former DA raised a conflict of interest for our office and required us to appoint a special prosecutor to act in our stead. I observed the murder trial as every other resident of the state of Wisconsin did and used the resources available to the public to write this book.

Second, you should be aware that some disturbing evidence is in this book. Some of it was deemed inadmissible in the murder trial. The rules of evidence are meant to ensure that only relevant and not unduly prejudicial evidence is presented to the jury. But these rules only apply to proceedings in court, since that is the forum where a defendant's liberty is at stake, not in the writing of a book. As they should, these rules err on the side of caution in order to protect the liberty of a person charged with a crime. But neither Steven Avery nor Brendan Dassey's liberty is at stake through the writing of this book. I have included these facts because when considered in light of all the other evidence, they have a bearing on whether or not Mr. Avery committed the murder. To ignore them would be to ignore evidence that might bring us closer to the truth, which is the ultimate aim of this book. It is worth noting that *Making a Murderer* did the same thing, with regard to evidence favorable to Mr. Avery and Mr. Dassey.

Nonetheless, caution must be exercised in determining the weight to assign to this evidence. Much of it was deemed inadmissible during the trial because of its tendency to elicit a strong emotional response and lead some jurors to conclude that because Avery acted in a certain way before, he probably did so again. To say the least, this evidence is not complimentary to Mr. Avery and if it is true, he is not the kind of man you want hanging around your daughter or your wife. The aim of this book is to appeal to reason, and as with the rest of the facts presented in these pages, it is hoped that readers will give to this evidence only the weight it truly deserves.

Readers should also know that I changed names of some of those involved to a lesser degree, including witnesses and victims in an effort to protect them. The three-decade-long Steven Avery case has caused enough harm over the years. The last thing I want to do is add to its impact by making known the identity of those who have to date largely avoided the public eye.

This book's subject matter is a court case entitled *State of Wisconsin* v. *Steven Avery*, and like the case itself, its focus is on the factual and legal issues relevant to determining the defendant's innocence or guilt. While Teresa Halbach and her family play an obvious role in the book, they are not its primary focus. This is by no means to suggest that the author does not care about Ms. Halbach or her family. No matter what one believes about Mr. Avery's guilt and whether the police planted evidence to wrongly convict him a second time, one thing is sure—Teresa's loved ones will never again see her walk through their front door. On another level, that fact makes all the rest nothing but white noise.

CHAPTER 1

"In on It Too"?

I sat there, frozen, staring over the open file. I couldn't move. How could I have forgotten? I prosecuted the case myself. Did we do it again; did we wrongfully convict an innocent man? *Twice!*

The troubles began almost immediately after the documentary aired. It started with social media; the bomb threats came later. *You're an utter fool,* pronounced the first message on my book's Facebook page, *either that or you're in on it too.*

"Utter fool," I could live with. Everyone's an utter fool sometimes, some of us more often than others. But "in on it too"?

The documentary—such an innocuous-sounding word—that had upset my former Facebook friend had just been released on Netflix, but it would soon become an international smash hit. It was, of course, *Making a Murderer,* about the Steven Avery case.

Avery is the wrongly convicted Wisconsin man who, two years after his release from prison for a crime he did not commit, perpetrated one of the most horrific murders in the history of Wisconsin, a state with a long and ignominious past of horrific murders.

At least that's what the majority of Wisconsinites and the few who paid attention to the story outside our borders thought before *Making a Murderer* turned the case upside down. All but the most conspiracy-minded agreed with the jury's verdict: that Avery and his sixteen-year-old nephew and accomplice, Brendan Dassey, were guilty of the unspeakably brutal murder of Teresa Halbach.

Still employed as an assistant district attorney in Manitowoc County, Wisconsin, where these events occurred, but not directly involved in prosecuting either of Avery's cases, I had written my own account of this now thirty-year crime saga in a book entitled *The Innocent Killer.* The American Bar Association published it in the summer of 2014—I began writing it more than seven years earlier—long before *Making a Murderer* was even a glimmer in the eyes of its Hollywood producers. The confidence I expressed in the final chapters of my book—Avery was guilty as charged of murdering Teresa Halbach, and that the police had not set him up a second time—was the source of my Facebook messenger's anger. I knew this because he admitted he enjoyed *The Innocent Killer* when he read it several months earlier, but after bingeing his way through all ten episodes of the documentary, his opinion had changed, and as I would soon find, he was not alone.

I had minced few words when describing the gross misconduct of the former sheriff and former district attorney in Manitowoc County. Steven Avery and his family were the victims of an injustice, horrific in its own right, in his 1985 wrongful conviction. Depending on whether you count the six year sentence Avery was serving concurrently for another unrelated but lawful charge, or not, he served either twelve or eighteen years in prison for a crime he did not commit. Either way, it's one hell of a long time to be sitting behind bars for something you didn't do. The county's top two law enforcement officials had intentionally, or at the very least recklessly, sent an innocent man to prison.

I wrote the book because I believed, and still do, that the three-decade-long Steven Avery saga is the best example of what can go wrong when police and prosecutors lose sight of their calling by seeking convictions instead of justice, as required by their oaths of office. An injustice that began in 1985 has festered ever since, leaving many victims in its wake and nearly destroying a local justice system that is still reeling from renewed exposure.

Steven Avery's arrest and trial for Teresa Halbach's murder in 2005 figures only into the final chapters of *The Innocent Killer*, and then only in the context of how his murder trial became intertwined with his wrongful conviction two decades earlier, nearly resulting in his acquittal. The book's treatment of the Avery saga was the opposite of *Making a Murderer*'s, which concentrated heavily on the murder case, exhausting its treatment of the 1985 wrongful conviction case by the end of the first few episodes.

I thought I had been about as even-handed as anyone could be when writing a book. I spared no sympathy for Avery and his family in recounting the wrongful conviction in 1985, nor condemnation of the sheriff and the district attorney who were responsible. But at the same time, except for drafting the initial search warrant, I was not involved in the murder investigation or its lengthy trial. I experienced it from the same perspective as nearly every other Wisconsinite: from the media. After observing the murder case unfold, I had no doubt that the jury got it right that the innocent man had turned into a cold-blooded killer. *Making a Murderer*, despite its creators' claim that it takes no position on Steven's guilt, takes the opposite view.

My impression from watching the trial from afar was that the trail of evidence in the Teresa Halbach murder case led directly to Steven Avery. There was no way of escaping it, at least that's what I had assumed at the time. Those who chose the other direction, I believed, had taken a misguided trip through the brambles and smoke-filled brush laid down for them by the defense in the form of claims of evidence-planting and a police frame-up.

I also believed that the trial judge, Mr. Avery's skilled and devoted defense team, and, yes, even the prosecutors had provided Steven Avery with an exceedingly fair trial. The issues had been joined, and after carefully considering their verdict over the course of three days of deliberations, the jury members had followed where the evidence objectively led.

* * *

Since I had called out my predecessors for inflicting on Steven Avery and his family an inexcusable injustice, you might think viewers of the documentary, incensed at what they believed was a second wrongful conviction perpetrated upon Mr. Avery, would think twice before assuming I was "in on it too." But you would be wrong. Nor did it matter that during the past several years I had become an advocate for criminal justice reform, presenting frequently at conferences and other public forums on the topic of wrongful convictions, and particularly on those where police and prosecutor misconduct played a role. I'd written published articles on the topic and had become none too popular among a subset of my colleagues as a result. But none of that seemed to matter to those who were convinced after watching *Making a Murderer* that I was part of a corrupt, local law-enforcement community that did the unthinkable by convicting an innocent man not once, but twice.

I had spoken out extensively on radio, television, and print interviews about how Steven Avery was, to use a colloquial term, screwed over by the former sheriff and DA. Dean Strang, co-counsel with Jerome Buting, for Avery in the murder trial, served as a panelist in a presentation I moderated in Milwaukee, just a few months before *Making a Murderer* aired. As did Walt Kelly and Steve Glynn, who were Avery's attorneys in his thirty-six-million-dollar wrongful conviction lawsuit. I also serve on the advisory board at the Wisconsin Innocence project in Madison, a rarity among prosecutors but not enough to convince the conspiracy theorists that I was not "in on it too."

So why had my former Facebook friend and thousands that would follow in his social media wake become so angry at anyone who disagreed with *Making a Murderer*? What kind of spell had the documentary cast over its viewers that over five hundred thousand citizens would sign two separate petitions, one to President Barack Obama and the other to Governor Scott Walker begging for Steven Avery and Brendan Dassey's release? Why would legions of Netflix viewers all but convict local law-enforcement officers—some of them my friends, and none of them here when Avery was wrongly convicted thirty years earlier—of planting evidence to wrongly convict him again? And finally, how had one documentary so profoundly inflamed the nation's passions that dozens of troubled individuals threatened my life and that of several others who work in local law enforcement?

What was it about *Making a Murderer* that so firmly convinced people that lightning had struck twice, that Steven Avery had been wrongly convicted a second time? And why were they so mad?

There was only one way to find out. I had to watch the show.

CHAPTER 2

WRONGFULLY CONVICTED

W hen I first met Laura Ricciardi and Moira Demos, the film-makers and creators of *Making a Murderer,* they were gradu-ate students from Columbia University's prestigious film program. Laura was also an attorney. I had interviewed with them nearly a decade earlier in 2007, not long after the Avery and Dassey trials. Although I was already a veteran prosecutor and a good deal older than they were, I shared their enthusiasm for the Avery case's enormous potential to expose to a large audience the infir-mities of a criminal justice system badly in need of reform, more so, I thought, than any other case that had or is likely to come along again. But none of us, least of all Laura and Moira, I sus-pect, had the slightest idea that the skill and tenacity with which they approached their work would result a decade later in a worldwide television phenomenon. I'm not even sure that Netflix had introduced streaming video to their customers back then.

Fast-forward to autumn of 2015, a few months before *Making a Murderer* aired. I received an e-mail from Ricciardi, and later a call from someone working on her behalf. She was giving me a heads-up that their persistence had paid off. At long last, she and Moira had found a home for their film, though they did not dis-close to me that their producer and distributor was the mother of all streaming-video giants—Netflix!

I was well into my obsession with the Avery case by the time I'd met the future Netflix documentarians, and when I interviewed with them in 2007, it was a cold and bitter time in northeastern Wisconsin, as nearly every scene depicted in their documentary. I was halfway through writing the manuscript for *The Innocent Killer*'s self-published precursor, with the title *Unreasonable Inferences*.

I aimed to focus my book on Steven Avery's wrongful conviction in 1985 and not on what at that time I confidently believed was his rightful conviction for murder twenty years later. The murder case is the more sensational part of the story—mayhem and murder trump everything else in the world of true crime. But Avery's wrongful conviction spoke much more directly to the criminal justice system and how it can so badly misfire, which is where my interests lay. I knew, too, that anything that brought more public attention to Teresa Halbach's murder would be difficult for her badly shaken family to bear. A book that concentrated on the lessons for the criminal justice system from Avery's wrongful conviction would be the lesser of two evils for them versus a cheap true-crime thriller about her gruesome death.

A week or so before my interview, Ricciardi, Demos, and I had shared our admittedly sanctimonious disgust at the former sheriff's and district attorney's misconduct when they railroaded Steven back in 1985. In retrospect, this is why I was under the impression that my interview with them was to focus almost exclusively upon the wrongful conviction case, and not the murder.

Our opinions about the murder differed sharply. The physical and circumstantial evidence reported by the media had convinced me—not just beyond a reasonable doubt, but any shadow of a doubt—that Avery and Dassey were guilty as hell. I was confident then that the defense team's evidence-planting accusation was nonsense, an unfounded allegation that unfairly besmirched the reputation of Lieutenant James "Jim" Lenk and Sergeant Andrew "Andy" Colborn, the two most directly targeted officers whose character was defamed. I had known and worked with Lenk and Colborn for years. They were two of the least likely law enforcement officers I could think of to be involved in any type of misconduct, much less planting evidence to frame an innocent man. I thought Steven Avery had received an exceedingly fair trial, which in the filmmakers' minds was really the only question that mattered, not whether he was innocent or guilty. At least that's what I thought at the time.

The interview started predictably enough. They asked me to recount the brutal assault of Penny Beerntsen on an isolated stretch of Lake Michigan shoreline about ten miles north of Manitowoc. Penny was the victim in the case for which Avery was wrongly convicted in 1985 and is one of the unsung heroes in a case lacking many others, unsung or not. I spoke extensively about the misconduct of the former sheriff and the district attorney who led the charge to falsely convict Steven back in 1985, about three minutes of which would make the final cut for the film

But halfway through the interview the mood shifted dramatically. Maybe I was overreacting, but I sensed that Ricciardi and Demos believed Avery had been wrongly convicted a second time or, worse, that they would adopt that narrative even though they had to know he was probably guilty. Either way, they appeared virtually certain that local police had planted evidence to strengthen their case, and it seemed to me that they were doing their level best to get me to agree or, short of that, to say something on camera they could later manipulate so it would look that way.

Now it was less than a week before Christmas, and only a few days after *Making a Murderer* initially aired. The discomfort I had felt so poignantly during the second half of my interview not quite ten years earlier flooded over me again as I prepared to spend the next several nights, watching the Netflix series that was about to turn our previously unknown little Midwestern town into the center of the Netflix universe.

* * *

I sat spellbound as I began watching episode one—not because of its content, but from seeing the places and faces I have contact with nearly every day. It was an audio and visual masterpiece complete with a pitch-perfect piece of haunting music. The effect was *Fargo*-ish in a way, but more emotionally complex. If only I had not been involved in the Avery story myself, perhaps then I could have simply enjoyed the craftsmanship that made the film so engrossing rather than turn into an increasingly nervous wreck.

In one of dozens of national media appearances that Laura Ricciardi and Moira Demos would make in the upcoming weeks, Ricciardi told an interviewer that "truth is elusive" in the Steven Avery case, and in some respects she is right. Even the title they, or someone at Netflix, chose could be interpreted in different ways. It might suggest that spending eighteen angry years in prison for a crime he did not commit made Steven Avery into a murderer. Or it may signify a belief that police and prosecutors made him into a murderer by planting evidence to frame him for Teresa Halbach's murder. The ambiguity of the title seemed to foreshadow a fair-and-balanced account of the Avery story.

It was an emotionally powerful beginning: Steven Avery, walking out of the prison gates in his red flannel shirt, sporting a shaved head, long beard, and twinkling bright blue eyes, reunited with his family on a clear September day, with green grass still covering the gently rolling hills of east-central Wisconsin. His extended family had turned out in full force to greet him at home as Steven's father, Allan, drove up with Steven in the backseat, smiling from ear to ear. The Avery Salvage Yard, which was also home to Steven's parents, Allan and Delores, was not filled with darkness and death on that warm September day. Instead, it was filled with happiness and life.

"I missed you," said Steven's cousin as they embraced. "It was like the same old Steve was back," chimed in a voice-over from the same cousin. "He was happy. He was smiling." Laughter, hugs, and kisses all around, and a genuine heartfelt excitement filled the air at the salvage yard that day. They may not have slaughtered the fatted calf for Steven, but Allan and Delores Avery's prodigal son had come home!

The tone shifted less than a minute and thirty seconds into the documentary. "This was one of the biggest miscarriages of justice I ever saw in twenty years in criminal defense work and thousands of cases," intoned Reesa Evans, Avery's public defender from previous charges.

"But I did tell him be careful. There was just something I felt, Manitowoc County's not done with you. They are not even close to being finished with you," added his cousin Kim Ducat as the video cut to a flock of geese taking flight into a gloomy and threatening-looking sky. As the night wore on, I grew increasingly fond of the birds' mysterious honking, expertly mixed in with the vaguely foreboding theme music, which together made for an excellent opening and closing to each episode.

Referring to his client's pending lawsuit, Walt Kelly succinctly stated the law as it applies to police misconduct. "There is a distinction in the law between simple mistakes, for which officers like that are immune," Kelly explained, "and purposeful conduct that violates constitutional rights, for which they're not immune." Steven Avery appeared on camera, speaking to reporters, and was heard voicing patience and restraint: "Just a little bit more waiting. I waited long enough. A little bit more ain't gonna bother me." The video then cut away to court document highlights from Avery's wrongful conviction lawsuit: *targeting Steven Avery, personal hostility, obstruction of justice*.

For the few remaining viewers whose hearts had not been sufficiently filled with sympathy for the protagonist, the camera turned to Judge Fred Hazlewood, who presided over Mr. Avery's 1985 trial. "The family sticks together. They have a very strong sense of family. They support each other. They do a number of things that are quite admirable," Judge Hazlewood explained from inside the very courtroom where Avery was wrongly convicted so many years ago.

I knew the focus of the series was the murder case, but I was surprised how little of the earlier case was included. No doubt my perspective played a role in my surprise. Avery and Dassey's arrest and conviction for Teresa Halbach's murder only figures into the last section of my book, and then only in the context of the wrongful conviction twenty years earlier. Still, why would they tread so lightly on the egregious abuse of power by the sheriff and the district attorney in the first case?

Past midnight, and with a busy day at work slated for tomorrow, I decided to go to bed. I'd have to watch a few more episodes of *Making a Murderer* to appreciate why its creators were not satisfied with rehashing a thirty-year-old injustice that had already been resolved. Why would people get riled up over that? The hacker group Anonymous doesn't threaten to reveal ten-year-old e-mails to prove a conspiracy, unless they think something can still be done about the supposed conspirators. Hollywood stars Alec Baldwin to Khloé Kardashian don't make fools of themselves trying to outdo each other weighing in on an ancient injustice, with "ancient" defined as more than two weeks old. Thousands of obsessed citizens don't spend untold hours and considerable energy contriving conspiracy theories, some of them spewing hatred and threats of violence against anyone who has the nerve to disagree. Nor do demonstrators take to the street three stories below my courthouse office shouting for justice for Steven Avery and Brendan Dassey. None of this happens unless people are mad as hell and they think they can do something about it.

I heard Steven Avery's familiar, folksy voice from somewhere off camera: "I really ain't got much on my record, two burglaries with my friends. We just rode around, get something to do, and we decided to rob a tavern and that . . . was the first time that I got busted with them friends."

The camera zoomed into highlights on a court document:

crawled into the bar through a broken window, $14.00 in quarters, two six packs of Pabst beer, and two sandwiches.

Avery's cousin Kim put an even kinder spin on her cousin's run-ins with the law: "Stevie did do a lot of stupid things. But he always, always owned up to everything he did wrong.

"He was always happy, happy, happy, always laughing," she continued, "always wanted to make other people laugh. I think the people in the outside community viewed him as an Avery, you know, viewed him as [a] troublemaker. You know, 'There goes another Avery. They're all trouble,'" she summed up as the camera panned to bleating sheep and crying seagulls off in the distance.

The documentary went on to offer an example of what kind of trouble a young twenty-year-old Steven Avery would get into: "Another mistake I did . . . I had a bunch of friends over, and we were fooling around with the cat . . . and, I don't know, they were kind of negging it on and . . . I tossed him over the fire . . . and he lit up. You know, it was the family cat. I was young and stupid and hanging around with the wrong people."

I have heard this excuse many times before. When a criminal defendant minimizes his conduct by saying he was hanging with the wrong crowd, the hangers-on usually say the same thing: "I wouldn't have done it, Judge, if I had better friends." It isn't a very good excuse and almost never finds sympathy with a judge.

I thought back to the police report where I had read about this incident years earlier and remembered that there was more to the story than *Making a Murderer* was letting on. Not quite ten years earlier, I had spent months researching Steven Avery and his family for my first book, and I knew that the cat-burning incident was much more than a childish prank.

The police report stated that Avery took a cat, poured gas and oil on it, threw it in a bonfire, and then watched it burn until it died. A friend who was present at the time told police that the cat jumped out of the fire, and Avery caught it and poured more gasoline on it before the animal died.

Thousands of Netflix viewers would never know that Avery intentionally threw the cat in a fire, and watched it burn and suffer a miserable death, managing to score two of the most common psychological signposts for potential homicidal behavior—animal cruelty and a fascination with fire—into a single act. As far as they would know, the cat mistakenly ended up in the fire when Avery was messing around with some friends. Happens all the time, right?

Avery told the documentarians that he missed his first daughter's birth because he was, as he put it, "locked up for that cat incident. . . . It kinda sucked. You know, you're supposed to be bringing your kid into the world . . . and then you gotta miss it."

Hmm, I thought as I scratched my head. *Interesting way to end a segment about burning the family pet.* They had just transformed a deliberate and disturbing act of animal cruelty into nothing more than a harmless accident and suggested that it happened when he was an adolescent when he was actually twenty years old.

I wondered if ordinary viewers, whose only familiarity with the case was what the documentary chose to show them, would view Steven Avery as favorably as the filmmakers intended. Like every human that ever was or will be, Steven Avery is not some biological specimen that can be placed under a microscope and pronounced as either all good or all bad.

In fact, on the few occasions I met him, he struck me as polite, even sincere, and with a hint of lightheartedness about him. However, there is another side to Steven Avery that I came to know while researching my book—a darker side that includes his propensity toward violence and sexual deviance. So far, it seemed that the documentarians were trying to redefine Steven's trouble with the law, and I thought they were smart to do so early on.

He certainly had racked up a considerable record prior to his wrongful conviction in 1985, and his next brush with the law was a bit more serious.

He had graduated from torturing an animal to endangering a person's life, and I was eager to see how *Making a Murderer* would depict that incident. I'd also read the police report on this case and was familiar with the facts.

It was January 3, 1985, less than seven months before his arrest in the wrongful conviction case, when Avery rammed his 1978 Ford LTD into the side of a light green Plymouth Volare driven by his neighbor, Sandra Morris, as she drove past his residence. When Morris stopped her car and was getting out, he approached and held her at gunpoint. Morris, by the way, was the wife of a Manitowoc County deputy sheriff. Morris lived right up the road from Steven and his wife, Lori, and she had to drive past their house on her way to work at five-thirty a.m. Her troubles with him had started a few months earlier. He would get up early, grab his field glasses, and peer down the road to see when Morris was leaving. Then he'd wait for her to drive past and, depending on how messed up he was that day, he'd either rub himself on the hood of the car or expose himself. One time he was wearing nothing but his shoes.

The January incident was a continuation of his prior behavior, and *Making a Murderer* gave us a watered-down version I'd soon see. Sandra Morris pulled out of her driveway at the usual time and started driving down the road past Avery's house. She had her infant daughter in the car that morning, and she planned to drop her off at her parents' house in town. Just past the Avery residence she looked in her rearview mirror and saw lights approaching from behind. The car seemed to come out of nowhere. It began passing on her left, and then without warning it struck the side of her car, causing her to careen back and forth in the road, but eventually gaining control without sliding into the ditch.

She came to a stop on the side of the road, thinking that someone had lost control and hit her accidentally. Before she got out of her car, she looked up and saw Steven Avery walking toward her. He was pointing a rifle at her head. He ordered her to get into his vehicle, but she motioned to her daughter on the front seat, and told him that her baby would freeze to death if she left her alone. He then looked inside the car and told her she could go.

Three deputies arrested him within the hour, and when they searched his house, they found a .30-06 rifle stashed under one of the kids' beds with a live round in the chamber. Steven Avery even confessed. Yes, he rammed his car into Mrs. Morris's car. Yes, he pointed the gun at her. And yes, he planned to force her into his vehicle.

This certainly wasn't the story I was observing being played out in front of me. Ignoring many of the facts outlined above, *Making a Murderer* was using unscripted, but edited, video footage from Sandra Morris's deposition to cast her as the villain and Steven Avery as the victim. The storyline seemed to be implying that he acted out of frustration and rammed into her car because she had been spreading lies about him while out drinking *at all* of the local taverns.

To say I was taken aback would be an understatement. It is not often that the victim is blamed when recounting a past crime, especially in today's climate. But this is the impression I got.

DA Denis Vogel, who would be responsible for Steven Avery's wrongful conviction less than a year later, rightly threw the book at him this time, charging two counts of endangering safety by conduct regardless of life as a repeater, one count for the mother, Sandra Morris, and one for her child, and another charge of felon in possession of a firearm. By virtue of Avery's prior convictions, he was a "habitual offender" under state law, so the prosecutor dutifully tacked on the appropriate penalty enhancer, increasing the maximum sentence on each count by six years. Avery faced a maximum sentence of forty-eight years in prison, but bail was set at only two thousand dollars and Avery's mom and dad posted it right away. Judge Fred Hazlewood, who would sentence him to thirty-two years in prison for what would become the wrongful conviction case more than a year later, gave him six years concurrent at the same hearing. Routinely, if not understandably, overlooked by most of the media accounts, from the moment Steven Avery was exonerated until this very day, he would have served six of the eighteen years in prison for his wrongful conviction even if he had not been wrongly convicted.

Avery had committed some stupid crimes over the years, but accosting the wife of a deputy sheriff was one of the most foolish. The men and women in blue, or brown in the case of the Manitowoc County Sheriff's Department, pay close attention when one of their own is the victim of a crime. Right or wrong, you don't victimize the wife of a deputy sheriff and expect it to go unnoticed. Cops are like family, they have to be, given what we ask them to do, and part of being a family is to watch each other's back. But the close-knit nature has its downside, an example of which was made tragically clear in our sheriff department's investigation of the assault and attempted murder seven months later that resulted in Avery's wrongful conviction.

With his crime against Sandra Morris still fresh in their minds, the sheriff and a few others jumped to the unwarranted conclusion that he was the perpetrator in that case, too. As one of the deputies put it in a deposition twenty years later, there was "talk among the officers" that Steven Avery might have been the assailant. As I will show later in this account, the sheriff, the female deputy who spoke first with the victim, and the department's eccentric police sketch artist took their suspicion far beyond talk.

I was looking forward to seeing how the documentary would handle Avery's wrongful conviction in 1985. I'd spent the better part of three years on weekends and in the early-morning hours before going to work, researching and writing about Manitowoc law enforcement's darkest hour. Up until recently, Wisconsin enjoyed a reputation as a clean state with little corruption, at least compared to our neighboring state to the south with its corrupt Chicago political bosses and their connection with the mob. To me, Avery's wrongful conviction remains one of the grossest miscarriages of justice in Wisconsin.

I also knew I would be in this part of the documentary. Having my fair share of vanity, but hopefully not more, I was anxious about how I'd come off. It's not that I had high expectations. Borrowing the words posted on my Facebook page from another viewer, I would be satisfied as long as I did not make an "utter fool" of myself.

Photo taken July 28th, 1985, read the on-screen caption, referring to a photo of a beaming Steven Avery, posing with his family and new twin boys, taken one day before the assault of Penny Beerntsen. The camera panned to rolling waves on the shoreline, as I began recounting a series of events that would forever change the course of so many lives. I explained how Penny went to the beach with her husband, Tom, and their two young children that day. I explained how in addition to managing the couple's charming candy store and ice-cream parlor in Manitowoc's touristy downtown, she was also a physical fitness instructor at the local YMCA. On this day she started off on a six-mile jog along an isolated stretch of Lake Michigan shoreline around three o'clock. I told the viewers about the man wearing a black leather jacket and how odd that was on what was probably an 85-degree day. He made a comment to her as she passed him, about a half mile into her run. I finished my part, describing how she could see him up ahead on her way back, but this time the man was standing directly in her path.

"To get away from him, she ran into the water, but he grabbed her and dragged her off into the woods. He knocked her down. She was clawing at him and he attempted to rape her, but he didn't succeed in penetrating her," continued an attorney that would represent Avery years later. Reesa Evans, his public defender, could be heard next, describing the more graphic details of how the man ripped Penny Beerntsen's clothes off, sexually assaulted her, beat her up, and then basically left her for dead.

Having adequately described the terror Beerntsen encountered on the beach that day, the documentary then shifted to Avery's wrongful conviction and depositions being taken in preparation for his subsequent thirty-six-million-dollar lawsuit. His attorneys in his wrongful conviction lawsuit, Walt Kelly and Steve Glynn, were featured prominently in this part of the program.

After Penny Beerntsen was taken to the hospital, it turned out that Sandra Morris's friend Judy Dvorak was the deputy sheriff who was assigned to go to the hospital. This is where the Sandra Morris matter made a difference. When Penny Beerntsen described her assailant, Judy Dvorak said, "That sounds like Steven Avery." Walt Kelly said this observation into the camera, in his engaging voice, accompanied by his equally engaging personality. It looked like they were filming in the same conference room in Kelly's office where I'd spent the better part of an afternoon with him and Glynn several years earlier in preparation for writing *The Innocent Killer*. Prosecutors or not, they gathered from our earlier conversations that I shared their opinion that what happened to Steven Avery back in 1985 wasn't just a mistake but the product of deplorable official misconduct.

I was, and remain, grateful to them for their openness and for so generously sharing their time.

Making a Murderer's use of unscripted audio from recorded jail telephone calls and police dispatch tapes, as well as video from court hearings and depositions, is part of what makes it so captivating, and the next scene did not disappoint.

Former Manitowoc County detective Gene Kusche was deposed in Steven Avery's wrongful conviction lawsuit on October 26, 2005, just ten days before the discovery of a partially concealed RAV4 at the Avery Salvage Yard would catapult the Avery case into national headlines. Thanks to *Making a Murderer*, I was now watching Detective Kusche's videotaped deposition ten years later in the comfort of my living room at eleven-thirty on the Monday night before Christmas, 2015.

Walt Kelly was questioning Kusche, who had met Penny Beerntsen at the hospital just a few hours after she was brutally assaulted. He had developed a composite sketch of her assailant.

With eyes nearly swollen shut, the victim's vision was blurry, but the sheriff, who knew Penny and her husband, and should have stayed out of the investigation, was determined to find her assailant as fast as he could so he could bring him to justice. Having leapt to the conclusion that Steven Avery was the assailant based upon her description, which it turned out did not match Avery that much at all, the sheriff ordered one of his deputies to retrieve Avery's most recent mug shot taken seven months earlier. The deputy brought it to the hospital, where the sheriff stuffed it into his pocket approximately thirty minutes before Detective Kusche started working on his masterpiece composite. I could almost feel Kusche's blood pressure rising as I was watching the former detective squirm under Kelly's blistering interrogation.

"I have one large framed composite drawing, if we could bring that up on the table and put it in camera range," Kelly instructed as he asked Kusche whether he was the one who framed it.

"It was the only one I ever did that was used in a court case. And I thought it'd make an interesting display in my office."

"Would you agree with me," Kelly continued, "that it's pretty remarkably coincidental that that would depict Steven Avery's January 1985 mug photo, which was available to you that evening?"

Kusche tried to deny it, but the photos, when placed side by side with his trophy, belied his denial.

Those of us who have closely examined Steven Avery's wrongful conviction case are convinced that Detective Kusche drew the composite sketch off Avery's mug shot. He had little training and even less experience. Fred Hazlewood, the presiding judge in the 1985 wrongful conviction case, referred to the two images as bearing an "uncanny resemblance" to each other, made all the more strange since Avery's hair was different on the day Penny Beerntsen was assaulted, and the drawing looking more like his mug shot taken six months earlier. Kelly put it this way in *Making a Murderer:*

> *"We were able to present, embarrassingly, the difference be-tween an older photograph and what we then had, which was the photograph from that night as to how Steven Avery actu-ally looked. That opened the door to us being able to argue that Kusche drew the composite from the photograph of Steven Avery that was already in their files. And to argue that . . . that never would've happened without the sheriff's participa-tion as well. In other words, they made the case against Steven Avery that night themselves."*

Watching all of this unfold on television was an odd experi-ence for me. It was fascinating and disappointing at the same time. Fascinating by virtue of seeing the faces of the main charac-ters in the wrongful conviction story and a visual portrayal of the various roles they played, but disappointing that some of the most compelling facts were left out. I imagine it's how authors whose books have been made into movies feel—the movie did not do justice to the content in their book.

There was no mention, for example, of Penny Beerntsen re-ceiving disturbing telephone calls from a man who, in hindsight, she suspected was the real assailant, and not Steven Avery. Or the day when the district attorney told his staff that Gregory Allen, the real assailant, could not have been the perpetrator because he was on probation with an airtight alibi, a statement that turned out, like so much in the wrongful conviction case, to be a mis-statement of fact, and a serious one at that. The list goes on, but more on that later.

Still, *Making a Murderer* was a visual masterpiece, and the next scene in episode one drew me in further.

A short clip was shown from September 11, 2003, the date Avery was released from prison after DNA proved his innocence.

"I feel free!" he said, laughing, to a throng of reporters on a clear late-summer day at the moment of his release while the prison gate buzzed in the background.

"When I left the prison, the anger left," he said somewhere off camera as the moving scenery suggested that he was on his way home after eighteen years. "It was gone. It stayed there behind them gates. It didn't come out with me," he continued, in my view, untruthfully.

The video returned to his welcome party, outside in the country, on that same gorgeous late-summer day.

"How you doing?" asked a male friend or relative.

"Oh, hello," Avery replied sincerely.

"How's it feel?"

"It feels wonderful."

When a television reporter asked Avery whether he forgave the victim, he replied both graciously and accurately:

"It ain't at all her fault, you know. Honest mistake, you know. I mean, most the time, I think the cops put it in her head more."

Episode one was almost over. With another busy day at work tomorrow, I decided to turn in early. I still had a lot of hours left to watch, but already I was surprised by how engrossed and fascinated I was. I looked forward to sitting down after work tomorrow night to a *Making a Murderer* marathon.

As the final scene played out, I didn't realize that I'd had a pretty good idea of what the answer was to my question from just minutes earlier, and I had it before the credits had even started rolling.

"They weren't just gonna let Stevie out," one of Avery's cousins said into the camera. "They weren't gonna hand that man thirty-six million dollars. They just weren't gonna do all that. And something in my gut said they're not done with him. Something's gonna happen."

"Do we have a body or anything yet?" An officer's call to dispatch was overheard over his siren wailing in the background.

"I don't believe so," the female dispatcher replied.

"Do we have Steven Avery in custody, though?"

CHAPTER 3

HIJACKED

The courthouse was abuzz all day with office workers hovering around their colleagues who had watched enough episodes of *Making a Murderer* to have its desired effect. I was swamped with preliminary hearings and plea dates, so I only caught bits and pieces of conversations. But between the little I did hear and the excited tones of voice and body language from those engaged in the conversations, there was no doubt that the documentary series had struck a chord.

After work, but before settling in with *Making a Murderer* for another night, I checked my book's Amazon page. I was curious what impact, if any, *Making a Murderer* was having on my reviews and, I'll admit it, my sales, too. I had put two and a half years into researching and writing it and was interested in seeing what readers thought and if opinions had changed since the series debuted. I noticed that sales were up, but what caught my eye even more was that about a dozen reviews had been posted in the last few days. Typically, one or two had trickled in every other week.

It was the beginning of a deluge of negative reviews, all of them one star and many of them saying the same thing. It would drive *The Innocent Killer*'s Amazon customer review ranking, a key factor for sales, from four stars, where it had steadfastly remained since its release eighteen months earlier, to barely over two—all in the space of three or four weeks after *Making a Murderer* aired.

That the book was a waste of time and money was a common theme.

Don't waste your money! If I could give this no stars, I would! wrote one reviewer, who had to settle for clicking the one star button since zero was not an option.

Waste of time unless you want fiction, 0 out of 5 stars, wrote another, also thwarted by the inability to select zero.

I was also a liar:

The only truth to this story is Griesbach is a liar.

Lies, lies and more lies. Doesn't deserve even one star!!!

Guy proves himself to be a liar by the end.

And one reviewer simply wrote: *Worst book ever.*

Amazon added, *7 of 12 people found this helpful.*

It came as no surprise when I found out later that these and a slew of similar reviews to come were part of an online campaign to sabotage my book. A member of the Justice for Steven Avery and Brendan Dassey Facebook group, who may or may not have actually read the book, obviously did not like what I had to say. He posted a call to action on the group's Facebook page, urging its members to write a damaging review to deep-six my book.

Posts on other forms of social media were more personal, with not a small number of them filled with venom and hate. Here's an exceptionally enlightening post, that besmirches the character of both myself and special prosecutor Ken Kratz, who was appointed to handle the trial owing to our office's conflict of interest from the 1985 wrongful conviction case:

> *You know what Mr. Griesbach, you're a scumbag! I just watched your interview on* Dateline. *You are perpetuating the disinfo against Steven Avery. You do not dare say a word about the dishonest methods used by Kratz. I pray you all face justice and I pray Steven and Brendan get a front row seat. We all reap what we sow. And remember Mr. Griesbach that the*

love of money is the root of all evil. Enjoy your interview earn-
ings. I pray they put you in the same cell with Kratz.

Another person who posted on Facebook more quickly got to
the point: *Get fucked Michael Griesbach. I wouldn't take your book for*
free.

They even hijacked my book's Facebook page and turned it
into a forum to discuss their conspiracy theories and attack me
for having the nerve to disagree with them. Such was the venom
and hate that was one of many unforeseen consequences of *Mak-*
ing a Murderer.

I was less angry than amazed at their intolerance and their unwillingness, or perhaps inability, to consider arguments to the
contrary. Figuring I should be able to express my opinions on my
own Facebook page, I replied to a few of their accusations early
on. I thought, naively, that reason and logic might change a few
of their minds, or at least show that there might be another side.
But rational thought carried little weight with those who developed such deeply personal views about Avery's and Dassey's guilt.
They were on a mission. They had become zealots.

When I wrote my book years earlier, I spent much more time
researching Steven's 1985 wrongful conviction than I did on his
arrest and conviction for murder two decades later—and then
only in the context of how Steven was nearly acquitted because of
the actions of the former sheriff and former district attorney. I
considered the murder only as it related to the earlier wrongful
conviction. It was not the story I was interested in.

Besides, I thought Avery's and Dassey's guilt was so obvious
that there was no need to dig deeper into the murder case to confirm their guilt. In a dramatic press conference almost four
months after Avery's arrest, special prosecutor Ken Kratz had all
but destroyed Avery's defense that the police had planted evidence in an attempt to wrongly convict him again.

Kratz, who was never one to shy away from the media, spared

none of the gruesome details of a confession the police had elicited earlier that day from Brendan Dassey, Avery's nephew and accomplice. It was the most dramatic event since Teresa Halbach's RAV4 and charred remains were found at the salvage yard and it was carried live on TV.

The prosecutor's words were unlikely to reach the tender ears of children, since they were broadcast in midafternoon during soap opera hours, but he suggested that anyone under the age of fifteen should leave the room, ensuring no doubt that the few kids who were watching would do just the opposite.

The details could not have been more horrific. Police had long suspected that Dassey knew more than he was letting on, and after months of denials he finally came clean. As police and prosecutors uncouthly refer to defendants' confessions, Dassey had puked all over himself. It was the stuff of a cheaply made horror film, except this was real.

Kratz recounted the events as Dassey described them to the investigators. Dassey got off the school bus at the usual time, about three forty-five and found a letter addressed to his uncle in the mailbox. As he walked up to his uncle's trailer, he heard a female voice inside screaming, "Help me!" When he answered the door, Steven Avery was "covered in sweat." He invited his nephew inside and asked him if he wanted to "get some of that stuff."

Brendan Dassey walked into the bedroom and saw Halbach naked and bound faceup on the bed with handcuffs and leg irons. Avery told him he already raped her and wanted to continue, encouraging him to join in. Halbach cried and pleaded with him, begging him not to do it, to let her go, and to get his uncle to stop. But instead, Dassey got on top of her and raped her for about five minutes while his uncle watched from the side.

Then if it's possible, it got even worse. The two of them went into the living room and watched TV for ten to fifteen minutes, Kratz explained. "That's how you do it," Avery said, telling his nephew he was proud of him. While the TV played, Avery talked about killing Halbach and burning her body. He returned from the kitchen a few minutes later, carrying a knife with a six- to eight-inch blade. Then they returned to the bedroom, where Avery told his victim he was going to kill her. He stabbed her in the stomach and handed the knife to his nephew and told him to cut her throat. After he did as he was told, Avery told him to cut off some of her hair.

Having given up trying to keep his emotions in check by this point, Kratz told viewers that Avery then went over to Halbach and strangled her. Uncle and nephew took off the shackles and tied her with a rope and took her to the garage, where even though Dassey believed she was already dead, his uncle shot her about ten times with a rifle, including a couple of times in the left side of her head. The duo then threw Halbach's body onto a fire pit, hardly twenty yards outside of Avery's bedroom window, behind his garage, which was already burning when Dassey had come home from school.

They put tires and brush on top to accelerate the fire, and while her body burned, they drove her RAV4 to the edge of the salvage yard and hid it from view. Avery later told Dassey that he returned to the fire pit within days and broke up some of her bones with a shovel, and he then buried them two to three feet from the fire toward the garage. He also used a bucket to carry some of her remains and put some by a steep hill at Radandt's, a neighboring quarry pit.

The prosecutor concluded his remarks by telling viewers that Dassey admitted he should have done something to stop his uncle, but he forced him to do it and threatened to stab him if he told anyone. When one of the detectives asked why he participated, Brendan Dassey replied, "I wanted to see how it felt . . . sex."

A decade earlier I had watched the press conference with my colleagues at the office on a television set in our conference room. Our thoughts went immediately to the Halbach family. When Teresa Halbach's remains were found in the fire pit, it was obvious that she'd met a horribly violent end, but other than Brendan Dassey and Steven Avery, nobody knew precisely how she died or the extent of her suffering. The fact that she had been raped by her assailant was a safe assumption, but the details of the assault and her subsequent torture went beyond what anyone imagined.

Had Teresa Halbach's family watched the press conference? I couldn't imagine that Kratz or his victim witness coordinator hadn't first met with them in person to tell them the news. Or had they requested months ago not to be informed if the details of her final hours ever became known? That would be impossible, given the extent of the media coverage, and besides, I'm sure they wouldn't want to remain in the dark: "Better the devil you know than the devil you don't."

Brendan Dassey's excruciatingly detailed account of the madness and horror Teresa Halbach faced in the final hour she spent on this earth, how two depraved souls had tortured, raped, and murdered her, and then disposed of her body in a fire, changed everything. After hearing Kratz's press conference nobody with an ounce of common sense bought the evidence-planting claim of the defense any longer—except those who knew something about false confessions.

Such was my mind-set when I sat down and waited for episode 2 to start streaming on Netflix, for what I thought would be an interesting but not terribly revealing evening at home.

October 31, 2005 Teresa Halbach, on a phone, read the caption as *Making a Murderer* began.

"Hello, this is Teresa with *Auto Trader* magazine. I'm the photographer and just giving a call to let you know that I could come out there today, um, in the afternoon. It would probably be around two or even a little later. . . . Again, it's Teresa. If you could please give me a call back and let me know if that'll work for you."

When I look back at it, this was the point in the documentary when my focus shifted and would mark the beginning of a steady deterioration in my confidence level of Steven Avery's guilt. I would soon find myself doubting much about the Avery case that I'd assumed for years to be true.

Notwithstanding the impression the documentary had just left by playing the recording of Halbach's call, Avery had lured her to the salvage yard that day—at least that's what the state had argued at trial, and what I believed to be true. Avery called her employer and requested "that photographer who had been out here before" and then followed up with three calls to her cell phone, blocking his identity on two of those calls with the *67 feature on his phone. But the waters were being muddied—as only a good defense lawyer at closing argument or a recording showing tone of voice and inflection can accomplish. It had become evident that Teresa Halbach knew exactly where she was going and whom she was meeting at the salvage yard that day.

The fact that Halbach left a message that day doesn't disprove the prosecution's contention that she was afraid of him. It's nothing out of the ordinary for someone who is providing a service to confirm with her customer that she will be available at a certain time. But still, the tone of her voice and the very fact she called suggested that perhaps she was not as afraid of Steven as I had come to believe.

I had the impression from media accounts, and from what I'd heard from some of the detectives, that she was apprehensive about going to the salvage yard that day because on a prior occasion Avery had come outdoors wearing only a towel. Would I have been less certain about his guilt, had I known that Teresa Halbach left him a message that morning and did not sound nervous at all?

If guilt or innocence was decided on the basketball court instead of a court of law, some trials would be called before the opening tip-off, because one team, usually the prosecution, would have the clear advantage in size and strength, while the opposing team would be left to play scrappy defense with no plays to rely on for its offense. Cases with overwhelming evidence of guilt rarely go to trial, and when they do, it means that one or both parties were being unreasonable in plea negotiations and refused to settle the case. Either that or the defendant had nothing to lose.

Not so with the Avery case. From the very beginning the game was destined to go into overtime. The defendant actually had a case, and he had hired a dream team of attorneys who could pitch to the jury a credible theory of the case. Oddly, much of their argument would be derived from the same pieces of evidence the state would use to prove Steven Avery was guilty. Where the state would introduce evidence of a key, a bullet, and some spots of the defendant's blood in the victim's car as proof of his guilt, the defense team would use the same evidence and, to continue the basketball analogy, cry foul. I could almost hear the defense lawyers proclaiming, "It's a frame-up, ladies and gentlemen, the cops are up to their dirty tricks again. It's obvious they planted this evidence and are trying to wrongly convict Mr. Avery again!"

But Steven Avery and Brendan Dassey had been found guilty nearly a decade earlier and the Wisconsin Court of Appeals had affirmed their convictions, in both of their cases. So why did it matter if a TV documentary suggested they might be innocent, or that I'd learned a few things myself that night that I wished I'd known before writing my book—a few that made me scratch my head and wonder if I really knew the truth for sure? Were Steven Avery and Brendan Dassey guilty or not? As I would discover as the night wore on, I no longer felt entirely sure.

As the night slowly crept into morning, scene after scene depicted in the documentary made me wonder even more. Here was Avery on the phone speaking to an unknown party on the other end.

"I'm doing good. I been working every day almost, waiting for Jodi to get out. She got locked up . . . drinking, you know, driving. I hollered at Jodi quite a few times to stop drinking. I guess it sunk into her because she did stop and she's a different person now. I gotta give her a lot of credit. When Jodi gets out, hopefully, we can set a wedding date." (Jodi Stachowski was Avery's loyal girlfriend and fiancée at the time of his wrongful conviction lawsuit and subsequent murder charge.)

Then Avery was heard speaking on a more recent phone call from jail, to the documentarians, most likely.

"A lot of people told me to watch my back. Most of the time I didn't even believe 'em. But then, sitting and doing depositions, I don't know, it kinda changed my mind. They were covering something up. And they were still covering something up. Even with the sheriff who's on there now, he's . . . covering something up."

By the end of the night I had seen clips of videos from several of the officers' depositions and, I had to admit, they looked like they were being defensive. They were not happy about being grilled by a roomful of attorneys concerning a very black mark on their department, especially not with Steven Avery sitting there, watching them squirm. It's a rare cop who does well when the tables are turned, when they are the one on the receiving end of a blistering interrogation by their accusers.

Most people do get nervous when being deposed. It's not much different than testifying in court, especially with the lens of a video camera peering into your eyes from three or four feet away. You are sworn under oath and intense lawyers start by grilling you about uncomfortable topics that you may or may not know anything about. But as I tell witnesses before they testify during trials, if you stick only with what you know and tell the truth, you have nothing to fear. If you don't understand the question, say that. If you don't know the answer, say that. And by all means, don't let the lawyers get under your skin!

On the other hand, nearly all of them looked more defensive than they should have if they had nothing to hide—at least in the video clips the documentarians chose to include in the series. When I later watched the complete video of the depositions of the officers who were most directly accused of wrongdoing—either in the first Avery case or in the second—my concern that they had something to hide, though significantly reduced, was not completely alleviated. This was not simply a case of only selective editing to make them look bad.

They say lawyers are the worst witnesses on the stand. We're either too wordy, too full of ourselves, too prone to analyze questions before we respond—or all of the above. But lawyers can have their fair share of these occupational hazards, and still be a halfway decent witness on the stand. On the three or four occasions I had to testify, I did not find it difficult at all. It helps, of course, if you have no skin in the game, which is the position I was in when it was my turn to be deposed in Steven's wrongful conviction lawsuit.

Almost a year to the day after Steven Avery was exonerated, my boss, DA Mark Rohrer, and I were both subpoenaed to appear for depositions at the local branch of a large Milwaukee law firm. Walt Kelly, one of Avery's lawyers who was prominently featured in the early episodes of *Making a Murderer*, would be our inquisitor that day.

Whether at trial or in depositions, when it comes to grilling reluctant witnesses, Kelly is one of the best. He's an aggressive attorney, but he's not just a hired gun. Kelly passionately believes in his client's cause, and to the extent he pushes the limits of civil advocacy, that's why. His gray beard and piercing blue eyes match the personality of this aging but still vibrant activist of the sixties, and although we'd never met, I liked him immediately. Besides, my feelings about what happened back in 1985 weren't a secret. I'd been open with the Wisconsin Department of Justice in the DOJ's independent review of the circumstances surrounding Steven Avery's wrongful conviction, and I intended to be the same the day I was deposed.

I walked into a not-big-enough conference room, where a crowd of red-eyed and weary attorneys were sitting around a table with pens and legal pads poised in front of them, ready to have at

INDEFENSIBLE

their next victim. In addition to Manitowoc County, the lawsuit named Denis Vogel, the former district attorney, and Tom Kocourek, our former sheriff, as defendants, both personally and in their official capacities as county employees. Since each party had his own attorney—including Walt Kelly for Steven, two each for Vogel and Kocourek, one for Manitowoc County, one for its insurance carrier, and one for Mark and me provided by the DOJ— when I started adding up the legal fees I gave up when I reached over twenty-five hundred dollars an hour.

I sat down in the witness chair—the one with the video camera positioned three feet in front of my face—and readied myself for battle. Steven Avery was sitting right beside me, and he appeared to be in good spirits. Who wouldn't be? His thirty-six-million-dollar lawsuit was picking up steam.

Kelly methodically covered the basics first: name, occupation, dates of employment at the district attorney's office, that sort of thing. Then he zeroed in on what I knew about Avery's wrongful conviction. So I told him about finding a criminal complaint charging the real assailant, a sociopathic sex predator by the name of Gregory Allen, in the Steven Avery file. Allen had lunged at a woman after dropping his shorts to his knees on the same stretch of Lake Michigan shoreline where he did the same thing in the case for which Avery was wrongly convicted two summers later.

Then DA Denis Vogel had prosecuted the case himself, and it's difficult to see how he failed to make the connection—especially since the complaint he signed charging Allen was in the Avery file. I told the roomful of attorneys about a series of telephone conversations I had with Vogel after the crime lab results came in showing that Gregory Allen, not Steven Avery, had committed the crime.

I'd been forthcoming with my answers, so when Kelly turned me over to the defense, they had very little to hone in on and I escaped pretty much unscathed. They'd each received a summary of my interview with the investigators from the attorney general's office and they knew where I was coming from. I noticed as I walked out that the attorneys representing the county, Kocourek, and Vogel seemed none too pleased with my answers. But what did they expect?

The events I recounted at my deposition that day brought back memories, most of them not very good, about what had happened two years earlier. They had deeply troubled me at the time. No longer wanting to be a prosecutor—not after seeing what Vogel and Kocourek and a few cronies had done to Steven Avery—I seriously considered leaving my job and hanging out a shingle, though having to put bread on the table squelched that plan before it got very far.

But until recounting the events that morning at my deposition, I'd moved on to other challenges at work and happier events, like birthdays and Christmas celebrations at home and camping trips in Wisconsin's North Woods. I'm not sure time heals all wounds—certainly not the loss of a child. But this wound, though deep, was not nearly as personal to me as it was to those who were directly affected—Steven Avery and Penny Beerntsen, the victim of Gregory Allen's vicious assault, primarily. Besides, with a family to support, there were not a lot of options.

Today it was different, though, and as I walked along our city's pier that juts out into Lake Michigan and ends at a historic-looking lighthouse, my thoughts drifted back to the events of the previous September.

On the morning we presented him with the stipulation and order granting Steven Avery's release, Fred Hazlewood, the trial judge in Avery's wrongful conviction case, asked me to call Denis Vogel. He thought it was only fair that we should give the former district attorney a heads-up to give him time to digest the news before the media started hounding him. That sounded reasonable to me, so I called Vogel at his law firm in Madison.

We had met on a few prior occasions, but we didn't really know each other, so our conversation was brief. I gave him the short version: the crime lab had retested some evidence and the DNA results made it clear that Gregory Allen, not Steven Avery, had been Penny Beerntsen's assailant. Denis Vogel didn't even try to feign surprise. I had just finished telling him that he'd sent an innocent man to prison for eighteen years, but he wasn't bothered in the least—or if he was, he sure didn't show it.

Now it was the following Monday. I was in court all morning and Vogel had left a message on my voice mail asking me to give him a call. It must have been serious because he called again that afternoon before I had a chance to return his call. Again, he was all business. He said an analyst from the crime lab had testified at the trial and his recollection was that her examination of some hairs had tied Avery to the crime. *Yeah, right, Denis,* I thought, *you're still relying on the "science" of hair examination.* Then, almost mechanically, Vogel asked me a question I'll never forget.

"Is there anything on Allen in the file?"

I feigned ignorance and mumbled something inconsequential about the case instead. Then I told him that my boss, Mark Rohrer, and I had turned the file over to the attorney general the previous Friday, which I'm sure wasn't news to him, since the media had already extensively covered Rohrer's request for an independent review.

I hung up the phone and just sat there in my office for a while, reflecting upon our conversation. Vogel's question—"Is there anything on Allen in the file?"—implied he knew that Allen, not Avery, was the assailant, didn't it? He was covering his tracks, and he must have thought I'd go along. How else could I take it?

Despite their reputations, most attorneys possess as much integrity as the next person, and maybe even more. Denis Vogel appeared to be one of the exceptions. How could he prosecute someone he knew was innocent? And how could he let somebody as dangerous as Gregory Allen go free? Among his other terrifying acts that summer, Allen had held a seventeen-year-old girl at knifepoint after he stalked her and broke into her house.

Being sanctimonious is a temptation for prosecutors, one I'm not immune from, so I tried to temper my judgment about what

35

Vogel had done with an understanding of why he did it. Part of the problem, I thought, was that by rushing the decision to arrest Avery without consulting the district attorney, the sheriff had put into play a course of action that would have been difficult to reverse.

I suppose Vogel could have cut Avery loose at the bail hearing and summoned him in later if he thought the case was strong enough to charge. But with such a prominent victim and with the media paying such close attention, letting Steven Avery go free would have been politically difficult. After all, district attorneys had to run for reelection every two years back then.

It also would have been nearly impossible to convict the real assailant, Gregory Allen. After Sheriff Kocourek and Detective Kusche's ridiculously suggestive eyewitness identification process achieved its objective of having Penny Beerntsen identify Steven Avery as her attacker. It would have been nearly impossible for Vogel to bring Allen to justice. Beerntsen would have to explain to the jury how she was now certain that it was Gregory Allen, although she had on three prior occasions positively identified Steven Avery as her assailant—in a photo array, a live lineup, and at a preliminary examination in court—before the state dismissed the charges against Avery and refiled them against Allen.

When the sheriff sent out his deputies to arrest a man from the wrong side of the tracks, a man whom nobody at the sheriff's department liked, and who just seven months earlier had rammed his car into a vehicle driven by the wife of a deputy and then held her at gunpoint—and when the sheriff did this, on the strength of nothing more than an eyewitness identification that was manipulated—he rang a bell that was impossible to *un*ring. This was a bell that would rise from the ashes and ring in more pain and sorrow for the next three decades and counting.

Regarding Vogel, was it possible he didn't know? The more I tried to convince myself that Vogel didn't know, the more convinced I became that he did. The more I thought about why he did it, the more I realized there was nothing that could possibly justify it. No doubt, the office of district attorney is fraught with political pressure, but you can't play politics with an innocent man's life. Ever.

Then I recalled my conversation with some of the office staff a few days after the crime lab called with the DNA results, about how all three staff members who worked there at the time thought that Gregory Allen, and not Steven Avery, was the assailant. They even approached Vogel with their concerns. However, he told them they were mistaken. He had checked with Allen's probation agent, who said that Allen had an airtight alibi, a statement that, like so many other statements made by the authorities in the first Avery case, turned out to be a big, fat lie.

I hadn't stayed up all night in thirty years, but I sat spellbound that night watching *Making a Murderer* until six-thirty in the morning when the sun made its low, reluctant rise in the Wisconsin winter sky.

The night was exhilarating and maddening at the same time. Exhilarating, because I'd been obsessed with the Avery case for more than a decade and the entire saga was being played in my living room on video and audio, instead of static black words on white sheets of paper.

Maddening, too, because as soon as my confidence in Avery's guilt was restored—at times by something as simple as a guilty and sinister expression on his face—the next scene would send me into a panic, convinced again that the police had set him up and had taken down his emotionally vulnerable and intellectually challenged sixteen-year-old nephew as collateral damage in the process.

Take the discovery of Teresa Halbach's vehicle at the salvage yard, for example. In *real life* it was the break investigators had been looking for. Had the RAV4 not been discovered by two volunteers from a search party two days after police had first been on the property, Steven Avery likely would have disposed of it in a "car crusher" on the premises the following day, and Halbach's murder might never have been solved.

I was especially curious about how the documentary would portray the discovery of the RAV4 because I was there shortly after it was found. DA Mark Rohrer and I were called out to the scene that Saturday, five days after Halbach had last been seen. Rohrer had called me at home, and from the tone of his voice, I knew it was serious.

Could I meet him out at the Avery Salvage Yard, he asked. A volunteer search party had just found the SUV of a freelance photographer from Calumet County who was reported missing two days earlier, and the police needed a search warrant for what they feared would be her remains.

"Where'd they find it?" I asked.

"At the edge of the junkyard near the woods. Whoever did it, [they] threw a bunch of branches on top to conceal it."

"Do we know anything else yet?"

"Well," Rohrer replied, "her final shot that day was of a used car for sale at the salvage yard, and guess who called to set up the appointment?"

"Oh, shit," I replied.

I hopped in our minivan and sped out to the scene, where more than a hundred police officers from several jurisdictions, including sixty state troopers, would later converge for a massive search while television helicopters circled overhead for what everyone feared would be Teresa Halbach's remains. I remember gathering information from detectives for a search warrant and wondering where in the midst of the countless skeletons of junked cars, each surrounded by tall grass and weeds, the killer had hidden the body. The scene has been permanently etched in my mind.

As darkness fell, a light drizzle that started in midafternoon turned into a cold, driving rain. A mobile unit from the state crime lab, equipped with a few floodlights and a space heater, served as the command post and a refuge from the dark and the wet and the cold. The rain got heavier as the night wore on, and the flimsy, transparent plastic that served as the canopy for the Crime Lab Unit flapped noisily in the gusty wind. I'll never forget the eerie feeling evoked by the shrill sound of police dogs loudly barking as the search continued late into the night.

Still, there was no body. Finally one of the dogs, a Belgian shepherd named Brutus, alerted on a burn barrel approximately one hundred feet behind the residence of Steven Avery's sister, Barb Janda, and her son Brendan Dassey. Although four different types of human bone fragments would later be identified inside one of four burn barrels, it wouldn't be until days later. In the meantime all four barrels were sent to storage for safekeeping.

A few days later, Special Agent Tom Sturdivant would identify bone fragments in the fire pit. He testified at Avery's murder trial: "Deputy Jost was standing in front of what appeared to be, in my opinion, a piece of bone fragment. It was approximately one inch in length. And, um, my opinion was, and I think we kind of agreed, that it was a piece of bone fragment. And after looking at that, I looked at this so-called burn pit at the end of that pile of gravel and also noticed other—what in my opinion were bone fragments . . . that were obvious around that, uh, pile of debris."

Three agents from the Wisconsin Crime Lab converged at the scene and began sifting through the contents of the burn pit and the grassy area around it. It didn't take long before they found pieces of charred bones and teeth fragments. Later a forensic anthropologist would confirm that these belonged to an adult human female not older than thirty-five.

The premise that Teresa Halbach was murdered there was confirmed by the lengthy investigation that followed. It uncovered evidence proving that she never left the salvage yard that day—at least not in one piece. At the very least, she was held against her will, shot, and her body burned. At the very worst, she was tied up, raped, and stabbed, too.

Our office's role in what turned out to be the Avery and Dassey cases began and ended the same day that the RAV4 was found and Brutus alerted on what would eventually be entered into evidence and referenced as "Burn Barrel No. 2." When a search for a missing person changed to more of a criminal investigation, Rohrer and I both felt that with the wrongful conviction lawsuit still pending, there'd be a conflict of interest if we continued to be involved.

As the investigation progressed in the weeks and months that followed, I knew no more about the Avery case than what was being shown almost daily on local news broadcasts. My regular caseload was more than enough to occupy my time, but like everyone else I paid attention as the investigation unfolded.

I occasionally thought back to that Saturday afternoon and what might have occurred between the day Teresa Halbach went missing and the day her vehicle was found. Had the police developed any leads? Had they come upon any information that gave them even a clue?

I'd always assumed that whatever leads they developed in those couple of days had gone cold and that finding the RAV4 at the salvage yard was the break they were looking for. But I was about to learn that my assumptions might have been wrong.

"Manitowoc County Sheriff's Department, this is Lynn," the familiar voice of one of our dispatchers announced.

"Lynn?" Andy Colborn's even more familiar voice said in reply.

"Hi, Andy."

"Can you run Sam William Henry five-eight-two?"

"Okay. Shows that she's a missing person, and it lists to Teresa Halbach. Okay. Is that what you're looking for, Andy?"

"Yup, okay, thank you."

"You're so welcome. Bye-bye."

I'm sure I wasn't the only one who conjured up a vision of Sergeant Colborn sitting in his squad car, or even standing behind Teresa Halbach's RAV4, staring at its license plate and calling it in.

And now Dean Strang, standing in for Jerry Buting as the bad cop, was in my living room—well, sort of—grilling Colborn about why he would be calling dispatch to run a check on the plates for Halbach's car two days before it was supposedly found.

"But let's—let's ask . . . establish this first," began the exceptionally well-spoken lawyer, who was caught by the court reporter posing a question in less than his typically clear and crisp style, "do you remember making the call?"

"Not really, no," Colborn replied in a not very confident tone.

"Were you looking at these plates?" Strang asked, after which the witness looked around nervously without providing an answer.

Then Strang went in for the kill: "Well, and you can understand how someone listening to that might think that you were calling in a license plate that you were looking at on the back end of a 1999 Toyota?"

Weeks later I would parse Colborn's entire testimony with a fine-tooth comb, but what I—and everyone else in the world who was watching that night—heard was merely: "Hm, yes."

I nearly jumped off my seat. *No way, no way!* Andy Colborn would never lie on the stand, much less plant evidence in a murder case.

"I didn't see them plant evidence, with my own two eyes," said Dean Strang in a later episode. "I didn't see it. But do I understand how human beings might be tempted to plant evidence under the circumstances in which the Manitowoc County Sheriff's Department found itself?. . . . Do I have any difficulty understanding what human emotions might have driven police officers to want to augment or confirm their beliefs that he must have killed Teresa Halbach? I don't have any difficulty understanding those human emotions at all."

And so it was for the rest of the night as I watched one episode after another of *Making a Murderer* hinting at police misconduct that, taken together, all but convicted Andy Colborn, Jim Lenk, and an unspecified number of unnamed others of planting evidence to frame Steven Avery for Teresa Halbach's murder.

41

The RAV4's ignition key found in Avery's bedroom? Planted, of course, by Colborn and Lenk.

The six spots of Avery's blood found in her car? Also planted—from a vial still kept in evidence from a post-relief conviction motion following his wrongful conviction.

And the bullet fragment found in the garage, the one fired from Avery's gun with traces of Halbach's DNA? Planted again, this time by Lenk, but perhaps with the assistance of Detective Dave Remiker, who happened to be in the garage the day it was found.

The cumulative effect of watching one disturbing episode after another was emotionally draining. A smoking gun—or, in this instance, a spot of blood with a preservative—that definitively proved the police planted evidence to frame Avery would have been easier to take. Like hundreds of thousands of other viewers, who were most likely in the same miserable hell I was, we were left hanging for hours, drawn in with the promise of an answer. In the end, we were left with more questions than answers, along with utter exhaustion and despair.

Some people can deal with uncertainty more comfortably than others. I think I can, at least concerning the big questions in life—questions of philosophy, religion, politics, and that sort of thing. I don't need ironclad certitude, for instance, to believe in the existence of God.

But *Making a Murderer* wasn't musing about life's ultimate questions. It was exploring a few practical questions and was inviting its audience to go along on the trip: Did the police plant evidence to frame Steven Avery for Teresa Halbach's murder? Was he wrongly convicted again? Considering Avery's pending lawsuit against the county, the involvement of the Manitowoc County Sheriff's Department early on in the murder investigation, and the series of what I had hoped were merely uncanny coincidences in how some of the evidence was found, these were very appropriate questions. A documentary is the ideal medium in which to raise these issues.

However, an unintended consequence of *Making a Murderer* is that it has invited the world to take part in a brainteasing adventure that is enormously harmful to real people with real lives. For these people, it is not an academic or cinematic exploration of the shortcomings of the criminal justice system.

Teresa Halbach's parents and her brothers and sisters, who have borne a greater burden than most of us will ever be asked to, now have to bear more. Penny Beerntsen and her family, who have dealt with the Avery case since it began thirty years ago, are bearing more pain, too. And even Sergeant Colborn and Lieutenant Lenk have been negatively and irrevocably impacted. Their sterling reputations have been forever tarnished on a scale perhaps never seen before.

These heroes—and in my mind they are exactly that—knew from the start that their personal tragedies could never be kept completely private. But they never expected that their burdens and that of their families would be shared with the entire world. They never asked for that. Nobody ever would.

CHAPTER 4

STICKS & STONES...

Threats to the sheriff's department started pouring in two days after *Making a Murderer* aired. Viewers were outraged by the documentary's not-so-subtle contention that police in some forsaken town in Wisconsin planted evidence and conspired with prosecutors to send a rough-around-the-edges but likeable man and his sixteen-year-old nephew to prison. Citizens from around the world took to their computers and cell phones to express their anger. Nor did they discriminate when choosing the objects of their disgust. Every member of the Manitowoc County law enforcement community, even those who had nothing to do with the case, was worthy of their disdain.

The sheriff's department bore the brunt of the anger. After *Making a Murderer* aired, the law enforcement office received over two hundred angry e-mails and telephone calls in the first week or so. Six of the calls contained threats directed at specific targets that were serious enough to warrant investigation by state agents and the FBI.

Jim Lenk and Andy Colborn, all but convicted by the documentarians of planting evidence to frame Avery and Dassey, were the most common targets by far. One of them received a threatening call at home on Christmas Day. He had hoped to spend a peaceful day with his family, who still loved him even if hundreds

44

of thousands around the world thought him the dirtiest of cops. Instead his and his family's Christmas Day was ruined by the call.

Some of the rage was misdirected. The City of Manitowoc Police Department, oftentimes confused with the County of Manitowoc Sheriff's Office, did not participate in the investigation of Teresa Halbach's murder, but dispatchers there were also fielding calls. Someone from Australia even sent an e-mail to the mayor, calling out the corruption in his despicable little Midwestern town. Even the county historical society took some heat as its rating on Facebook plummeted after scores of Netflix viewers posted negative ratings and ranting reviews about the city.

"Our entire review section was tarnished," said the society's executive director, "it was getting tainted by the minute."

Why would ANYONE want to call this place home? rhetorically asked one of the reviews. The exasperated executive director complained to a reporter, "They don't look at the great things we're doing."

Others knew precisely where to direct their rage.

Certain that governmental corruption was afoot, one of several Anonymous groups—self-appointed guardians of American citizens' constitutional rights—announced they'd hacked into the sheriff's department's computers and found a treasure trove of incriminating e-mails proving that evidence had been planted. They promised to make the e-mails public in two days. However, either they came up empty-handed or the illustrious group of hackers had been bluffing, since the day came and went without any disclosure.

A few weeks later one of their masked sympathizers, donning the traditional Guy Fawkes mask, managed to join a crowd of demonstrators at the courthouse to scold the local police and to chant slogans and carry signs demanding Steven Avery's and Brendan Dassey's immediate release.

"What do we want?"

"Justice!"

"When do we want it?"

"Now!"

Afraid the demonstrators might disrupt court proceedings, the three judges cleared their calendars, so I pitched my suit and tie in favor of jeans and a hooded jacket. Call me a coward, but I avoided being near the officers in charge of security when small groups of demonstrators occasionally came inside to either use the restrooms or to get out of the cold.

With the exception of a yelling match initiated by a pro-police counterdemonstrator, which nearly turned into a fight, the march was angry and loud, but never got out of control. To ward off trouble and to show national-news television audiences that Manitowoc was a friendly and kind Midwestern town after all, nearby businesses provided hot cocoa and cookies to demonstrators on both sides.

But the lawful expressions of protest did not last long. The FBI was contacted a few weeks later when a sheriff's department officer received a suspicious package in the mail with a note attached that said, *For Steven Avery.* When the hazmat team opened the package, a tube exploded with glitter. Nothing else was in the package, but the invasion of privacy upset the officer and his family and made them wonder what was next. In an atmosphere filled with hate, who is to say what people so driven by anger were capable of doing?

It didn't take long to find out.

"If you don't do it yourself, I'd do it for you—with a bullet to the head," came the answer in the form of a telephone call to the sheriff's department a few days later.

A man called joint dispatch a few weeks later and announced that sheriff's department officers and the county prosecutors would be executed in their homes on Sunday, January 31. The same message was called into our office later that day. The sheriff promptly informed the FBI, and was told they'd "open a file."

"Announcing plans ahead of time to execute the nonbelievers," my colleagues and I joked, with no small amount of bravado.

I had received a few threats on social media, and a particularly deranged citizen said he was going to make my boss, the current district attorney, watch as he murdered her children and then did away with her. The endless string of police shootings that summer and fall had raised the level of anger, by several notches, to one of rage against police and prosecutors, which only added to our uneasiness.

I had received dozens of angry messages in response to my criticism of *Making a Murderer* and support for the police in several media interviews. One woman named Billie, for instance, whose cover shot on her Facebook page included a blissful picture and the words *John 15:12,* wrote some rather unholy words I won't share here. I didn't have to bother looking up that Bible verse, either. It was right there on her page: *My command is this: Love each other as I have loved you.* It's a pretty safe bet that those sentiments didn't apply to me.

Amidst this kind of insanity, anything seemed possible, so with caution the better part of valor, a few of us made plans to be out of town that weekend—just in case.

The appointed day for our execution passed without incident, but as *Making a Murderer* catapulted into a national, even international, phenomenon in the weeks that followed, it became clear that concerns for our safety were not misplaced.

On February 3, 2016, six and a half weeks after *Making a Murderer* was released, two bomb threats were phoned into the sheriff's department. The first caller claimed there were bombs inside the sheriff's department and that he was getting "Justice for Steven." Two hours later, at a little after nine p.m., a second caller said there was a vehicle packed with explosives in the parking lot between the jail and the courthouse and there would be a "huge massacre" when the bomb went off.

Officers from surrounding police agencies and a bomb-sniffing dog meticulously searched the sheriff's department and the courthouse throughout the night. No devices were found, and the buildings were declared safe to open for business the next day. Still, though, the threats had caused plenty of disruption and rattled all of our already shaken nerves.

A police spokesperson told reporters there was a good chance the threat came from outside the state. "I can't say I'm totally surprised at it," he said, "I was hoping nothing like this would occur. We will prosecute this to the fullest when this person is caught."

The callers had employed a complicated calling route to phone in the threats, so city and state police set out to backtrack through the layers of calls to find their origin. As the officer in charge put it, the calls were "intricately spoofed." In the end they proved too convoluted to trace.

At the same time the bomb threats were phoned in that night, SWAT members were dispatched to the residence of one of the officers castigated by the documentary. A Lifeline emergency signal had come into the sheriff's department and was followed by a phone call from a purported neighbor of the officer reporting that a man with a rifle was outside his neighbor's front door.

SWAT members arrived and discovered it was another hoax. The officer and his family were fine, nobody in the house owned a Lifeline alert system, and there had never been a man with a rifle at the door. State police and the FBI later tried to trace how the emergency alert was routed through the officer's residence. Again, their efforts were unsuccessful.

For several more weeks the city continued to be on edge. It was a particularly difficult time for third-shift officers who had to deal with the backlash on the streets from *Making a Murderer*. Like most small towns in Wisconsin—medium and larger cities like Madison, Milwaukee, and Green Bay, too, now that I think of it— Manitowoc has its share of taverns, with more than a few street corners having two or three allowing those who had tipped a few too many to stumble from one to the next without getting into their car.

Several police threat referrals came across my desk with requests for charges. In one of them an officer arrested a man after a fight broke out at Revolutions Bar on the city's north side. The man started screaming "Avery" from the backseat of the squad car on the way to the jail and then threatened to kill the officer and his "entire family" during a string of expletives that were difficult to make out.

In another incident, an officer was dispatched to the south side at three forty-five in the morning in reference to a man sitting in the front seat of the neighbor's pickup truck. Asked if he knew whose vehicle he was sitting in, the man said with a dazed look on his face that it was Teresa Halbach's and he was going to rape and kill her and then frame Steven Avery.

It was very evident the subject was under the influence at this point, the officer dryly noted in his report. The officer didn't hazard a guess about which drug the man had used to blow away his mind on that particular night. Given the recent scourge that was visited upon our city, heroin would be the safest bet.

Working in suits and ties from nine to five in buildings designed to instill a modicum of dignity and respect—and where only the most hardened drug and alcohol addicts are nervy enough to show up drunk or high—threats to prosecutors are rare, at least compared to those made to cops on the streets. Still, owing to my book's firmly expressed position that Steven Avery and Brendan Dassey were rightly convicted, I was on the receiving end of plenty of venom and anger myself.

One woman made it very clear that she was not my friend. She posted in the commentary section of a news article concerning the lack of progress in finding the source of the bomb threats made a few weeks earlier: *Ask prosecutor Michael Griesbach—he practically accuses everyone who asks why he has published false facts in his book of being some form of terrorist—making the same false equation. Obviously threats are wrong, but this article with the obtuse "Justice for*

Steven" is more insinuation publicity, the same corrupt PR used to convict Avery and Dassey out of court.

In compliance with the newspaper's policy for posting comments, the woman gave her name and identified herself as a film producer at an outfit called Fear the Hills. I Googled it at that time and discovered that Fear the Hills Facebook page had 6,066 likes. That is a list to which I would not have added my name for a number of reasons, not least of which is there are one too many sixes for my comfort level.

Those who publicly express anger and threaten to inflict physical harm are a small percentage of the number of people in any movement or cause, and the Avery and Dassey supporters were no exception. Over five hundred thousand people signed an online petition asking President Obama to pardon them and to hold Manitowoc County officials, who were complicit in their wrongful convictions, accountable to the highest extent of the law. Tens of thousands of Wisconsin residents signed a similar petition for Governor Walker to sign.

The White House released a statement noting the president had no power to issue a pardon for people convicted in state criminal courts, so a pardon for Avery and Dassey would need to be issued in Wisconsin. *While this case is out of the Administration's purview,* the White House added, *President Obama is committed to restoring the sense of fairness at the heart of our justice system.*

Not quite an endorsement of the movement, but close enough. Four months after dropping out of the presidential race, Governor Walker issued a statement, too. After pointing out how he had never issued a pardon during his five years in office, the governor said he was not going to start with Steven Avery.

As I finished watching the documentary, my own certainty about the guilt of Steven Avery and Brendan Dassey had been compromised even more so. Ever since, it continued to vacillate whenever I heard something new, as did the level of discomfort that accompanied my uncertainty. People don't demonstrate in front of a Wisconsin courthouse in the middle of winter for nothing. Nor do half-a-million people sign petitions asking the president of the United States to pardon a man convicted of murder, especially one as senseless and ruthless as Teresa Halbach's.

After finishing the documentary, I settled into a resignation of sorts. I didn't like it, but I could live with my lack of certainty concerning their guilt. Our conflict of interest applied to appeals and possible retrials, so we were not responsible for their cases going forward. I figured the court system would sort it all out while I sat comfortably by and watched the whole mess unravel from a distance.

But I figured wrong.

CHAPTER 5

CONVOLUTED CONCERNS

If Steven Avery and Brendan Dassey didn't murder Teresa Halbach, then who did? The creators of *Making a Murderer* tried, and failed, to give viewers a credible alternative—as did Avery's lawyers, who faced the same problem closing the deal with the jury at trial. The frame-up defense nearly succeeded. We know that because the jury deliberated for three days before reaching a verdict. According to one juror, their initial vote was seven to five in favor of acquittal. But all that was about to change—the missing piece of the puzzle may have been found.

From a concerned citizen, read the subject line of an e-mail I received at work just days after the documentary aired—the kind of e-mail you're not supposed to open because its source is unknown and you might spread some untoward virus. I opened it anyhow.

The message was brief. In fact, there was none—just a link to a blog that I also opened, probably breaking a techie's second golden rule. The blog's author went by the name of "Convoluted Brian," and his blog boasted a subtitle of "The Importance of Understanding." Whether his blog adds to or subtracts from his readers' understanding of the world is in the eye of the beholder, but convoluted or not, Brian McCorkle was clearly a smart guy who had done his homework concerning the Avery case. The blog contained a wealth of what appeared to be accurate information about both the Avery and Dassey cases, but at the moment I was only concerned with the page I'd been directed to.

Posted two years after their trials, the page was entitled "Alternate Suspect." It offered up a previously unknown suspect, a German national by the name of Wolfgang Braun (pseudonym), who I would soon learn was not unknown to me during the trials. The source of the dirt on Wolfgang Braun was his wife, Sophie (pseudonym), although at this point I knew neither of their names since Convoluted Brian had not provided them on his blog, presumably out of concern for Sophie's safety. As I read through Convoluted Brian's account of what Sophie allegedly had told him, I did so with a growing fear.

The couple had separated and Sophie was moving from Bonduel, Wisconsin, to Maribel, where she had signed a lease with an effective date of November 1 for a country home six miles from the Avery Salvage Yard. Wolfgang was acting strange at the time, Sophie explained, sleeping in their attic and exhibiting other bizarre behavior. One day he told her he'd gone to the rental property and spoke of visiting an auto salvage yard. Sophie claimed she later found out it was October 31, the day Halbach was last seen. Wolfgang said that he felt the photographer was "stupid" and that she asked him if she could take some pictures of the rental property while he was there. Sophie also said that Wolfgang had a cut on his finger, which was intermittently bleeding, and she noticed he had scratches on his back that night.

Continuing what I assumed was a made-up story, Sophie claimed that a few days later she discovered a can of lighter fluid in one of the outbuildings on the rental property with a bloody fingerprint on it. Wolfgang told her he'd burned a doll crib, but when Sophie checked, the crib had not been burned. She described bizarre behavior that grew steadily worse as the week of Halbach's disappearance unfolded—culminating in Wolfgang's arrest for a domestic violence incident on November 6 in the early-morning hours after Halbach's RAV4 was discovered at the salvage yard.

That last bit of information concerned me. Wolfgang Braun's arrest would be easy to verify, which made it unlikely she was making it up—at least that part. Sophie said a few months later he was arrested again—this time for burglary, intimidation of a witness, criminal trespass to a dwelling, resisting an officer, and bail jumping when he struck her after being released from jail, which was in violation of the no-contact condition of bail.

Per Convoluted Brian's blog, Sophie claimed that months later she opened a closet at the base of the stairs and discovered a pair of women's jeans, a top, and a pillowcase with red stains on it. In another location she discovered a pair of women's underwear with red stains on it. Suspecting her husband may have been involved in Teresa Halbach's disappearance, she contacted the sheriff's department. According to Sophie, the detective steered her away from her suspicions and told her they already had their suspect locked up, which was exactly what Wolfgang told her would happen if she reported her suspicions—the police would just laugh and never believe her.

I hoped this was simply a case of someone seeking attention by claiming she had information regarding a very publicized case or that the owner of the blog had taken things out of context. But what if it's true? It might mean that Steven Avery and Brendan Dassey were innocent, or at the very least, it could re-open the case and maybe even result in a new trial. Either way, the prosecution of Avery and Dassey was in serious jeopardy if Sophie Braun was telling the truth.

This can't be happening, I thought. I had felt for nearly a decade—no, I *knew*, for nearly a decade—that the jury got it right; that Avery had not been wrongly convicted a second time. Avery and Dassey were responsible for Halbach's murder, I was sure of it. No way had *Making a Murderer* gotten it right.

I stared blankly out the window behind my desk, not even trying to gather my thoughts. Then I walked into the hallway and descended the three flights of marble stairs in a building where I'd spent most of my waking hours for the last twenty-five years. The familiar took on the unfamiliar, and nothing looked the same. People I've known and worked with for years even seemed different somehow. I was stunned. I walked back up the three flights of stairs and returned to my work, but for the rest of the day, I wondered why.

Lawyers, scholars, and judges call it exculpatory evidence—a legal term for evidence that suggests may be helpful to the defense. Or as more formally stated in the law: *Evidence that tends to negate the guilt of the accused.*

The rule, which goes to the heart of the constitutional right to a fair trial, is straightforward enough: If a prosecutor knows of exculpatory evidence that is material, he or she must promptly turn it over to the defense. In Wisconsin, prosecutors have a further duty to turn over all exculpatory evidence, regardless of whether it is material.

While not uncommon, exculpatory evidence exists in fewer cases than you might expect. If we are doing our jobs as prosecutors, we aren't charging people with crimes unless evidence of their guilt is clear—as in "proof beyond a reasonable doubt" clear. And if guilt is clear, then there shouldn't be much, if any, evidence that the defendant is innocent. If there is, we need to turn it over to the defense, right away. It's that simple.

If the new evidence makes us prosecutors doubt the defendant's guilt, then we regroup and dismiss the case—at least that's what we are supposed to do. In fact, even if we still think the defendant is guilty despite the new evidence, if we don't think we can prove it beyond a reasonable doubt, we're supposed to dismiss it. There are always other fish to fry, and, more often than not, the fish that got away will be back before long.

Exculpatory evidence is ordinarily easy to spot. And if it's not, there are more than enough federal and state court decisions to provide prosecutors with guidance when it's a close call as to whether a particular piece of evidence or information is exculpatory or not. If after reviewing the case law, we're still uncertain, then on the theory that it's better to err on the side of caution, one would hope that most prosecutors would cough it up. If upholding a defendant's constitutional right to a fair trial is not incentive enough for prosecutors, the possibility of losing their licenses to practice law should suffice.

Wolfgang Braun's statement to his wife Sophie is without doubt exculpatory evidence. And if the prosecution knew about it, they had to turn it over. And they should have known because Sophie said she relayed the same information she gave to Convoluted Brian to the police. If the prosecution team had her statement, I was sure they disclosed it to the defense. Unless they followed up on Sophie's information and discovered there was no doubt she was making it up—which would also be fine.

But what if the officers from the sheriff's department who interviewed Sophie—it just had to be the sheriff's department again—never passed the information on to the prosecutors? It's not their call, but what if they thought it wasn't true, so why bother the prosecutors with such nonsense when everyone knew that Steven Avery and Brendan Dassey murdered Teresa Halbach, not some German national who just recently moved into the area and, as far as they knew, never even met Halbach.

Worse, what if the county sheriff's officers thought there was something to it and intentionally failed to pass it on? That road led to disaster and a conclusion I did not want to draw.

If all that weren't enough, the prosecution's problems did not end there.

First, when it comes to exculpatory evidence, prosecutors

don't get to hide behind the police. We are deemed by the law to know what they know—even if we don't. So if the sheriff's department failed to tell Kratz and his team about Sophie and Wolfgang Braun, it would not alleviate the problem.

Next, what if the prosecutors knew about Sophie's statement, but did not disclose it to the defense? The day would only be saved if they had followed up on Sophie's information and found out she was obviously lying, maybe to get back at her husband for something he'd done or perhaps because she was delusional.

But unless it was very clear that she was making up her story, this road would likely also lead to disaster because neither cops nor prosecutors get to judge whether potentially exculpatory evidence is reliable. We're not the gatekeepers of reliability of witnesses and the truth. The law, the judge, and ultimately the jurors are the gatekeepers of this realm—not the prosecutor.

This last scenario presented an especially complex problem, the answer to which is not very clear in the law. Despite its well-earned reputation for being overly complex, the law generally makes sense. Judges and legal scholars have had hundreds of years to develop ways to deal with issues that invariably arise in conflicts between individuals or groups. Whether the fight is about money or kids, who's at fault when someone gets hurt—or for our purposes, what rules apply when the government accuses someone of a crime and wants to put them in jail—the law has already answered most of the questions that might arise. And if it hasn't fully answered a particularly thorny question, it is sure to have given it a good going-over and written its musings down.

What happens when a prosecutor comes upon new and arguably exculpatory evidence after a defendant is convicted—like I just did when I was reading Sophie Braun's explosive statement—is one of those complicated questions, the answer to which, like the devil, is always in the details.

So I did what most lawyers do when they don't know the answer—I opened a book, *The Wisconsin Statutes,* and specifically the section entitled "Special Responsibilities of a Prosecutor." In relevant part, here is what I found:

When a prosecutor knows of new, credible and material evidence creating a reasonable likelihood that a convicted defendant did not commit an offense of which the defendant was convicted, the prosecutor shall promptly disclose that evidence to the defendant.

Furthermore, [if a prosecutor knows of] *clear and convincing evidence establishing that a defendant in the prosecutor's jurisdiction was convicted of an offense that the defendant did not commit, the prosecutor shall seek to remedy the conviction.* Meaning, I assume, we have to dismiss.

New, credible, and material—but just how new, how credible, and how material? And exactly what is a "reasonable likelihood," anyhow? Your reasonable likelihood might very well not be mine.

Lawyers love words like these because they give them wiggle room to spin their arguments whichever way suits their clients' interests that day. But as prosecutors, we have no business spinning arguments, at least not on issues of law, and especially not on the fundamental issue of innocence and guilt.

I was fairly confident even without researching the issue that if Braun's statement was not known to the prosecution team because the sheriff's department kept it to themselves, it would qualify as "new" under the statute. And there was no question that, if true, her statement about Wolfgang's behavior and statements during the week that Teresa went missing were "material."

It came down to the third squishy word in the statute—"credible." Was Braun's statement credible? Was she telling the truth? If she was, then under the rules—even a decade after Steven Avery and Brendan Dassey were found guilty, after both of their convictions had been upheld in the court of appeals, and after ten years of the Halbach family believing that Teresa's killer had been brought to justice—her statement had to be turned over to the defense. A new trial would follow, and the prospects for a conviction would be slim, assuming the state would even refile it.

INDEFENSIBLE

* * *

As concerned as I was about Braun's statement that her husband might have been Teresa Halbach's killer, and what that might mean for the Avery and Dassey cases, owing to our continued conflict of interest, it was not our office's job to figure it out. I could do all the thinking I wanted, but I could do nothing to investigate whether she was telling the truth. I knew Sophie had provided enough detailed information that it could not be ignored, I forwarded it to the special prosecutor in charge.

That night at home, I tried to figure it out. The possibilities of how the police and prosecutors in the Avery and Dassey cases could have handled Sophie's information seemed endless, and almost all of the scenarios ended badly.

Sophie would not be the first spouse in a dysfunctional marriage to spin a yarn to get her spouse in trouble with the police. Why did she tell her story to Convoluted Brian several years after the events occurred? Was she still bitter and not willing to give up the anger and hate, even after they divorced? Did she contact Convoluted after searching online for a pro-Avery blog?

On the other hand, in the last twenty-eight years I've prosecuted over two thousand domestic violence cases. The "Battered Women's Syndrome," as domestic violence experts refer to it, is real. I've seen it in action.

Domestic violence is far more prevalent than most people realize and they have no idea what victims go through. Bouncing back and forth between wanting to escape their abuser and not being able to leave him for fear, for financial reasons, or other factors, they tell police the truth one day and recant their statement the next, sometimes explaining away their swollen face and bruises as the result of a fall. Occasionally they exaggerate the beating to keep the abuser in jail so they can escape before he returns to make good on his promise to beat her worse next time or even to kill her.

But rarely will an untrue or exaggerated story be as detailed as Sophie Braun's. If Sophie's story was a lie, it was a whopper!

* * *

The next morning I sent an e-mail to Tom Fallon, the one remaining member of the prosecution team. I attached Convoluted Brian's rendition of Braun's statement, along with a short note that I was not vouching for or against its credibility, but that it included enough detail that it should probably be looked into.

After not hearing back from Fallon, I spoke with my boss and we left a voice mail requesting that he give us a call. I was in court when he called back, but he told my boss he was unable to open up my e-mail for some reason so I should send it again. I did and he confirmed the receipt of same.

There was comfort in knowing I had fulfilled my obligation under the law. I passed the information, as I understood it, on to the person in charge and now he would have to decide what to do with it.

The comfort lasted for no more than a week. How did I know Fallon was going to follow up? He was in the middle of moving back to the attorney general's office after transferring to the district attorney's office in Madison for a few years. I'm sure he was swamped at work. Besides, I thought, he was probably none too pleased about being stuck with the Avery case, especially now that *Making a Murderer* had catapulted the case into the national spotlight. He was the only member of the prosecution team left. Kratz was no longer working or living in the area, and the other prosecutor, Assistant DA Norm Gahn, had retired. Fallon was solely responsible for both the Avery and Dassey cases—the entire mess.

I figured there'd be no harm if I found out more from Convoluted Brian. Up to this point I did not even know the woman's and the suspect's names—Brian had omitted them to protect Sophie. I wanted to verify if Wolfgang was arrested in a domestic violence incident, as Sophie said he was, including when and where, to see if it matched up with what Sophie had claimed. But without their names I could verify nothing.

Convoluted Brian was hard to track down, but shortly after I sent him an e-mail asking for the names of the suspect and the suspect's wife, he sent a reply. Without any commentary the names of both individuals and the case numbers for the two domestic violence arrests appeared on my screen. I went on the Circuit Court Access Page (CCAP), our state's online database for every criminal charge filed going back twenty-plus years, and after entering the first case number scrolled down to find out who had prosecuted Wolfgang Braun. It was me—as it was for the second set of charges two months later. The charges and the dates and the places where the offenses occurred matched up, too. At least with regard to the domestic violence cases, Sophie was a reliable reporter of events.

But that she was telling the truth about where she and Wolfgang lived and when and where he was charged with unrelated crimes—no matter how close in proximity and time to Teresa Halbach's murder—did not mean she was not lying about everything else. To find out more, I would need to retrieve the files.

We have a subscription in the office for the *Manitowoc Herald Times Reporter,* which included a story about the Avery case nearly every day for months after *Making a Murderer* aired. Before leaving for the day, I picked up the "Distorter"—as many of us in town somewhat fondly refer to our local paper—to check out that day's installment on the Avery case. Brendan Dassey had written a letter from his prison cell and the paper had copied the handwritten note in full just as Dassey had scribbled it down.

To The People of the World, the letter began, *I am writing to let you know that me and my uncle Steven are innocent. The investigators tormented me until I said what they wanted me to say. . . . They tricked me. The investigators lied through their teeth on the stand. If I would get a new trial the truth would come out because I am not afraid of them anymore. They ruined me and my families lives.*

Dassey signed it, *Sincerely yours, True and innocent, Brendan Dassey.*

I could hardly wait to get my hands on the 2005 Wolfgang Braun files! On my way out of the office, I asked our receptionist to retrieve them from our off-site storage facility. As I drove home that night, it occurred to me for the first time that Brendan Dassey and Steven Avery might really be just that—true and innocent.

CHAPTER 6

MERRY CHRISTMAS

The tree had been up for a week, the decorations hung, the college kids back in the nest, the Nativity set displayed, cookies baked, and plenty of hot chocolate and schnapps on hand—all the traditions that make Christmas such a peaceful and joyful time for our family were finally in order. The next day the comfort of family would be replaced by fear, not by means of an unknown substance sent in the mail, as one of the officers received, but by information I would soon learn about Wolfgang Braun.

No matter where I went or whom I talked to, I could not escape *Making a Murderer.* Extended family, neighbors, colleagues, friends—that was all anyone wanted to talk about. Having heard that I appeared briefly in episode one the documentary, a few of them assumed I shared its point of view. The media coverage was incessant, too—though after I began speaking out against what I considered the series' obvious bias in dozens of radio, television, and print media interviews all across the country, I was hardly in a position to complain.

It was not a surprise, then, when I came home after reading Brendan Dassey's letter "To The People of the World" on the way out of the office, and I saw my wife, Jody, and the kids in the living room, already several episodes into *Making a Murderer.*

"Hi, guys." No answer.

"Can you believe it—Christmas is only two days away!" No answer again.

"The courthouse blew up today." Still, no answer.

I couldn't blame them. The documentary was so absorbing that a friend told me that he and his wife watched the entire series straight through one night.

I threw something into the microwave for dinner, and took the dog for a walk. I managed to catch Jody between episodes long enough to tell her that Convoluted Brian had e-mailed me Wolfgang and Sophie's names and that I had been the prosecutor on the files. Jody has an excellent memory and she immediately recognized Wolfgang's name—I probably forgot it an hour after he entered his plea.

That meant there was something highly unusual about Wolfgang Braun because I rarely discuss cases at home. It's not that I mind talking about my job or that I can't—other than the juvenile cases, they are almost all a matter of public record. But most of my days are pretty boring, at least at this point in my career. Naturally patient, Jody is almost always willing to listen, but the kids will only pretend to listen to me for so long.

Besides, my job is not exactly uplifting. As cops and prosecutors, we spend most of our time dealing with people when they are at their worst, when they have done something that will only make their already-difficult lives more difficult. Many of them wish they could take it back—until they get drunk or stoned the next time and repeat their criminal behavior, or maybe even take it up a notch or two in its severity. I suspect most cops feel the same way as I do—why bring all of that home?

Criminal cases divide roughly into equal parts of booze, greed, drugs, violence, and sex. Some of our defendants mix these ingredients together in a variety of dismal ways. You might think with this kind of material, the life of a prosecutor would never get dull, but you'd be wrong. Pride, greed, lust, envy, gluttony, wrath, and sloth—Chaucer's seven deadly sins. None of us escape them, but peering into others falling prey to their temptations becomes tiresome after a while. We spend most of our day scrounging around in other people's lives, trying to figure out if we have enough evidence to prove their most recent transgression, and if so, what kind of punishment should be imposed and for how long.

There is also a great deal of repetition involved. If you've seen one drunk-driving case, you've seen them all—especially after more than twenty-five years in the business. A patrol officer stops a vehicle for weaving in or out of its lane. He approaches the vehicle and notices the driver has bloodshot eyes, slurred speech, and "the odor of intoxicants emanating from his person." They might as well have an AutoText program for these last three observations. The driver bombs the field sobriety tests—including a few that most people would fail stone-cold sober. The drunk is arrested without incident unless he becomes unruly with the officer and must be "decentralized" and then "assisted to the ground." After a quick stop at the hospital to take a blood sample, forcibly if necessary, which comes back later at two or three times the legal limit, the driver is hauled off to jail. A well-trained monkey could handle the prosecution.

In a totally separate category, though, are the half-dozen or so cases every year that are serious enough or unique in some other way to warrant a discussion over the dinner table at home. Wolfgang Braun's cases fell into the second category—not because of the run-of-the-mill domestic violence offenses he committed, but because of an aura of danger, intelligence, and manipulation that was sufficient to place him in that year's fairly exclusive club of "I hope this guy doesn't kill somebody, someday" membership.

Jody remembered that I told her Wolfgang Braun was a German national and that he was creepy, but not much more. It was, after all, ten years ago. I recalled little more than what he looked like, and only after she reminded me how I'd described him to her after coming home from work after his plea hearing. He was a fit, trim, strong, middle-aged man, with close-cropped short gray hair and intelligent eyes—smarter than anyone else in the room, I thought at the time, as I'm sure he did, too. He was personable, if not outright friendly, with his attorney and everyone else in the courtroom before and during his sentencing hearing despite, or perhaps in part because of, his broken English.

But still, I remember thinking in court that day that there was something very disturbing about Wolfgang Braun's personality, but that's as much as I could recall. To find out more, I needed to review his files, hopefully the next day.

Having exhausted my memory of Wolfgang, I went up to bed and fell asleep to Steven Avery's plaintive voice wondering why the police were after him again, along with the documentary's foreboding theme music, as both sounds made their way up the stairs and through my bedroom door.

It was Christmas Eve and the courthouse was abandoned when I arrived at the office the following day. I'd asked our receptionist the day before if she could retrieve the Wolfgang Braun files out of storage, and I must have shown a sufficient degree of deference because both files were on the top of my desk when I arrived.

I started with the criminal complaints—the ones I'd filed a decade ago, but had long since forgotten the details. Wolfgang was arrested on domestic violence charges after Sophie called 911 a little after four in the morning on Sunday, November 6, 2005. That was less than eighteen hours after Teresa Halbach's RAV4 was discovered at the Avery Salvage Yard six miles away. He had punched Sophie on the right side of her head after she told him she would no longer help him get his green card—his visa had expired in August. As officers began escorting him from the house, he braced himself against a door frame and struggled until they were able to "decentralize him to the floor."

The second complaint proved more interesting. On January 19, nine days after he was released from jail, Wolfgang showed up at two forty-five in the morning outside Sophie's door. The bail conditions from his first case were still in effect, including that he have no contact with Sophie, so he was in violation of bail, a crime in itself. He forced his way into the residence and then shoved her around before taking her digital camera and wrestling her cell phone away.

But it was the resisting charge that jogged my memory of why I considered Wolfgang so emotionally disturbed. When police arrived, Sophie told them that after taking her camera Wolfgang ran out the door toward the northwest corner of the property. They eventually found him sitting in a grassy area in the midst of plowed fields with a pair of black socks and a digital camera at his side. This was at four twenty-one in the morning, in the middle of winter. As soon as he saw the police, Wolfgang tried strangling himself with the socks until they were able to subdue him with a few bursts of pepper spray to the face. He was taken into custody and hauled off to jail, where he remained on a one-thousand-dollar cash bail until his sentencing hearing two months later.

I leafed through the contents of his disheveled file and came across three photos of jailhouse graffiti written in thick, block-styled letters in pencil that jogged my memory even more as to why I thought Wolfgang was so disturbed. A note from a corrections officer indicated that Wolfgang had drawn the giant words on his cell's bathroom walls a few weeks before he was released.

WHAT IS FAIRNESS IN JUSTIFIED—EVER GUILTY, read one of the messages on a six-by-six-foot portion of one wall in half-inch-wide lines to form the letters. It was difficult to decipher, probably in part because his English was poor. Did he mean "What in fairness is justified?"

GOD BLESS YOU, read another.

The third message, written on the wall immediately to the right of the cell's stainless-steel toilet, but too large to have been accomplished while Wolfgang was doing his business, screamed DEAD IS FREEDOM. One or maybe two words were written above those, but they were too blurry to read—at least on the copy of the photo I was looking at in the file.

Wolfgang's writings on the jail walls and his behavior in the farm field that night, along with the vibe he gave off later at his sentencing hearing, explained why I told Jody about him a decade earlier. But that's not what I was looking for. I was there to find out if Sophie told the police or maybe even our office that she suspected he was involved with Teresa Halbach's murder. If she didn't pass on this information back then, when it was fresh on her mind, then she probably made it all up several years later when she spoke with Convoluted Brian. If that was the case, I could go back home and continue with our holiday cheer.

I checked the file notes next. We make entries on stapled pages on the left side of the defendant's file to explain what occurred at every court proceeding or to scribble settlement offers—there is no time to draft final settlement letters in most district attorney's offices. It's way too busy.

One of my colleagues did bail hearings that day and her notes indicated that Wolfgang Braun was a German national with an INS detainer. The fact that he had an INS detainer meant he was in the country unlawfully and would be sitting in jail until the feds deported him—unless for some reason they decided not to do so. The court commissioner set five-hundred-dollar cash bail, just in case.

I must have been on intake that month because I ended up handling both files and the next entry was mine: *MG should handle file, dangerous defendant with victim afraid he'll kill her if he's released. Look for max and/or deportation.* The victim witness coordinators or I must have spoken with Sophie to generate that note, so I rifled through the file to get to the victim witness, or V/W, section. If Sophie said anything about Teresa Halbach's murder, this is where it would be.

A memo written by Tammy Henrickson (pseudonym), one of the victim witness coordinators at the time, recounting telephone conversations she had with Sophie, was on top. Tammy had written the memo to DA Mark Rohrer, at my direction, and an unusual number of e-mails and correspondence filled that part of the file.

Captioned *State of Wisconsin* v. *Wolfgang Braun,* Case No. 2005CM810, and dated December 29, 2005, the memo was addressed to Rohrer and began as follows: *Per Mike's request, I am informing you of information the victim has told me over the telephone on the above entitled matter.*

It began by describing how frightened Sophie was of Wolfgang. Certain that Wolfgang would kill her if he was released on bail, she asked to be placed on the jail's victim contact list so they could immediately call to give her time to leave the area if he was let out of jail.

Ten lines down she moved on to the topic that generated my request that she draft the memo.

Sophie has stated that they live approximately 4 to 5 miles from Steven Avery's residence and that there have been some "suspicious" incidents happening, such as, she found a pair of women's panties that are not hers hidden in the house. Wolfgang Braun told Sophie with a suspicious grin that he burnt something. When she asked for an explanation, he said he burnt an old doll crib. She checked the crib and it wasn't burnt. Then she checked the burn barrels outside and they looked like they hadn't been used in a long time.

Sophie called Henrickson a few days later and said she found a gasoline can with "what looked like blood on [it] and some bloody surgical gloves" hidden in Wolfgang's tool box in one of the outbuildings.

Less than a month after Teresa Halbach was murdered, with the events fresh on her mind, Braun told our office that she suspected her husband was involved in the murder. Over the next few hours I would find out that she had provided more detail to us than she had to Convoluted Brian two years later, and we weren't the only ones in law enforcement she told. It made her account much more credible, and it threw my life into a tailspin. The rest of the file only added to the severity of the spin.

I sat there, frozen, staring over the open file. I couldn't move. How could I have forgotten, I prosecuted the case myself. Did we do it again; did we wrongfully convict an innocent man? *Twice!* I leaned back in my chair and looked out my office window at Lake Michigan's angry, cold, wintry gray waters. The lake turns clear blue in summer and even warms up enough for a swim in the latter part of July through the middle of August, at least for the brave-hearted. But I wasn't thinking of summer and I wasn't feeling brave-hearted. I was thinking of Wolfgang Braun.

It turns out that Braun had shared her suspicions about Wolfgang's involvement in the Halbach murder with the Manitowoc County Sheriff's Department, but she was met with resistance. According to Sophie, her first attempt via a phone call was met by a response that they were too busy and, as Henrickson quoted her in another memo, "didn't have time for such nonsense." Sophie provided statements and even physical evidence supporting her suspicions to two detectives, but again, according to Sophie, she was met with skepticism and her concerns were rebuffed. As luck—I fervently hoped—would have it, Dennis Jacobs was one of the detectives Sophie spoke with. Jacobs was famously heard in the documentary at the end of the first episode, asking dispatch, "Do we have Steven Avery in custody, though?"

No matter how I tried to tame the ill winds I confronted in the Wolfgang Braun file, they were headed straight in my direction in a swirling, dark, and devastating cloud—and they were coming in fast. Did the sheriff's department pass on to Kratz what Sophie told them? If they did, was Sophie's information followed up on, and were the results of the follow-up investigation disclosed to the defense?

And what about me? Why did I tell Tammy to document what Sophie had told her? Was it just a cover-your-ass memo I wanted for the file? If it was, it wasn't a very good one if it just sat in the file. Or did I make sure that a copy of the memo was sent to Kratz?

Next came the most obvious and largest question of all. Was it possible that lightning had struck twice? Had Steven Avery been wrongly convicted again, framed by the same sheriff's department that had already taken eighteen years of his life and was apparently willing to take down his sixteen-year-old disadvantaged nephew as collateral damage?

I didn't want to believe it. Everything I thought I knew about police and prosecutors and human nature itself would be turned on its head. I'd quit my job rather than continue to be a part of the process. Jim Lenk and Andy Colborn were two of the finest police officers I knew—the last cops I'd suspect of planting evidence. If there's anything such as honest to a fault, Colborn, in particular, would fit the bill. Lenk, likewise, was as solid as a Wisconsin winter is long. There's no way these guys would plant evidence, and there's no way the entire sheriff's department would follow their lead. Even the prosecutors would have to have known, because when you try a case like this, you work intimately with the police and you know every detail of the case. If evidence was planted, they would have known.

But if Sophie Braun was telling the truth, her husband, Wolfgang, not Steven Avery, was probably Teresa Halbach's killer, especially when the information she provided to Convoluted Brian is added to what she told the police. Given what Sophie told the police, I could not see how it could be any different. To find out more, it would take more digging, but it was Christmas Eve and the digging would have to wait.

I'd been obsessed with Steven Avery's case since September

2003 when a telephone call from the crime lab proved his innocence of one crime. But not that night—I would not allow a crime saga that began on a summer day in 1985 on the shores of Lake Michigan to ruin one of the most sacred nights of the year. For three decades this crime saga had festered, and no matter what I found out, it was sure to fester more.

CHAPTER 7

DEAD END

The Christmas spirit was alive and well when I returned home late that afternoon. A snowstorm was howling outside, with five inches already on the ground and seven more in the forecast before the storm moved on. With a foot of snow expected, and sustained northeasterly winds of thirty-five miles per hour off Lake Michigan, the storm fit squarely within the category of an official blizzard.

Looking forward to a relaxing evening with plenty of holiday fare to eat and drink, I went into the kitchen and started telling Jody about Sophie Braun. I was determined to avoid discussing the Avery case for the rest of the day and that night, but I knew she would ask me for the short version of what I had found in Wolfgang's files.

Jody and I met in law school, but it took us five years to figure out what was apparently obvious to our friends and our families all along—that we were made for each other. There are few of law's, or life's, complicated scenarios that don't eventually find their way into the middle of one of our conversations. I value my wife's judgment more than anyone I've ever known, with the possible exception of my dad, who taught philosophy for years at Marquette University. Dad is long gone, although when I stop long enough to quiet my mind and bother to listen, I have no doubt that he's still here to share his comforting wisdom like he always did.

I started talking, calmly at first, while I handed Jody the pile of documents I brought home from the office. I told her about Sophie reporting her suspicions that Wolfgang might have something to do with Halbach's murder to both the police and to our office during conversations with Henrickson. I mentioned that when Sophie first called the sheriff's department, they told her they were too busy and "didn't have time for such nonsense." Later, Sophie turned over some physical evidence to one of the detectives, who seemed none too interested in following up. The main point, though, I explained to Jody, was that Sophie's statement to Convoluted Brian a few years after Teresa Halbach was murdered wasn't some yarn she had spun after the fact. If Sophie was perpetuating lies, she started perpetuating them almost immediately after Halbach went missing.

"So what do you think?" I asked two minutes after giving her a stack of documents that had taken me nearly three hours to wade through at work. "Did Wolfgang do it? Was Avery wrongly convicted again? Did the cops set him up?"

She continued reviewing the paperwork without looking up and ignored me like she always does when I ask multiple questions without waiting for her reply.

"This is insane, not Colborn and Lenk, they'd never do this—they're two of the most honest cops I've ever known," I continued.

Twenty minutes later, having carefully reviewed the documents, Jody told me she really didn't know—and then she methodically went through the competing scenarios, commenting on those facts that supported and detracted from each. I wish I had an organized mind like that. It would save a great deal of time.

She thought it was likely—not 100 percent certain, but likely—that if Sophie Braun was telling the truth and, equally important, if Wolfgang was telling Sophie the truth, that Wolfgang was the killer. I had to agree: if you treat the facts in Sophie's statements as true, it's hard to reach any other conclusion.

However, Jody also felt that Sophie's description of Wolfgang sounded "off." The report was extremely detailed and expertly written. It seemed more clinical than you'd expect, almost as if it was written by a psychologist or other professional evaluating a patient rather than by a distraught victim who is so afraid she can barely think. She thought that Sophie, who was highly educated and obviously intelligent, could either keep her composure under very nerve wracking conditions and write an exceptional and accurate report, or she was fabricating the story in order to get her husband deported and permanently out of the picture. We both agreed it was difficult to tell if Sophie was telling the truth, but we needed to approach the case as if she was and analyze what it meant about the guilt or innocence of Steven Avery. Braun was at a salvage yard on the day Teresa Halbach disappeared. According to his own words, a "stupid" female photographer wanted to take pictures of their rental property out in the country. He had scratches on his back and a cut on his finger, which was still bleeding that night. She found a pair of yellow lace women's panties, which weren't hers, hidden in a closet. Before Halbach's SUV and her remains were found at the salvage yard, he told Sophie with an "unusual grin" that he burned something. When she asked what, he said he burned a doll crib, but the crib was not burned. Four or five days after Halbach was murdered, Sophie found a bloodstained surgical glove in his toolbox in one of the outbuildings, along with a gas can with a bloody fingerprint on it.

"Either one or both of them were lying," Jody succinctly concluded, "or Wolfgang Braun is your killer." Like I said, my wife has an organized mind.

Calling a halt to their Spoons competition in favor of finding out what their dad was so concerned about on Christmas Eve, the kids joined our discussion in the kitchen. The oldest started poring over some of the documents and quickly learned that Wolfgang Braun was not just a "typical" disturbed individual—he was as dangerous and depraved as they came. Whether or not he murdered Teresa Halbach, Sophie had provided ample documentation proving that her husband was a severely mentally unstable and dangerous man.

The incident, which occurred on November 6, 2005, was not an isolated incident, Sophie wrote in one of her letters, *but rather a continuation of a long history of aggressive and abusive behavior committed by Wolfgang Braun. Mr. Braun is a serious and immediate danger not only to me, but also to all women, children and animals.*

She said he once laced her food and drink with Klonopin, a major central-nervous-system depressant, and then cleaned out her bank account when she was in the hospital. On another occasion he beat her so severely that her left eardrum was shattered, resulting in some permanent hearing loss. They lived in Pittsburgh at the time, and after his arrest in that incident for assault, "terroristic threats," and unlawful restraint, he was deported.

In the throes of the vicious and confusing cycle of domestic violence, she accompanied her husband to Germany, where she spent five years "living in horror," Sophie explained. He often sexually assaulted her there after "very severe beatings" and drove her to remote areas in both Germany and Austria and beat her. The abuse continued when they returned to the United States, up to the most recent incident on November 6, one week after Teresa Halbach went missing.

Not atypical in domestic violence relationships, Sophie worked full-time while Wolfgang was rarely employed and stole what he needed from his victim—if you can term prostitutes and Internet and cable-TV pornography as needs. He destroyed plumbing and damaged windows, doors, and walls in their apartments, resulting in their eviction from several apartments. He cut electrical cords, slashed her clothing, and threatened Sophie and others with knives. He burned her important personal documents, including her driver's license and Social Security card and her children's birth certificates. He stole her passport, too.

Not unlike Steven Avery, Wolfgang Braun dabbled in animal abuse and fire. He frequently burned his wife's clothing, and she once found him sitting near the basement furnace, dousing his body with paint thinner and charcoal lighter fluid. When a former girlfriend ended their relationship after he threatened her with a knife, he doused himself with gasoline and ignited himself at her door. He was no stranger to animal abuse, either. Three of Sophie's house pets vanished or died when she lived with Wolfgang. A few months before Teresa Halbach was murdered, Sophie's German shepherd puppy "suffered a mysterious double leg fracture."

At least this is what Braun said about her husband.

If even half the information Sophie provided about her husband's criminal and mental health histories was true, it evidenced an extremely depraved mind capable of murder. It did nothing to prove he actually committed a murder—much less Teresa Halbach's murder. However, when combined with other circumstantial evidence tying him to the murder—their crossing paths at the salvage yard the day she disappeared, his odd statements to Sophie about Teresa's disappearance, and the incriminating physical evidence she found—his twisted, perverse mind and criminal history made a convincing case that Wolfgang was the culprit. The police must have taken a very close look at Wolfgang Braun, and they would have a great deal of explaining to do if they didn't. And if Steven Avery and Brendan Dassey did not murder Teresa Halbach, which is what half the country believed—at least the half that watched or read about *Making a Murderer*—then Wolfgang Braun was almost certainly the killer.

But it was all useless speculation if Braun was lying, and the only way to figure that out was to dig further into the documents I passed over in the office but now had at my side. On one side of the ledger was the accompanying documentation that Sophie provided with her statement. It corroborated much of her information, including dates and locations of prior arrests, along with the names, addresses, and telephone numbers of four mental health hospitals in Germany and Pittsburgh where Wolfgang had been treated, paired with the name of at least one of his physicians. Such detail was either ironclad proof that Wolfgang was certifiably crazy and capable of murder—or Sophie was the best manipulator I've seen. And with over twenty-five years in the business, I've seen more than my share of manipulators.

But still, there was plenty of reason to doubt Sophie's credibility. Tammy Henrickson noted in her memo that she had a "strange feeling" about Sophie. *I'm not sure if she's sincere, or maybe she's very angry with the defendant and wants revenge, or if she's just very manipulative,* she wrote.

Calling her husband a psychopath, Sophie angrily threatened to go to the media, the governor, and "whoever else she has to, in the state of Wisconsin, if he's set free." And in another call to Henrickson a few weeks later, she said our office would be held responsible if Wolfgang was released and came and killed her, adding that we don't "have a very good track record of convicting the right people."

Later, when I had to dismiss a felony charge in return for Wolfgang's agreement to plead in on two misdemeanors, because she showed up twenty minutes late for a preliminary hearing, Sophie had to admit that she was the one who contacted Wolfgang after his release from jail, and not the other way around—and then only after I told her the defense had two witnesses ready to testify to prove it.

It was maddening. As soon as I was convinced Sophie was lying, something she said, with accompanying proof, changed my mind. They were classic statements of a domestic violence victim in the throes of fear and despair. It's not unusual for a victim in an abusive relationship to initiate contact with the perpetrator soon after he beat her—sometimes the victim even posts his bail. The detail and sheer volume of the information, much less the extent of the abuse she suffered at his hands, showed she was terrified of her husband. Either that or she went to the most extraordinary lengths I've seen in twenty-eight years on the job to make it seem that way.

I have experienced being held as his captive, he first destroys all telephones or cuts the phone line, he disconnects the electricity, and he tortures the victim with physical and mental abuse, she told Henrickson in an e-mail. If Mr. Braun is allowed to go free, he will certainly hunt me down and hurt me or kill me.

Obviously, I had believed her at the time. Wolfgang's lawyer had filed a motion to modify bail from cash to personal recognizance. For some inexplicable reason the INS had dropped his detainer, so if the motion was granted, Wolfgang would be released from jail. In what I thought was a pretty decent argument at the motion hearing, I pointed out the obvious flight risk, and the even greater risk to Sophie's safety, even making a few of Sophie's letters outlining his violent history and mental health treatment part of the record. Despite my objection the presiding judge granted the motion. When Sophie learned that Wolfgang was free to move around as he pleased, she sounded genuinely terrified that he would find her and kill her.

There was, of course, another possibility. Sophie could be truthful about Wolfgang's past and the abuse he inflicted upon her over the years, but lying about his apparent connection to Teresa Halbach's murder. It wouldn't be the first time a domestic violence victim exaggerated or even concocted a story to make certain her abuser was held in jail longer than he otherwise would be. By doing so, she would get some breathing space or more time to arrange things in order to flee.

To come up with such a detailed account of why she thought Wolfgang may have been involved in the murder, Sophie would have had to follow the news about Teresa Halbach's disappearance extremely carefully. But many of the details of her story matched what was objectively true, including the proximity in time and distance between Halbach's murder and Wolfgang's beating of Sophie after she refused to help him obtain legal status in the country—the only way he could leave the country without being stopped at the border. The incident occurred less than eighteen hours after Halbach's vehicle was found only six miles up the road.

Concern over his immigration status also led to Wolfgang's second arrest, two and a half months later, when he barged in and ransacked Sophie's house looking for his papers. He asked the deputies to check for his paperwork before they took him to jail. In the words of the police report, *he appeared to become more agitated after no paperwork was found.* He braced his feet against the kitchen's door frame and had to be pepper-sprayed in the face by the deputies before they could haul him out of the house.

I had reviewed every document and note in both of Wolfgang Braun's files and talked the meaning and import of their contents to death with anyone in the house who was willing to listen. But in the end it proved impossible to answer the question upon which the entire Avery case seemed to hinge: Was Sophie Braun telling the truth? If she was, her husband was almost certainly the killer.

Well after midnight, when everyone else had gone up to bed, I sat in the living room, turned off all but the Christmas tree lights, and reflected about what had happened in the last week. A television documentary and a German national with an expired visa had transformed what for ten years I thought was an open-and-shut murder case into a classic whodunit. Millions—perhaps tens of millions worldwide—believed Steven Avery and Brendan Dassey were victims of a local justice system rivaling a banana republic in its corruption. Now I wondered myself if they might be right. Had I gone mad?

Making a Murderer was leaping onto the national and even international stage—most notably in the United Kingdom and in the Far East, where it made front-page headlines in Beijing. Confirming its cultural import, it made its way into late-night television comedy shows and even the music industry in the form of the rock band The Arcs' not-so-smashing hit, "Lake Superior," and several others that followed. Legions of Netflix viewers who were transformed into online sleuths parsed through the minutiae of a case that took eighteen months to investigate and six weeks to try and formed unshakeable opinions about Avery's and Dassey's innocence or guilt. If the O.J. Simpson case defined the last century's obsession with American crime and its system of justice, *Making a Murderer* was making its own case for owning that distinction in this one.

All of which meant exactly nothing for those of us at ground zero. With unyielding sympathy for its protagonists and considerable contempt for the police and prosecutors who sent them to prison, it added yet another layer to an already tragedy-laden crime story that had bedeviled my hometown for thirty years. In a narrative widely accepted by nearly everyone whose only familiarity with the Avery case was the documentary itself, local police were all but convicted of planting evidence to frame Steven Avery a second time and taking down his sixteen-year-old cognitively delayed nephew as an unfortunate but necessary bit of collateral damage.

The success of the series heaped additional suffering upon two families that had already endured more pain than any family ever should. Any hope of privacy for Penny Beerntsen and her family vanished within a week's time. But worst of all was the indifference with which the series treated a life-filled beautiful young woman named Teresa Halbach, whose memory was lost amidst the white noise of *Making a Murderer* and whose family was left to wonder if it could possibly get any worse.

A week earlier I had sat transfixed, captivated by the telling of a crime story I'd been obsessed with for years, but also threatened by its challenge to everything I thought I knew. The revelation or, more accurately, my rediscovery of an alternate suspect in the person of Wolfgang Braun had added to a growing doubt that

I could no longer ignore. My efforts to determine whether Sophie Braun was telling the truth, though aided by my family, had reached a dead end.

While clinging to claims of objectivity in one interview after another in the coming weeks, the creators of *Making a Murderer* would correctly point out that truth is elusive in the Steven Avery case. But elusive or not, I aimed to find out. I went to bed that night determined to find it. With as open and unbiased a mind as possible, I would start over from scratch. I would revisit the investigation and prosecution of Steven Avery and Brendan Dassey from beginning to end and follow the facts wherever they led. If they ended with a conclusion that Wolfgang Braun was the culprit, then I would come forward and notify the court of what I had learned. If not, my original beliefs were confirmed.

CHAPTER 8

THE RAV4

Before setting out on what turned into a two-month journey through the ins and outs of the Avery case, I had to set some ground rules. First, what facts would I consider? Which of the trees in the forest were fair game to rely upon as I navigated my way through the thickets and the thorns of the Avery case? Should I limit myself to only the evidence the jury was allowed to consider at trial? Did I need to ignore everything else I knew or was able to find out about the case and about Steven Avery, including his past?

There are good reasons for the law's exclusion of certain evidence at trial. After all, a jury is entrusted to decide a defendant's fate, sometimes for the rest of his life, and in some states his life itself. But I wasn't deciding whether Steven Avery and Brendan Dassey should be imprisoned for life, or in Dassey's case for the next thirty-two years. Two separate juries and judges and courts of appeal have already decided all that.

I decided that my test would be the same question that is at the root of most of the rules of evidence that apply in trials—whether the evidence was reliable. I would approach the evidence with skepticism, but if it appeared reliable after due diligence and careful consideration, I would treat it as fair game. If not, it would be out of bounds or, in keeping with my chosen metaphor, not to be used as a guidepost in my journey through the Avery woods. Endeavoring to find the truth as best as I could, I would not be constricted by the rules of evidence, but would consider whatever common sense dictated, as long as it was reliable.

Making a Murderer failed to contain itself to just the evidence admitted at trial. If I were to truly discover the whole truth behind Teresa Halbach's murder, then I would have to consider all of the reliable but inadmissible evidence out there, not just the evidence the documentarians chose to present. Others would have to judge for themselves the reliability of the facts I chose to include. I would present the facts and let my readers decide.

My other ground rule—and this one would be more difficult to follow—was that I would do everything in my power to prevent any preconceived notions from getting in the way. I had privately condemned the filmmakers for doing just that during numerous media interviews in the preceding weeks, and I did not want to make the same mistake. We are all susceptible to developing agendas or preconceived notions that blind us from the truth. It would not be easy, but I would need to be constantly on guard against this tendency to which none of us are immune.

After hearing Special Prosecutor Ken Kratz recount Brendan Dassey's confession in graphic detail at his breaking news press conference, a decade earlier, I had fallen into the trap myself. I turned off the critical thinking switch after that, even when I wrote Part 3 of *The Innocent Killer. Why waste the time and effort?* I thought. *Steven Avery was obviously guilty.*

But I had missed a few important details and, as several Facebook commentators and Amazon reviewers pointed out after *Making a Murderer* aired, I had inaccurately stated a few of the facts. None of substance that would have affected my view of Avery's guilt at the time, but it was sloppy and understandably upsetting to readers convinced after watching the documentary that Avery and Dassey were innocent. For some of them, it was evidence that I wrote the book as a tool of the state in order to cover up police and prosecutor misconduct.

The accusation is nonsense. On the other hand, our minds are easily confused when we are overly confident about what we think we know. This time I was determined not to let that happen. Once we assume something to be true, by an unintended but skewed perspective from what we do for a living or stubborn habits of thinking, our false assumptions and opinions are difficult to dislodge. It is human nature—a weakness from which none of us are exempt—but it was completely at odds with what I was determined to accomplish: to once and for all find the truth, the whole truth, and nothing but the truth about the Avery case, so help me, God.

I needed to do one more thing before I set out on my journey. I ask juries to do it all the time: Don't lose the forest for the trees because you are sure to get lost amidst the fog. Concentrate on one bit of evidence to the exclusion of the rest, and you will never succeed in finding the truth. Like the other two ground rules I set before heading out on my journey, this rule had to be applied equally to both sides—to the facts and circumstances suggestive of innocence, and to those supporting guilt.

In practice this meant that I had to keep two conflicting ideas in mind at the same time. Ever mindful of the defense theory that police had conspired to plant evidence in an effort to frame Avery and Dassey, I had to do so without forgetting the prosecution's argument that the very physical evidence the defense claimed was planted pointed squarely to their guilt.

I stood back for a few minutes and took in the size and basic shape of the Avery and Dassey cases. The trail wove through plenty of thickets and thorns, but even from this distance it looked well marked. This would be no easy journey, but not an insurmountable one, either, as long as I kept my wits about me and paid close attention to where I was going.

* * *

I began where all journeys do, at the trailhead. But in this case it was difficult to find. The prosecution maintained it was when Teresa Halbach's RAV4 was discovered at the salvage yard on November 5, five days after she was murdered there on Halloween Day. The defense, however, insisted it began two days earlier when they claimed Manitowoc County sergeant Andy Colborn called in the RAV4's license plates to dispatch after finding it somewhere out in the county before he, and presumably some of his partners in crime, planted it at the salvage yard to set up Steven Avery.

To be fair to the defense, I had to start my journey where they claimed the trail began, so my task at this early stage was to find out if there was anything to their accusation, parroted by *Making a Murderer,* that Colborn had seen the RAV4 somewhere other than the salvage yard two days before it was found. But I had to do so without losing sight of the entire forest, which required, as it did in most cases, that I hold two contradictory possibilities in my mind at the same time. First, that Steven Avery hid the RAV4 partly concealed under branches and another car's hood at the edge of his property after he and his sixteen-year-old nephew murdered Teresa Halbach. And second, that Colborn, probably with help, planted the RAV4 at the salvage yard as part of a grand conspiracy to frame Avery for Halbach's murder in retaliation for his thirty-six-million-dollar lawsuit against Manitowoc County.

Was the RAV4 planted or not? The answer lay in the clumsy language of the law. When deciding questions disputed by the parties, the trier of fact is to consider the "totality of the facts" and "circumstances and the reasonable inferences therefrom." To do so, I needed to compare two transcripts—one from *Making a Murderer* and the other from the trial—both of which, thanks to crowdsourcing efforts of interested and concerned citizens, were available online.

I assumed as I sat down and compared the transcripts that the answer would be a close call—that, as is typically the case, both sides had marshaled facts in support of their position, leaving the answer hidden among different shades of gray. Maybe the facts would be so convoluted that I would not feel comfortable enough to make the call one way or the other and, if so, I'd have to move on to the next stage of the journey.

What I found, instead, was an instance of selective editing that would make any propagandist proud. First, portions of Colborn's actual trial testimony (bracketed below) were removed from the documentary, to make it appear he answered a question in the affirmative that he never answered at all. Second, a question that would have helped explain his side of the story to the viewers is never heard. If you follow along carefully, you will see what I mean.

> *Strang: Well, and you can understand how someone listening to that might think that you were calling in a license plate that you were looking at on the back end of a 1999 Toyota. From listening to that tape, you can understand why someone might think that, can't you?*
>
> *[Kratz: It's a conclusion, Judge. He's conveying the problems to the jury.]*
>
> *[The Court: I agree, the objection is sustained.]*
>
> *[Strang: This call sounded like hundreds of other license plate or registration checks you have done through dispatch before?]*
>
> *Colborn: Yes.*

Whoa! The documentarians had literally spliced testimony to manipulate and distort the truth.

And that wasn't all. Colborn explained to Kratz on direct examination that a detective from Calumet County had given him the plates of the missing young woman's vehicle earlier that evening, and the purpose of his call into dispatch was merely to confirm that he had the right information before he started look-ing. But the documentarians chose not to include his explana-tion—just like they chose not to include his redirect examination, noted below, when he made the purpose for his call even clearer:

> *Kratz: Mr. Strang asked whether or not it was common for you to check up on other agencies, or perhaps I'm—I'm mis-phrasing that, but when you are assisting another agency, do you commonly verify information that's provided by another agency?*
>
> *Colborn: All the time. I'm just trying to get . . . You know, a lot of times when you are driving a car, you can't stop and take notes, so I'm trying to get things in my head. And by calling the dispatch center and running that plate again, it got it in my head who that vehicle belonged to and what type of vehicle that plate is associated with.*

I noticed when I watched the documentary that the inclusion of cross-examination and rebuttal during the Avery and Dassey trials appeared to depend upon whether doing so would advance or detract from the defense theory. At times it was as though the viewers were jurors who were only shown the case for the defense. Initially I had no idea the editing was this extreme.

Colborn had provided a reasonable explanation for calling in the plates that the filmmakers took great pains to prevent me and millions of other viewers from knowing. As I looked back on how I felt watching the documentary, I realized they had done it with great skill. Colborn's call into dispatch, along with his sketchy and unconvincing testimony, had shocked me if not into disbe-lief, then at least into having serious doubt. But having reviewed the trial transcript, it was obvious they were trying to pull the wool over everyone's eyes.

In a moment of high drama and with a spring in its step, *Making a Murderer* had jumped on the defense bandwagon with reck-less abandon when it played the dispatch tape to conjure up an image of Colborn calling in the plate after finding the RAV4 somewhere out in the county other than at the salvage yard. They followed up with carefully edited portions of Colborn's not very successful efforts to stay cool under the blistering cross-examination of Dean Strang, who had uncharacteristically taken over the bad-cop role from his partner, Jerry Buting, to whom the job came much more naturally.

The documentary hinted at Colborn's answer as to why else he might have called in the plate, but only in the most oblique and unconvincing way. Add the foreboding music and footage of geese taking flight from a dismal-looking, fallow farm field—and the fact that they omitted the entire redirect examination of Colborn by Kratz, where he explained himself in a direct and clear answer to an equally direct and clear question—and you have an impressive, though pitiful, instance of unadulterated propaganda.

It was far too early to draw any firm conclusions about Avery's and Dassey's guilt or innocence and what, if any, evidence was planted by the police. But the documentarians had deliberately distorted the truth, and to be fair to the prosecution—as well as to Colborn, whose reputation the documentary has forever tarnished—I decided (reasonably, I think) to keep this in mind going forward as I evaluated the rest of the evidence.

Making a Murderer's manipulation of the evidence alone did not prove that Colborn, and possibly others, did not plant the RAV4. I had promised myself not to give the cops or anyone else the benefit of the doubt. There's a reason most states and the federal courts don't permit the results of lie detector tests into evidence at trials—it's simply not possible to tell scientifically, with 100 percent certainty, whether someone is telling the truth.

Also, it's not just the facts that tell the whole story. The law's clumsily worded rule puts it that "the totality of the facts and circumstances" are to be considered when deciding disputed issues. Maybe this oft-quoted rule of law is not as empty a phrase as it sounds. The more I considered not just the facts, but the circumstances surrounding the discovery of the RAV4 at the salvage yard, the more I was convinced that Colborn was telling the truth and was merely doing his job.

To many viewers, on one side of the equation was what appeared to be Colborn's nervous, defensive appearance while testifying in court, but we all have different demeanors on the witness stand. If we're a nervous sort, our discomfort is exaggerated under the glare of television lights in a packed courtroom hanging on our every word—especially if we happen to be an honest cop accused of serious misconduct that goes against everything we are trained to do.

You're a cop walking up to the witness stand dressed in your uncomfortably starched and stiff sheriff's department uniform. Your department-issued Glock, placed awkwardly in a holster at your side, scrapes against the microphone, emitting a loud screech as you try to maneuver it along with the rest of your body into the barely wide-enough witness stand. The defense has already accused you of being a corrupt cop out to get an innocent man. The case may very well hang in the balance, soon to tilt one way or the other, depending upon how you hold up under questioning by a highly skilled and intelligent defense attorney.

Now ask yourself, how would you feel? How would you do on the witness stand under the glaring lights of the camera and the watchful eyes of the jurors?

If you are blessed with being comfortable in your own skin, if you can rub shoulders effortlessly with anyone—anywhere— under any circumstance, if you're a well-trained actor or politician, then even if you're telling the biggest whopper you've ever told, you will come off as cool and collected on the witness stand.

In the end our appearance on the witness stand is much more a function of our personality than whether or not we are telling the truth. No doubt there are exceptions when a witness appears nervous because he or she is lying. In my experience, at least, people who perjure themselves on the witness stand, including the one or two cops I have suspected of doing so over the years, are accustomed to lying and come off just fine.

What about Colborn's motivation, then, to plant evidence and set up Avery in revenge, out of anger, to escape financial ruin, to avoid embarrassment, or any of the other reasons associated with Avery's thirty-six-million-dollar wrongful conviction lawsuit that the defense threw into the hopper? This was a recurring theme of the defense and of *Making a Murderer* in support of their entire frame-up defense. At first blush it was fairly compelling.

Sergeant Colborn and Lieutenant Jim Lenk had been deposed just a few weeks before Halbach disappeared, and they had reportedly taken a beating by Avery's lawyers. Looking back at it, I'm sure they wished they could have stayed away from the investigation.

Upon closer inspection Colborn and Lenk's connection to Avery's 1985 wrongful conviction was tenuous at best. They weren't defendants in the lawsuit because despite all the condemnation from the defense team at trial and in *Making a Murderer*, their sins were not even sins of omission, which is what Avery's lawyers were accusing them of and *Making a Murderer* was condemning them for. It turns out they did exactly what they should have done—as the jurors evidently concluded, and as most Netflix viewers likely would have, if they had been given all the facts.

The defense theory rested upon a telephone call that Colborn received from a Green Bay detective that could have led to Avery's release in 1995, ten years after Avery was wrongly convicted and eight years before DNA finally did set him free. The detective had called to report that an inmate in the Brown County Jail was claiming that he had assaulted a woman jogging on a beach in Manitowoc County ten years earlier, presumably Penny Beerntsen, the victim in Avery's wrongful conviction case. The inmate claimed that someone else had been convicted of the assault and was presently serving time in prison for a crime he did not commit. Gregory Allen, the real assailant, must have experienced a rare moment of shame.

Colborn was a corrections officer at the jail at the time, with neither the experience nor the authority to investigate any crime, much less a ten-year-old sexual assault and attempted he'd never heard of, where the court of appeals had already affirmed the defendant's conviction. On duty he took the call from the Green Bay detective and did exactly what protocol required. He passed the information up the chain of command. The information must have made it to the very top because word came back down from the sheriff telling Colborn to stay out of it—they already had the right guy.

Colborn's minimal involvement in the wrongful conviction— and the 1995 telephone call from the Green Bay detective was the extent of it—seems an unlikely motive to plant evidence and risk his entire career. Was it possible he was so upset by his recent grilling, at his recent deposition, or had some sort of a visceral reaction against Avery, who was present during most of the depositions? Was it possible that he was so loyal to his department and county that he would risk prosecution for evidence planting and perjury? Sure, but there was no evidence backing that up, and I had promised myself I would not engage in pure speculation on behalf of either side.

And there was another circumstance within the "totality of facts and circumstances" that made it less likely that Colborn had planted the car. While not impossible, it would be difficult to drive Halbach's RAV4 to where they allegedly hid it on the salvage yard without being seen by a passerby or being noticed by one of the many family members who live there. The property is difficult to access from the rear, which is where the vehicle was found, so it would have to be pushed or driven through the entrance, right past the Avery family homes. It would be difficult to remain undetected, even at night.

The vehicle was hidden in the ideal location for Steven Avery— or I suppose some other culprit in the family or connected to the salvage yard—who would need to hide it before disposing of it later in the "car crusher." The killer would have to put off that task until no one was around to wonder why he was destroying a relatively new and fair-conditioned vehicle. Also, the vehicle would need to be stripped of any identifying information, such as the VIN plate on the dashboard, possibly the engine, rims/tires, and also drained of all fluids, before being hoisted into the car crusher—all of it making plenty of noise.

Fairness for the defense required that I not allow my assumptions to cause a knee-jerk reaction. I knew and respected Colborn and Lenk for years, but I could not permit my gut instinct, which said they would never do such a thing, to affect my evaluation of the evidence.

For the prosecution, conversely, fairness forbade me to consider unwarranted speculation and attacks on the officers' character and motivation if these allegations did not stand up to close scrutiny.

For both sides, going forward, I would not forget what I had learned about the RAV4. If the police planted it, I would not have lost sight of that damning fact. But the evidence suggested they didn't. What's more, it appeared the defense team and the documentarians manipulated the facts to suggest they did.

In the end I chalked up round one as a win for the prosecution. But the game—or the journey—had just begun and I had a feeling the next round would be a much closer call.

CHAPTER 9

THE KEY

It was one of the most damning pieces of evidence in Steven Avery's entire trial. Not literally a smoking gun, the ignition key to Teresa Halbach's RAV4 was trumpeted as such to the jury by both sides.

But whom did it damn? The accused or his accusers?

Neither side disputed that Halbach drove her RAV4 to the Avery Salvage Yard on Halloween Day, 2005, but their opinions concerning what happened to the RAV4's ignition key after she arrived sharply diverged.

As the prosecution would have it, Avery tucked it into the back of a small bookcase cabinet in his bedroom after he and Dassey murdered her. It was the perfect place to hide the key until he could later retrieve it, when he had the time and the opportunity to dispose of the car. With the garage door shut and the RAV4 safely hidden from view, the theory went, Avery cleaned up the blood and anything else that might have drawn suspicion, until he could dispose of the final piece of evidence linking him to the murder—the RAV4. If he had succeeded, the volunteer search party would not have discovered the RAV4, and grounds for a search warrant would have been shaky at best. Teresa Halbach's murder might have never been solved.

Steven Avery had already chosen the method of the vehicle's

demise, went the prosecution's theory. He would flatten it out in the "car crusher," which, as I recall from the day I was there, was located almost as far away from his house trailer as one could get. It was about 380 feet away from where Pam Sturm and her daughter found the RAV4. With the ignition key tucked safely in the back of his cabinet, close to his bed, he would bide his time until he had the opportunity to dispose of the car. To the prosecution it all made perfect sense.

The defense cried foul, however. As luck would have it, it was Colborn and Lenk, *Making a Murderer*'s designated villains, who found the key. It wasn't just bad luck; it was dumb luck, too. Had it not been for the higher-ups' well-intended but unwise decision to allow Manitowoc County officers to participate in the search, as long as an officer from another jurisdiction accompanied them, they never would have been in Avery's residence. And opened themselves up to charges of evidence planting.

With Steven Avery's thirty-six-million-dollar lawsuit pending against the county and its former sheriff and DA, the sheriff's department had a clear-cut conflict of interest. In hindsight, it would've been better for both Colborn and Lenk if they had not been asked to assist in further searches, once the RAV4 was located at the salvage yard.

To make matters worse, a prior search to collect specific items in Steven Avery's bedroom had come up empty-handed.

The gift could not have been wrapped any better for the dream team defense of Buting and Strang. They took what in a normal case would have been a compelling piece of evidence for the state and turned it on its head. Based on how Buting described the discovery of the key, it was nearly impossible to believe it had not been planted. Here's an excerpt from *Making a Murderer:*

> *"That key does not fall from . . . you know, in between the backboard and the frame of that little bookcase and find its way underneath a pair of slippers. Yeah, it just does. . . . You know, things fall straight down, thanks to gravity."*

MICHAEL GRIESBACH

While permitting Manitowoc County officers to participate in the searches was perhaps not the best decision, it certainly doesn't prove Colborn and Lenk planted the key. Earlier, I had assumed they had an explanation about how they found it when previous searches came up empty-handed. After all, the jury heard *all* the evidence—not just the media accounts or what a pair of documentarians a decade later chose to include. They obviously must have accepted the explanation, since there's no other way to reconcile their verdict of guilt.

I assumed it was just one more in a series of uncanny coincidences in how the investigation unfolded, but it was just that—an assumption. Conflicted out of the Avery case and with my own caseload to keep up with, I knew no more about the Avery case than what the media reported. Now, though, I aimed to find out.

Gearing up for a deep dive into the details surrounding the discovery of the key, I turned to the trial and documentary transcripts, as I did concerning Colborn calling in the plates to the RAV4, but also to the video clips in the documentary itself. After three frustrating hours of searching for the relevant portions of the transcripts and tuning into the right episode of *Making a Murderer,* I waded in with eyes wide open to find out whether the documentary had at least presented both sides.

Aided again by two smart, determined, and detail-oriented Redditors as obsessed with the Avery case as I was, we were able to uncover what the documentarians were up to with regard to the key. The manipulation of Colborn's testimony regarding calling in the RAV4's plates could not hold a candle to its distortion of how he and Lenk found the key. It was the mother of all manipulations—at least up to that point in my review of the files. *Making a Murderer* had once again confounded the truth.

If a picture's worth a thousand words, then streaming video is worth more than a million. The documentarians took full advantage of their awesome power by showing close-up images of the key sticking out like a sore thumb on the floor of Steven Avery's bedroom and an empty cabinet *after* the key had been found and *after* the cabinet had been moved and emptied of its contents. Inserting these images into the midst of carefully edited testimony of police officers fumbling on the witness stand, trying to explain themselves, it was impossible to conceive how the key could have been missed during previous searches. The documentary effectively convicted Colborn and Lenk of planting the key.

Those who knew no more about the Avery case than what the documentary chose to show them would never know this, but both Colborn and Lenk did have an explanation for how they found the key. Running contrary to the documentarians' views, their explanations did not make the cut. Netflix viewers may or may not have been satisfied with the explanation, but they should have been given the opportunity to decide for themselves.

Here is Colborn's unedited testimony concerning the key at Avery's trial to help you decide.

> DA Kratz (K.): In performing that search, Sergeant Colborn, did you move or manipulate this piece of furniture at all?
>
> Colborn (C.): Yes, sir.
>
> K.: Can you describe that for the jury, please?
>
> C.: As I stated before, we were looking for specific printed [materials] or photographs. There is a narrow area between this cabinet and this desk, right there. And in order to make sure that there was no evidence or anything else that we needed lodged between there, I actually tipped this to the side and twisted it away from the wall.
>
> K.: If you can describe that further, I don't know if you can do it with your words, or show us with your hands, how you did it?
>
> C.: I will be the first to admit, I wasn't any too gentle, as we were, you know, getting exasperated. I handled it rather roughly, twisting it, shaking it, pulling it.
>
> K.: And that's the cabinet that you are talking about?

C.: Yes, this piece of furniture right here, a cabinet.

K.: I'm sorry. Sergeant, in shaking and twisting that particular cabinet, did you pull it away from the wall itself that you can see behind there?

C.: Yes, I did.

K.: After that process was complete, were the items— The binder that we can see in the lower left-hand corner of the cabinet; can you point to that, please? Was that, and the other items within that cabinet, removed and examined by yourself and your . . . other members of your team?

C.: Yes, sir.

K.: Did you have occasion to replace those items into that cabinet after having pulled it from the wall?

C.: Yes, sir.

K.: What was done with the cabinet after that thorough search of the . . . of those materials was completed?

C.: The items that we didn't use or collect as evidence—that binder and some of the other things there were kind of stuffed, rather forcefully, back in there. And other items that we were going to collect as evidence were—we had so many that we didn't have a container in the room large enough to hold them all. So Lieutenant Lenk exited the bedroom to get a larger container and I began to search this desk here.

K.: By a "larger container," what are you talking about?

C.: A box.

K.: Now, at this time, that is, as the search was completed, what was done with that piece of furniture; what was done with the cabinet itself?

C.: It was still kind of away from the wall, but it was more or less stuffed back into its original position.

K.: Now, other than the bedroom slippers being pushed to the side, had anything else changed, other than the pulling out and the twisting and the jostling of the cabinet?

C.: As we looked at the cabinet, it appeared that in the process of us stuffing everything back into the cabinet, we had separated the back of the cabinet, the small piece of paneling that would be the back of the cabinet, from the frame of the cabinet itself.

K.: Let me stop you there. Did you have occasion, then, to go look at the back of this piece of furniture, the back of the cabinet, after this key was processed?

C.: Yes.

K.: I know I'm jumping ahead just a little bit, but could you describe what you saw; could you describe the back panel of the cabinet?

C.: It would be made out of a . . . I'm trying to think of the right word, like a piece of wood, the same thickness maybe as a piece of paneling that one would put on a wall. You know, it's a thin piece of wood, it's not—it's not like it's a quarter-inch piece of plywood nailed to the back of the cabinet. It's a thin piece of wood. The piece of furniture itself is old and not in the best state of repair. And I believe it was just very small, short brads or nails that held the piece of paneling or the piece of wood to the back of the cabinet. And I'm sure that when we were putting things in, we exercised more than enough force to push it away. And there was a gap now between the back of the—the piece of paneling on the back of the cabinet and the frame of the cabinet itself.

Colborn is then cross-examined by Strang:

Attorney Strang (S.): Now, that thorough search, had you been working on the cabinet and on the desk?

C.: Yes, sir.

S.: You described yourself as being, I think you said, "none too gentle"?

C.: That's true.

S.: With the cabinet. And explained, "I wasn't any too
gentle, as we were getting exasperated"?

C.: Yes, sir.

S.: What was exasperating you about the cabinet, or
that bedroom, on November 8, 2005?

C.: The content of the material that we were collecting.

S.: So you felt exasperated and that caused you to take
it out on the cabinet?

C.: Didn't exactly take it out on the cabinet. It just
caused us to not be gentle in the handling of the
material.

While Colborn and Lenk's explanation of how they found
the key did not make the cut for *Making a Murderer,* carefully se-
lected portions of Calumet County deputy Daniel Kucharski's
testimony did.

Per the decision to permit Manitowoc County officers to participate in the search, as long as they were teamed up with an officer
from another jurisdiction, Kucharski was assigned to accompany
Colborn and Lenk on the day the key was found. With extensive
editing—at times even interposing words and phrases from different points in Kucharski's testimony—along with misleading
images of the key and the cabinet taken on different days and at
a different time than when the key was found, the documentarians beautifully set up the police conspiracy theory. And, of
course, they left out Calumet County deputy Kucharski's explanation of how the key was found. The documentarians may think
the explanation is bunk, but viewers and readers should have all
the facts in order to decide. Here, then, is Kucharski's response
from the witness stand when asked how the key came to be found.

*"We were searching the cabinet. Lieutenant Lenk and Sergeant
Colborn were searching the cabinet next to the desk. They were
pulling books in and out of the cabinet, photographs in and out*

of the cabinet. They were moving the cabinet, eventually putting the books and photographs and things back into the cabinet, banging things around, moving it. We believe it either fell out of the cabinet or from some place hidden inside the cabinet or underneath the cabinet, or in back of the cabinet."

With the key a major part of both sides' case, I wanted to learn as much as possible from the most reliable source. Calumet County deputy Kucharski seemed like an obvious choice. Not accused of being part of the Manitowoc frame-up, and in the room with Colborn and Lenk when the key was found, if anyone should be able to shed some light, it was Kucharski. Police reports are more thorough than court testimony, so that's where I turned.

On November 8, the day the key was found, the search team of Kucharski, Lenk, and Colborn were given specific and detailed instructions about what they were to look for. Kucharski's reports indicated: *[They were to] collect the HP computer in living room, any computer related storage devices, all pornographic material, and a swab of DNA testing of suspected blood in the bathroom.*

All three officers were together in the relatively small bedroom and in visual and verbal contact at all times while searching the bedroom, the report continued. *Kucharski photographed and collected pornographic material found in the bedroom along with misc. ammunition, a cloth rope and a pillow with a red stain on it.*

I was surprised to learn how close Kucharski was to Colborn and Lenk when the key was found: *Sgt. Colborn was approximately two to three feet away from me finishing up the search of a desk area, and Lt. Lenk was approximately one foot from me finishing up the search of a cabinet located next to the desk.*

Given the significance of the key and how it was found, here is Deputy Kucharski's unedited recounting of how the key was found:

LENK had gone through the cabinet and then he and COL-BORN moved the cabinet around looking for pictures stuck in the back of the cabinet. I was in visual contact when they were doing this as they were only a couple of feet from me. Sgt. COLBORN began to put the books that were taken out of the cabinet back into it. He was having some resistance against the books, they were caught on something, and he pushed on the books banging them into the back of the cabinet. Lt. LENK left the room to call the command post for some boxes for the pornographic materials that we had found. Sgt. COLBORN went back to searching through the magazines under the desk area. I was completing the search of the nightstand. After approximately two minutes, Lt. LENK came back to the room. He entered the doorway of the room approximately one foot away from me, pointed to the floor and said, "There's a key here." He pointed to the floor next to the cabinet by a pair of men's slippers.

It was strike two against *Making a Murderer.* The documentarians had done a masterful job. By repeatedly showing video clips of the key in plain view on the floor, with books inside the cabinet and items on top, and by carefully editing testimony from Deputy Kucharski and altogether omitting the details from Colborn and Lenk, they convinced Netflix viewers worldwide—beyond a shadow of a doubt—that Colborn and Lenk had planted the key.

Granted, had they included Colborn and Lenk's explanation of how they happened upon the key, viewers' opinions of their account's credibility would be split and, like every other issue in the Avery case, hotly contested. By choosing to hide the explanation of the police because it ran counter to their chosen agenda, the documentarians denied viewers the opportunity to decide for themselves. By skillful editing and their expert use of video and sound, they made the decision for everyone else, and not for the first time in the upcoming weeks did the word "censorship" come to my mind.

I had promised myself I would not let my favorable impression of Colborn and Lenk affect my evaluation of whether they were telling the truth. After all, I could imagine without justifying it for a minute that convinced of Steven Avery's guilt, but concerned there was not enough evidence to convict him, Colborn and/or Lenk could have planted the key to strengthen the case. Short of being in the room when they found the key, I realize it's impossible to know with 100 percent certainty. My opinion is just that— an opinion. But at least it's based upon the "totality of the facts and circumstances," as encouraged by the law—not just the ones pushed by the defense and fed to me by *Making a Murderer.*

CHAPTER 10

THE BLOOD

In one of the most dramatic turns of events since Teresa Halbach went missing, topped only by Ken Kratz's press conference where he recounted Brendan Dassey's confession in unnecessary and horrific detail, Jerome Buting proclaimed a "red-letter day" for the defense.

The defense had requested to examine the court file from Steven Avery's 1985 wrongful conviction case. It was the same file—actually a box full of court records and exhibits—the deputy clerk had found during Avery's appeal ten years earlier. Buting walked into the clerk's office at the appointed time and saw the box just sitting there, unattended, behind the counter.

Buting had stumbled upon an explanation for how Avery's blood found its way into Halbach's car—it was from the vial! The defense needed to tie the sheriff's department to the vial, but it helped if the alleged conspirators had conspired previously. The courthouse bailiffs were sheriff's department deputies with keys to the clerk's office and therefore access to the vial. They, or one or more of their colleagues, must have gone into the clerk's office after hours, opened the package of evidence from the 1985 file, and secreted some of Avery's blood from the vial. Local reaction to the blood vial defense varied with opinions largely depending upon the opinion holder's preconceived notions with regard to the police.

Half a block from the courthouse, right downtown, Warrens Restaurant has been the pulse of the community in Manitowoc for almost fifty years. It's one of those greasy spoons that grace most every American small town. With bottomless cups of coffee and a menu of breakfast items that are more than just passable, it's an early-morning gathering spot for local attorneys and anyone else who enjoys shooting the bull. Local, state, national, or beyond—there is no problem too large or too small for the folks at Warrens to solve. Mostly, though, it's a place of friendship and fellowship, where like at Cheers, everyone knows your name.

As a morning person and a hopeless coffee addict, I'm a semi-regular at Warrens, stopping in a few mornings every week. It opens at six and I like to get there around six-thirty to join the earliest of the early-morning crowd.

The Avery case was the chief topic of discussion at Warrens from the day Teresa Halbach disappeared until the end of the trials. From Mike the window washer to the county executive, everyone at Warrens had an opinion about the case, and given what I do for a living, they inevitably asked me about mine.

Opinions for the most part did not evolve. Some thought from the start that Steven Avery was guilty as sin, that the conspiracy theory was nothing but a pack of lies spewed out by a couple high-priced, out-of-town attorneys. Their opinions didn't change when Lenk and Colborn found the key; it was just more conspiracy-theory nonsense as far as they were concerned.

Take Joe, for instance, whose nephew was a sergeant at the sheriff's department. Each time I'd walk by, he'd sarcastically shake an imaginary blood vial. Then he'd ask if I'd been out at the salvage yard lately, helping the cops plant some more of Avery's blood, just to make sure.

Tammy, on the other hand, bought the defense wholeheartedly. Of course the cops set up Avery, Tammy explained; that department is corrupt from top to bottom. Just last month they nailed her teenage son for writing another forged check. And this time he didn't even do it and took the plea bargain only to avoid going to jail. She was 100 percent certain that the conspiracy theory was true.

My own reaction was one of astonishment and concern. The defense team's stumbling upon the blood vial could tip the balance in favor of an acquittal. It was bad enough that Colborn and Lenk were the ones to find the key. But now, with the sensational blood vial defense, there was a legitimate chance that the perpetrator of one of Wisconsin's most horrific murders since Jeffrey Dahmer could go free.

Ten years later, in a scene of magnificent suspense, *Making a Murderer* showed the lawyers in the clerk's office huddled around the vial as though it held, if not the secret mystery of how the universe was formed, then at least the answer to whether the police had set up Steven Avery again. Unbound by the rules of evidence, much less the duty of presenting both sides, *Making a Murderer* persuaded Netflix viewers worldwide into believing that the Manitowoc County Sheriff's Department had done it again. For the first time in history, an innocent man was wrongly convicted twice.

Viewers were treated to several close-up shots of the blood vial with a tiny, but distinct, hole on the rubber stopper on its top, similar to what would be left from a syringe. When considered in light of several other scenes supportive of the defense's blood-planting claim, it was for many viewers powerful evidence that the police had secreted some of Avery's blood from the vial and planted it in Halbach's RAV4. Not having previously heard about the hole in the vial, the imagery was so persuasive that it even left me perplexed for a while.

In exploring the blood vial defense, my first thought was: *What's with the hole on top of the vial? I don't remember hearing about that.* And with good reason I found out, because neither side paid much attention to it during the trial.

Twenty minutes of online research was all it took. There was nothing unusual about the hole on the stopper of the vial. What would be unusual, instead, would be its absence, because that's how blood gets into a vial. It was a red herring—a misleading piece of filmmaking if ever there was one, using an argument so outlandish that not even Avery's attorneys made much of it during the trial.

Asked on *Dateline* a month after *Making a Murderer* aired if the hole in the stopper should have been there, Dennis Ernst, the director at the Center for Phlebotomy Education in Corydon, Indiana, and chair of the committee that writes the standards on drawing blood samples, replied, "Well, it had better be there. There's always a telltale puncture mark in the tubes that are properly filled, so the presence of a hole means absolutely nothing."

Ernst had told *OnMilwaukee* magazine reporter Jessica McBride a few weeks earlier that there are two different methods by which blood vials are filled. In one, the nurse draws the blood with a syringe and then sticks the syringe into the rubber stopper top of the vial to insert the collected blood into the tube of the vial. The other method uses a "tube holder adapter," a device with needles on both sides. One needle goes into the person whose blood is being drawn and the other goes into the tube stopper to insert the person's blood into the vial. Ernst elaborated that in either method, "If it's properly filled, that stopper will always have a pierced marking."

It's hard to imagine that by then Jerry Buting was not aware of the insignificance of the hole, but he was still peddling the theory during his interview in the *Dateline* episode a month after the documentary aired. "And get this," he said to the host, "right in the center of the top of the tube is a little tiny hole, just about the size of a hypodermic needle." I'd put my money on the chair of the national committee that writes the industry standards rather than Jerry Buting.

Given the play afforded to the presence of the hole in the documentary, complete with a dramatic scene of the apparently astonished attorneys huddling around the vial in the clerk of courts' office, Netflix viewers might be surprised to learn that Buting and Strang presented no evidence concerning the hole during the trial. They knew it would be folly, because in an excellent bit of proactive lawyering, the prosecution had subpoenaed the nurse who had collected Avery's blood specimen and injected it into the vial.

Marlene Kraintz was the prison nurse who withdrew Avery's blood specimen on January 2, 1996, during his second appeal. She told prosecutors and was prepared to testify that she put the hole in the vial with the syringe while filling the tube with his blood in the ordinary course of her job. Knowing that Kraintz was waiting in the wings, and with no way to rebut her testimony, the defense conceded defeat by not presenting evidence about the hole to the jury.

But the hole in the stopper was not the only weapon in the arsenal of the defense. What about the blood between the stopper and the vial?

"You could definitely see that right up to the edge, there was blood around, in between the stopper and the glass," Buting insisted on *Dateline*. "The rubber stopper had to be removed from the tube after the blood was put in there, in some way or another, in order for blood to be trapped in there."

Dennis Ernst, the man who writes the national standards for blood draws, told *Dateline* that dried blood between the stopper and the vial is to be expected because the tube is not 100 percent airtight. "It's not sinister at all. That stopper is not a complete tight fit down at the lower ends of it," Ernst explained, "so it's typical and common to see blood gathering around the stopper on the inside of the tube."

The evidence tape around the packaging of the vial was also shown prominently in the documentary. Surely, that is a telltale sign of tampering with the vial. Or is it?

According to the clerk's minutes in the court record of the 1985 wrongful conviction case, DA E. James Fitzgerald was the last person to open the package. Fitzgerald opened it on June 19, 2002, at twelve twenty-five p.m., pursuant to a court order granting the Wisconsin Innocence Project's motion for additional DNA testing, and then closed it two minutes later with the vial still inside. The evidence tape had to be cut at that time in order to retrieve other items of evidence: fingernail clippings and hair. According to the prosecution, there was nothing suspicious about the evidence tape being broken.

Fitzgerald had opened the package in the presence of Avery's lawyers from the Innocence Project pursuant to the court's instruction to the parties to try to reach an agreement regarding which items of evidence should be sent to the crime lab for DNA testing. Ironically, the crime lab used this very blood vial, which had become so controversial, in his murder trial five years later.

It's possible, and in my opinion likely, that Fitzgerald simply forgot to refasten the evidence tape on the package after removing the vial. But the defense legitimately pointed out that the evidence seal not being reaffixed begs the question of whether it had been opened again. A few drops of Avery's blood could have been removed in some other way, including by an officer putting a syringe into the already existing hole or by simply removing the cap and failing to reseal the package.

Still, it was clear that *Making a Murderer* had badly manipulated the significance of the vial's condition—neither the hole in the stopper nor the dried blood were signs of tampering. But that still left the broken evidence tape on the package and the possibility that an officer could have accessed the blood by placing a syringe into the already-existing hole or by simply removing the cap.

I had reached a dead end without knowing for certain whether the police did or did not secrete some of Avery's blood from the vial. To find out more, I would need to turn to what freed Steven Avery in 2003 and what had apparently convinced the jury to send him back to prison four years later: hard, cold, objective science.

CHAPTER 11

EDTA

When a blood specimen is collected for forensic testing, a tiny amount of a chemical compound called ethylenediaminetetraacetic acid, or EDTA, is added to the vial so that the blood doesn't degrade over time. Blood in its natural form doesn't contain EDTA, which means there should not be any—not even a trace—in Steven Avery's bloodstains found in Teresa Halbach's car. Unless, of course, his blood was planted from the vial.

If it could be proven that there was no EDTA in the bloodstains, then Avery must have been "actively bleeding" when he was inside the car, especially because he had a fresh cut on his right finger when the police spoke with him a few days later. Having already dispelled the alleged signs of tampering to the vial— the hole in the rubber stopper and the dried blood between it and the glass tube—I considered the defense theory that the police had planted Avery's blood as less likely.

My confidence that Steven Avery had indeed murdered Teresa Halbach was growing by the day. Brendan Dassey's account of how the two of them murdered her and what his uncle did with her body afterward added weight to this conclusion, since Avery had to drive the vehicle to its eventual resting place and some of his blood was near the ignition switch.

With this backdrop, proof that Avery's blood inside the RAV4 was not from the vial would be enough to prove beyond a shadow of any reasonable doubt that he had indeed murdered Halbach, I thought, and probably in the manner recounted by Dassey.

With so much riding on the evidence that Steven Avery's blood was found in Teresa Halbach's car, both sides fought tooth and nail in shaping how the issue would be resolved. It was one of the most complicated and consequential legal battles of the entire trial, with the prosecution trying desperately to keep out any mention of the vial to the jury and the defense equally desperate to prevent EDTA testing. The road to get to a final decision was long and complex.

On January 3, 2007, just six weeks before the start of the trial, the prosecutors filed a "Motion to Exclude Blood Vial; or in the Alternative to Analyze the Vial of Blood." Arguing that the defense had presented only speculation and no actual evidence that police had planted Avery's blood in Halbach's car, the prosecution sought to exclude any mention of the vial. But if the Court disagreed and allowed the blood vial evidence in, then they wanted to test it to prove that while the blood vial contained EDTA, the bloodstains in Halbach's RAV4 did not. With Milwaukee County assistant DA Norm Gahn handling the motion for the prosecution, the hearing was held the next day.

As a nationally recognized DNA expert, Gahn said that EDTA testing would either dispel or confirm whether the blood was planted and go a long way toward proving or disproving the defendant's claim of innocence.

"Too many allegations have been made against people who are public servants or law enforcement officers," he added, "and we must have the opportunity to have the vial and do the testing that is suitable to meet the defense.

"There will have to be assumptions by the jury," the prosecutor explained, "that some law enforcement officer had access to this vial somehow. This isn't a case of negligence we're talking about here. It's an intentional crime committed by LEOs [referring to law enforcement officers] and possibly along with the clerk of courts.

"There are so many collateral issues that this evidence lacks probative value and would be a waste of time and confusion for the jury," Gahn continued. "The state is asking the court to not allow the evidence to come in."

Dean Strang handled part of the motion for the defense.

"The blood vial evidence goes directly to the integrity of some of the most damning evidence against Avery that the state intends to offer," Strang retorted, "the small amounts of blood that the state will say were found in Teresa's vehicle."

"Mr. Avery has been saying from the beginning to anybody with a microphone and TV camera, initially in early November 2005, that if his blood is in the Toyota RAV4, somebody planted it."

The defense had been playing cat and mouse with the vial ever since they became aware of it, at least seven months earlier—most likely because they did not want it tested for fear of not liking the results. It was only six weeks before the start of the trial and they still had not requested permission to admit evidence of their "frame-up" theory—including the vial.

So the judge ordered the defense to file its frame-up motion by January 12, if they chose to file it at all and reserved ruling on the state's motion to preclude the blood vial defense or, in the alternative, to test the blood in the RAV4 for EDTA.

In a bid to put an end to the cat-and-mouse game, he also ordered that if the blood was not tested, neither party would be permitted to make reference to the absence of a test during trial. His order applied to the defense, as well as the prosecution, because nothing had prevented Buting and Strang from requesting that the blood be tested.

A week later, under seal but on time, the defense filed its "Statement on Planted Blood," so the court and the parties convened again, on February 2, ten days before the start of the trial. Judge Patrick Willis, giving the conspiracy theory a major but not unexpected shot in the arm, agreed to allow the frame-up defense, including evidence concerning the blood vial.

Left in the balance was whether the state's request to permit EDTA testing of the defendant's blood found inside Teresa Halbach's car would be approved. Both parties staked out their positions again.

Referring to Colborn and Lenk, Norm Gahn pleaded with the court to permit the testing: "We have a responsibility to be able to restore their good names. They've protected this community and put their lives on the line. They are both good, decent family men. They deserve to have their reputations protected. The best we can do is to allow us the opportunity to test the vial of blood."

Gahn also sought to set the record straight concerning why the prosecution team requested permission to conduct EDTA testing only weeks before the start of the trial. "While the defense knew about the blood vial at the very latest in July," Gahn told the court, "they waited until December sixth to put this on us."

"Mr. Gahn is being disingenuous," Buting shot back, "if he is comparing this in any way to DNA, where you can look at one, look at the other, and say, 'Yes, there is a match.' There is no such test."

When the wrangling was finished, Judge Willis found it only fair to permit the prosecution to have the blood tested. "If there is probative evidence that can be derived from testing the blood in the vial, I think it's important to both parties that such evidence be presented to the jury," he explained, "regardless of which party the evidence supports."

Aiming to strike a balance of fairness for both sides, he also ordered that the blood samples be split so that the defense could pursue independent testing if that was their wish—and if they could find another lab to do it. But with the start of the trial only ten days away, the parties would have to move fast.

The significance of Judge Willis's decision to allow Dr. Marc LeBeau, the Unit Chief from the chemistry lab at the FBI, who developed the protocol for a test to determine the presence or absence of EDTA in blood stains, to testify about his results is hard to overstate. Would another judge have allowed the test and its results into evidence at the trial? Would another jury have discounted the results after an expert witness called by the defense testified that the protocol was not reliable? The likelihood that this particular jury discounted the blood vial defense hardly disproves it.

There are those who believe that despite its infirmities, the adversarial justice system is the best way to resolve conflicts that inevetibly arise, especially in a society as complex as ours. Pitting the opposing sides against each other, and letting them fight it out in front of a jury, proponents claim, is the best way to find justice and, theoretically, the truth. Whether it's the best we can do—for there are other kinds of justice systems in different parts of the world—our system has its downsides.

One of them is the vagaries of its results. Avery's trial is a good example. Judge Willis made a difficult decision in the heat of trial to allow the prosecution to use a recently developed protocol by the FBI to determine whether Avery's bloodstains in Halbach's car could have come from the vial. And he did so even though the state requested it just five weeks before the start of the trial. In part, he allowed it because the defense attorneys had known about the vial since July 2006 and could have sought testing themselves, but primarily he allowed it because it offered perhaps the best chance to find the truth.

If one hundred judges were presented with the same dilemma, some would allow the prosecution to proceed with the EDTA testing, and some would not. In fact, if you asked the same judges on a different day—perhaps when they were distracted by a difficult matter at home or their favorite sports team had blown a big lead the night before—some of them might have come to opposite conclusions themselves. Judges are human, and justice is not perfect.

To some extent, juries are crapshoots as well—though in my experience they usually get it right. If one hundred different

Photographer Teresa Halbach was last seen on October 31, 2005.

Members of a volunteer search party located Teresa Halbach's RAV4 at the edge of the Avery Salvage Yard on the morning of November 5, 2005. *(Photo courtesy of Calumet County Sheriff's Department)*

A smear of Steven Avery's blood was found on the interior of the RAV4 driver's side instrument panel. *(Photo courtesy of Calumet County Sheriff's Department)*

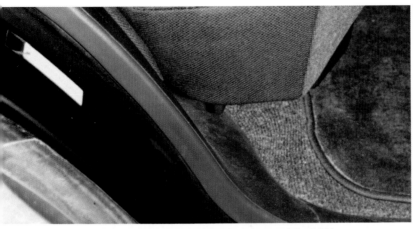

Avery's blood was found on the door frame of the RAV4.
(Photo courtesy of Calumet County Sheriff's Department)

Items found on the front passenger seat of Halbach's RAV4 included a CD case
with Steven Avery's blood on it. *(Photo courtesy of Calumet County Sheriff's Department)*

Avery's DNA was found on the hood latch of Halbach's vehicle after Brendan Dassey's
confession on March 1, 2006. *(Photo courtesy of Calumet County Sheriff's Department)*

The Avery Salvage Yard, located about ten miles north of Manitowoc, WI, was the site of what is believed to be the largest criminal investigation in Wisconsin history.
(Photo courtesy of Calumet County Sheriff's Department)

Steven Avery called *Auto Trader* magazine and asked them to send "the photographer that had been out there before" to take a picture of this Plymouth Voyager owned by his sister, Barb Janda. *(Photo courtesy of Calumet County Sheriff's Department)*

The car crusher at the Avery Salvage Yard. Numerous crushed cars can be seen in the background. *(Photo courtesy of Calumet County Sheriff's Department)*

Avery's defense lawyers argued that this tiny hole in the rubber stopper on the vial of his blood was indicative of tampering by the police. *(Photo courtesy of Calumet County Sheriff's Department)*

Avery's lawyers also cited this dried blood between the rubber stopper and the glass on the vial as further evidence of police tampering. Expert witnesses disputed the claims. *(Photo courtesy of Calumet County Sheriff's Department)*

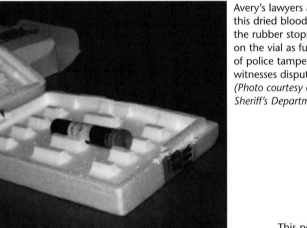

This police photo of a cut on Steven Avery's hand was taken on November 9, 2005, nine days after Teresa Halbach was murdered. *(Photo courtesy of Calumet County Sheriff's Department)*

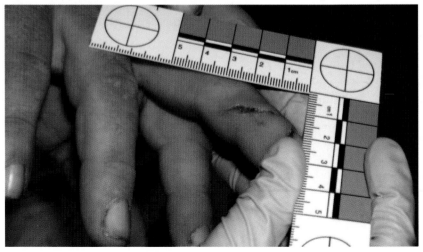

The key to the RAV4 with its blue fob was found next to a cabinet in Avery's bedroom.
(Photo courtesy of Calumet County Sheriff's Department)

The back of the book case in Steven Avery's bedroom where police believe he hid the ignition key to the RAV4. The key fell out when the paneling on the back separated from the wood frame.
(Photo courtesy of Calumet County Sheriff's Department)

A bullet fragment was found in a crack in Steven Avery's garage floor on March 1, 2006. The investigator who found it testified it resembled the head of a nail. *(Photo courtesy of Calumet County Sheriff's Department)*

The inside of Avery's garage is shown in a photo taken after the first bullet fragment was found. Marker #9 marks its location. *(Photo courtesy of Calumet County Sheriff's Department)*

A second bullet fragment was found underneath a green air compressor in the back of Avery's garage. *(Photo courtesy of Calumet County Sheriff's Department)*

Close up of the bullet fragment (Marker 23A) with Teresa Halbach's DNA on it. *(Photo courtesy of Calumet County Sheriff's Department)*

A .22 caliber rifle was found in Steven Avery's bedroom. *(Photo courtesy of Calumet County Sheriff's Department)*

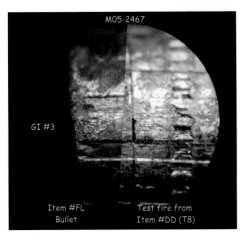

This photo shows a bullet comparison for Item FL against a test fire from Steven Avery's .22 caliber rifle. It also shows the bullet fragment containing Halbach's DNA, found in Avery's garage. *(Photo courtesy of Calumet County Sheriff's Department)*

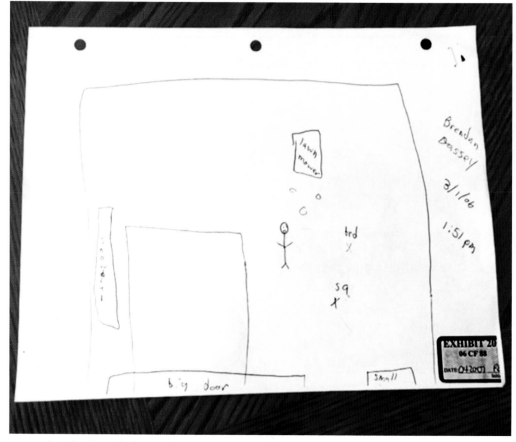

Brendan Dassey's drawing of Steven Avery's garage depicting Teresa, Steven and Brendan in their locations when Teresa was shot by Steven. *(Photo courtesy of Calumet County Sheriff's Department)*

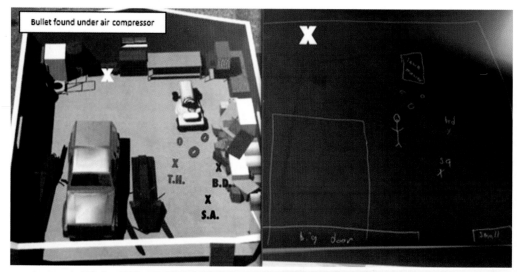

Side by side comparison of Trial Exhibit 107 with manual entries made next to Brendan Dassey's drawing of the garage on March 1, 2006.
(Photo courtesy of Calumet County Sheriff's Department)

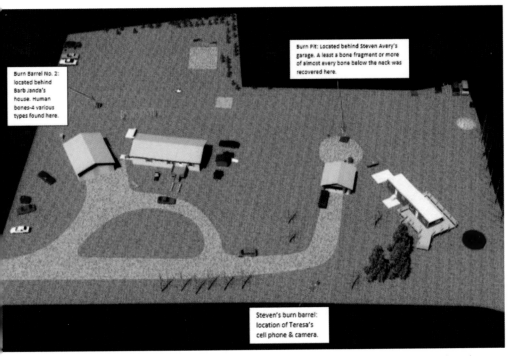

Animation showing the location of a burn pit behind Steven Avery's garage and two burn barrels. *(Photo courtesy of Calumet County Sheriff's Department)*

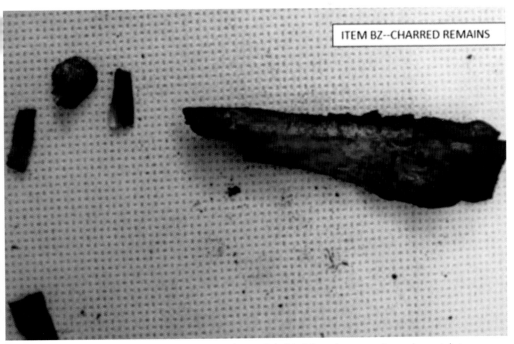

Testing on the charred remains found in burn pit behind Avery's garage showed a match to Teresa Halbach's DNA profile. *(Photo courtesy of Calumet County Sheriff's Department)*

Teresa Halbach's cell phone, PDA and camera were found, shattered and burnt, in a burn barrel in front of Avery's trailer home. The tire rim to the right was found on top of the other burned debris.
(Photo courtesy of Calumet County Sheriff's Department)

Avery's red trailer home, Barb Janda's van, and Avery's burn barrel (on the right), where Teresa Halbach's cell phone, PDA, and camera were found.
(Photo courtesy of Calumet County Sheriff's Department)

Retired Deputy Inspector Eugene Kusche testifying at his deposition in Steven Avery's wrongful conviction lawsuit on October 26, 2005, just five days before Teresa Halbach was murdered. *(Photos courtesy of Magne-Script Video Court Reporting)*

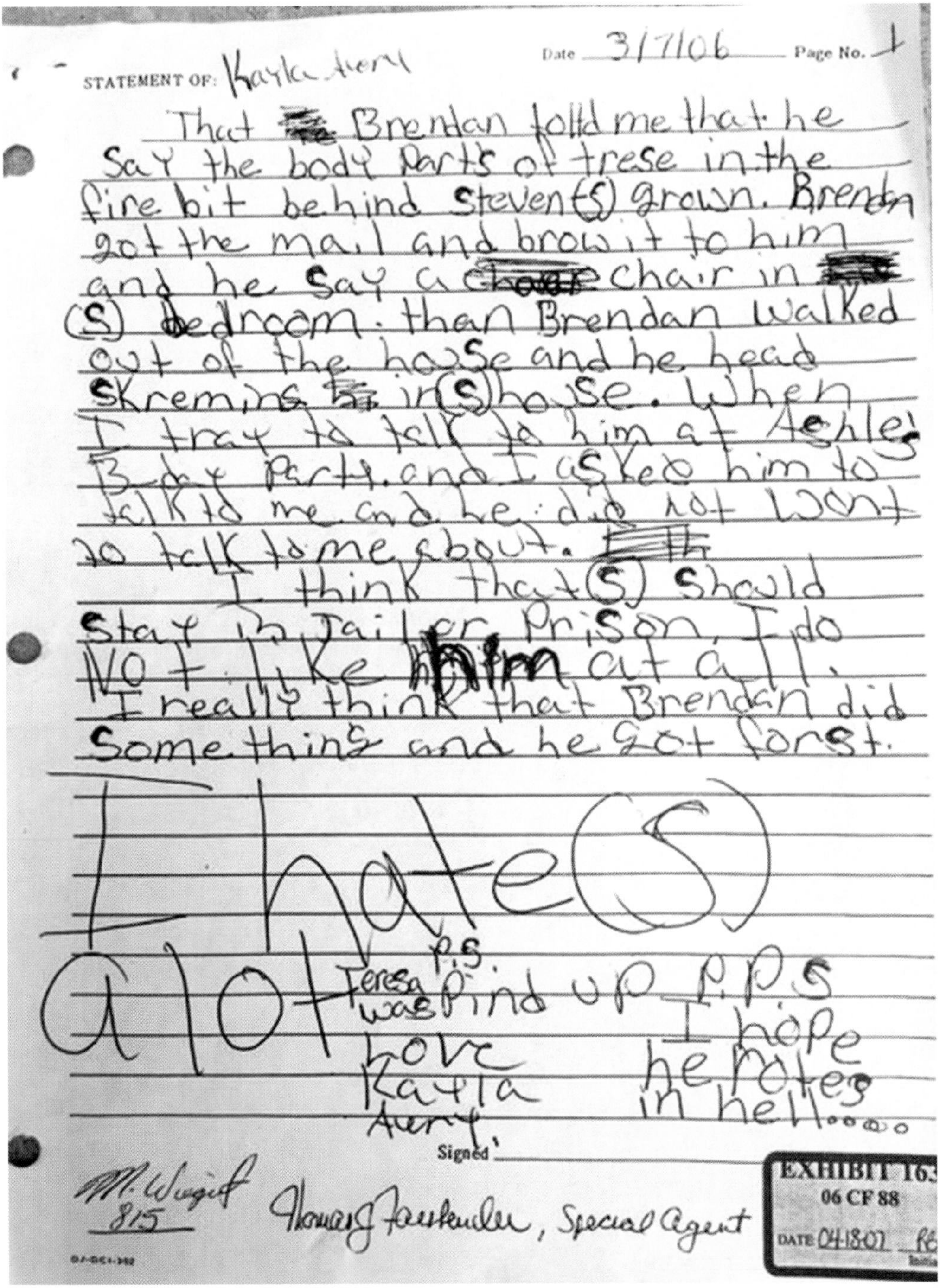

STATEMENT OF: Kayla Avery   Date 3/7/06   Page No. 1

That ~~the~~ Brendan tolld me that he
say the body parts of trese in the
fire bit behind Steven(S) grown. Brendan
got the mail and brow it to him
and he say a ~~close~~ chair in ~~the~~
(S) bedroom. than Brendan walked
out of the house and he head
skreming ~~the~~ in (S) house. When
I tray to tell to him at Ashlei
B day party. and I asked him to
talk to me and he did not want
to talk to me about. ~~I~~
        I think that (S) should
stay in Jail or prison. I do
NOT like **him** at all.
I really think that Brendan did
some thing and he got forst.

I hate (S)
a lot

P.S.
Teresa
was find up

P.P.S
I hope
he rotes
in hell...

love
Kayla
Avery

Signed _____

M. Wiegert
815

Thomas Fassbender, Special Agent

EXHIBIT 163
06 CF 88
DATE 04-18-07

DJ-GCI-302

From the Dassey trial: Written statement of Kayla Avery, Brendan Dassey's first cousin.
(Photo courtesy of Calumet County Sheriff's Department)

This picture accompanied a Tweet meant for Colborn and Lenk.

Colborn Which Bullet Should We Use Lenk One On The Right Grab Teresas Toothbrush Brains Dont Matter #MakingAMurderer pic.twitter.com/3FPxQUNnM6

— 0Hour1 ☿ (@0Hour1) December 29, 2015

Facebook call to action to sabotage *The Innocent Killer.*

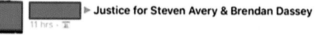 ▶ **Justice for Steven Avery & Brendan Dassey**

11 hrs · ☿

People – listen up to me if you want a shot at justice!

I have caught a prosecutor planting false evidence in his book "The Innocent Killer." You have been seeing that from people I have enlisted to help. He is an OFFICER OF THE STATE – This is direct VIOLATION of Avery's CONSTITUTIONAL RIGHTS and would warrant protection by the FEDERAL COURT to intervene and STOP A STATES OFFICER from PLANTING EVIDENCE – which would open the case back up.

But we need to make it happen, we are half way there – listen -- if his book is killed completely on Amazon the news and everyone else will take notice that the people are TIRED OF LIES by the PROSECUTION no matter how they do it. In this case by a tricky book. The federal courts and even his own brother will have to take note as there is no way to contstrue that it is ok to PUBLISH FALSE EVIDENCE (Need I remind you this case is about planting evidence) in a book or otherwise.

Go here to Amazon, sign up and review the book and tell the world it has FASLE EVIDINCE from a WISCONSIN STATE PROSECUTOR. Not someone posing as an author.

And go anywhere else you cans think of and do the same. This is a great opportunity to reveal their true colors. DO IT NOW>

The Innocent Killer: A True Story of a Wrongful Conviction and its Astonishing Aftermath
The story of one of the nation's most notorious wrongful convictions, that of Steven Avery, a Wisconsin man who spent eighteen years in prison for a crime he did not commit. But two years after he was exone...

amazon.com

The Manitowoc County Courthouse.

juries were presented with the exact same evidence heard by the jury in Avery's case, their verdicts would undoubtedly not be the same.

All of which is to say that I had more work ahead of me. The jury's guilty verdict, after all, is not proof that Steven Avery murdered Teresa Halbach. It means only that the twelve people chosen to determine his fate found beyond a reasonable doubt that he was the killer, and only after the judge, who happened to be on intake when the complaint was filed, permitted them to hear the results of a newly developed test conducted by the FBI.

I began by reading approximately five hundred pages of the trial transcript that dealt with the EDTA testing conducted by LeBeau, not to mention exhibit documents, to judge for myself the best I could whether the procedure for blood stain testing was legitimate and sound. In the process I learned much more than I'd ever hoped about EDTA, and what follows is what I found.

With the legal battle over the admission of the EDTA testing resolved only a month earlier, Norm Gahn called Dr. LeBeau to the stand on March 5. With Judge Willis, as is his habit, giving them an occasional break to stand up and stretch, the jurors listened attentively to LeBeau—as they did several days later to the testimony of the defense expert, Janine Arvizu, who challenged the method of detection in the FBI EDTA results.

LeBeau told the jury he is the unit chief of the Chemistry Unit at the FBI Laboratory in Quantico, Virginia. As the unit chief, he oversees day-to-day operations—including making decisions about the types of cases the unit accepts for analysis, assigning cases to the most appropriate personnel, and reviewing the results of final reports to make sure they meet the quality requirements of the Quality Assurance Department at the lab.

LeBeau testified that he has a Ph.D. in toxicology from the University of Maryland and four years of postdoctoral work at St. Louis University. He serves on the Board of Directors of the Society of Forensic Toxicologists, and is a member of the International Association of Forensic Toxicologists and the American Academy of Forensic Sciences. He has authored or coauthored fifteen to twenty peer-reviewed journal, professional, and scientific articles that are published in professional publications and is a frequent presenter at workshops and conferences.

Not only did LeBeau have impeccable credentials as an expert in his field, he also used nontechnical terms to explain matters of science and technology to jurors in a non-condescending and ordinary way. He was a trial lawyer's dream for an expert witness.

LeBeau explained to the jurors that he supervised every process of this particular case—the method development, the receipt of the evidence, the decisions that were made on which items were to be analyzed, when it was analyzed, and how it was analyzed.

"I took the results and compiled them," he told the jury, "formed an opinion as to what they meant, wrote the report myself, issued the report after it had been reviewed by an independent scientist that works within my unit, and, of course, came here today to testify."

He explained that EDTA is a chelating agent—a chemical that latches onto metals in their environment and removes them from that environment. It's found in many commercial products, such as shampoo, laundry detergent, fertilizers, and sodas, just to name a few.

Most blood vials, LeBeau stated, have some form of a preservative anticoagulant like EDTA to allow this blood to be stored for some time so it's still usable in the laboratory.

He told the jury that with the sensitivity of the method they devised for this case, they were able to detect a concentration of the EDTA as low as thirteen parts per million.

"And did you receive samples to test in this case?" prosecutor Norm Gahn asked.

"We received a number of swabs that were reported to us as having been taken from bloodstains out of a Toyota RAV4, as well as control swabs that were collected in the areas near where those bloodstains were," LeBeau answered. "And we also received a tube of blood in a purple-stoppered tube, an EDTA tube, which was collected from Mr. Steven Avery."

The specific bloodstains tested were the ones taken from the dashboard, the rear passenger door, and a CD case on the front passenger seat.

After LeBeau explained the testing process, Prosecutor Gahn asked if he tested the bloodstains for the presence of EDTA and, if so, what were the results.

"Yes, I did, or we did," LeBeau replied. "We were not able to identify any presence, whatsoever, of EDTA or the EDTA iron complex on the controlled swabs, any of the controlled swabs from the RAV4," the FBI chemist confidently replied.

On the other hand, "The purple-stoppered tube from the clerk of courts office that was reported to have come from Steven Avery," Dr. LeBeau answered, "did indeed contain significant amounts of EDTA."

Bringing the point home, Gahn asked, "Based upon your training and experience, and based upon your test results using the LC/MS/MS technique, and based upon all the data that you reviewed and all the compilations that were done in this case, do you have an opinion, to a reasonable degree of scientific certainty, whether the bloodstains from Teresa Halbach's RAV4 that you tested came from the vial of blood of Steven Avery that was in the Manitowoc County Clerk of Courts Office?"

"It's my opinion that the bloodstains that were collected from the RAV4 could not have come from the EDTA tube that was provided to us in this case," LeBeau replied. And with that, Gahn passed his witness to the defense, whose evidence planting claim had taken a major hit.

During his cross-examination of Dr. LeBeau, Jerry Buting demonstrated an impressive knowledge about EDTA testing and its short and not-so-successful use during criminal trials. After a few disarming pleasantries he sparred with the FBI chemist about his expertise in the specific field of EDTA testing and the reliability of his lab's testing process in the Avery case.

"Good afternoon, Doctor," Buting began.

To which, LeBeau offered an equally curt, "Good afternoon."

"I'm sure you're anxious to get back to Virginia, where it's not quite so cold."

"It would be nice, yes."

Then Buting launched into a headlong attack on the prosecution's expert witness, first on his credentials, then on the hastily developed protocol for his test.

"You said you authored or coauthored fifteen to twenty articles?"

"That's correct."

"How many of those articles did not involve drug-facilitated rape?"

"Seventeen."

"And how many of those involved postmortem fluids, analysis of postmortem fluids? Do you know what I'm talking about, from deceased bodies?"

"Yes, I know what you are talking about," LeBeau replied calmly but firmly, already aware of what kind of inquisitor he was facing in the courtroom that day.

Buting's point was that most of Dr. LeBeau's publications involved either drug-facilitated sexual assaults, also known as date rape drugs, or postmortem fluids—not EDTA testing.

"You also give quite a few presentations, just this year alone, out of . . . looks like out of nine times that you have gone around presenting talks this year, six of those involve drug-facilitated sexual assaults, right? Have you ever, in your life, been asked to give a presentation on EDTA interpretation in bloodstains?"

"No, I have not."

"You are not a sought-after presenter on that particular topic, are you?"

"No, sir, I'm not."

"Have you ever before testified, in a court of law, as an expert who is giving opinions about the interpretation of EDTA and bloodstains?"

"No," LeBeau answered, which surely raised eyebrows among a few of the jurors.

Buting moved on to attacking the testing itself, pointing out that the last time the FBI tested for EDTA was in the O.J. Simpson trial two decades earlier. Only two years on the job at the FBI at the time, LeBeau was not involved in the O.J. case, but that didn't stop Buting.

"And might the fact that the FBI had not tested for EDTA since the O.J. case be because your lab screwed up in the O.J. Simpson case?"

"No, we did not screw up, as you say, in the O.J. Simpson case," LeBeau replied.

A skilled cross-examiner does not give the witness a chance to elaborate and Jerry Buting is a very skilled cross-examiner.

LeBeau had explained in his direct examination that his lab at the FBI had agreed to take on the Avery case as part of its responsibility to investigate allegations of public corruption on the federal and state levels. If police officers had planted evidence in this case, it certainly constituted a crime of public corruption.

But the FBI rarely gets involved in state crime investigations, which opened up another line of questioning for Buting concerning LeBeau's "public corruption" rationale.

LeBeau had spoken about the seriousness of public corruption in his direct examination: "If an individual is truly in that political position or in a law enforcement position, and they are doing something illegal that erodes the public's trust in that agency or that individual, and we would want that, certainly, that individual out of that office or off the street.

"But additionally," LeBeau had continued, "if they are being wrongly accused, we want to be involved in that investigation to help set the record straight and hopefully clear their name . . . so again, the trust can be restored."

"Okay," Buting asked, "can you show me anywhere in that request (from the prosecution) where it says our purpose is also to find out if there might be any evidence that there's a corrupt cop in Manitowoc County?"

"No, I don't see anything of that nature," LeBeau replied, "but I can elaborate if you like."

Again, not giving LeBeau a chance to elaborate, Buting charged that the actual reason the feds got involved was to "eliminate the allegation that this vial was used to plant evidence, isn't that true?"

"No, sir. If I can elaborate, I will be happy to explain."

"You can elaborate later, sir."

LeBeau had conceded that given the prosecution's late request, his lab was "under a time crunch," as Buting had put it.

"As a matter of fact," Buting asked, "no one has ever presented to any jury, anywhere, not just you, no one has ever presented a test for EDTA in bloodstains in a criminal trial before, other than the O.J. Simpson case?"

To which, LeBeau said he wasn't aware of one.

Foreshadowing the position that would be taken by the defense's own expert witness in a few days, Buting ended by suggesting that "even with this brand-new test you devised," the prosecution could not prove with absolute certainty that there was no EDTA in the bloodstains.

"All you can say is that there is none detectable, given your limits of detection, correct?"

LeBeau believed that his test was "more than adequate," but again he had to concede that there is necessarily some limit beyond which any testing—including the one he had devised in this case—cannot go beyond.

Regardless of the concession their expert made at the end, the prosecution had struck a major blow to the evidence-planting claim of the defense. The basics of their argument remained intact—the blood in the vial contained EDTA, while his blood in the RAV4 did not. With no other source of his blood available to the police, Steven Avery must have been bleeding inside Teresa Halbach's car—powerful evidence, indeed.

No one knows except the jurors themselves, and most of them aren't talking, but having read Dr. LeBeau's testimony, I would not be surprised if he swayed some jurors who up to that point might have been sitting on the fence.

Buting may have done more harm than good for the defense. With my own caseload I was unable to attend the trial, so I didn't have the chance to observe LeBeau's demeanor. From the transcripts, however, he seemed to be an ideal expert witness—competent, credible, knowledgeable, fair—and, perhaps most important, able to convert complicated concepts into plain words that a jury can understand.

Buting's inquisitorial style might work with some witnesses, but it can backfire with others. It's one thing to beat up on and demean a nervous, overly officious cop two years on the force, but it's another to go after a witness with the credentials and intelligence of LeBeau.

Buoyed by LeBeau's convincing testimony, the prosecution rested its case the next day. They had called over fifty witnesses and moved nearly five hundred exhibits into evidence, and now it was time for the defense to present its case, should they decide. The presumption of innocence stays with an accused throughout the trial unless, and until, the state proves his guilt beyond a reasonable doubt. The burden of proof is upon the state, where it belongs, and the defendant need not put on a case at all. Additionally, jurors are instructed by the court not to consider the number of witnesses each side calls during the trial because it has no bearing upon the defendant's guilt or innocence.

Still, typically, the defense puts on a case, and Buting and Strang followed suit in Steven Avery's trial—though Avery himself chose to exercise his constitutional right not to testify. One of their key witnesses was an expert witness whom they had retained to challenge the EDTA testing conducted by Dr. LeBeau.

It often happens to jurors; and after reading the defense expert's testimony in the Avery case, it happened to me. Two hours earlier I was convinced—not 100 percent but close—that LeBeau's EDTA testing proved that the bloodstains in the RAV4 did not come from the vial. A few hours later, after reading the defense expert's testimony, I was no longer sure.

Working in the industry since the 1980s, Janine Arvizu was a laboratory quality auditor in Albuquerque, New Mexico, and it was obvious from her testimony that she was good at her job. As she explained, she did most of her work for the federal government because it is the largest consumer of lab results and makes important decisions based on those results.

"The people who use lab results—it's not like buying a pound of sugar or buying a pound of flour," she explained to the jurors, because the quality of data varies among the labs and they make very important decisions based on the results of the data.

"It's a very technically driven job to place quality control practices and measures in to ensure that you consistently and reliably produce good quality data," she stated.

"Experience has shown in the measurement in science business, that the best way to ensure the reliability and the validity of the results is to have a very rigorous, quality assurance program in place."

She testified that a protocol or a testing method might be acceptable for use in one application but "completely inappropriate" in another. "So it's really essential to understand exactly the scope of what you are trying to use the results for."

Arvizu was not impressed with the FBI's EDTA testing's protocol, nor with the operating procedure, nor with Dr. LeBeau's final report.

"The fact that EDTA is not detected in a stain does not mean that EDTA was not present in the stain," she told the jury. The test was fine for screening and detecting EDTA in a bloodstain, but according to Arvizu, it was inadequate to determine its absence.

"That's really the problem," she continued. "The issue with this procedure is not whether or not it's a valid result. If you were actually detecting EDTA, this is a good method. The problem really occurs when EDTA is not detected in a bloodstain."

She was referring to what scientists call a "detection limit"— the lowest concentration of a chemical's presence a test is able to detect.

"In the procedure employed in this case, EDTA is readily identified at a concentration of thirteen micrograms per liter. The common term is parts per million," she explained.

She told the jurors that the FBI's claimed detection limit was "theoretical" and did not account for "complicating factors associated with taking a real-world sample and getting it to the point where it's clean and pristine enough to be able to inject it into an instrument."

Among the complicating factors in this case, she said, were "the swabbing of the bloodstain and extracting the sample from that stain and diluting it before you get it into the instrument."

"The problem is you just don't know whether you didn't detect EDTA because there was none there or because your detection limit wasn't low enough to see it, even if it had been there. That's really the problem."

She also disagreed with LeBeau's decision to test only three of the six stains of Avery's blood found inside Halbach's car. When asked about this by Buting, she replied that she was "not in the business of just making guesses about what might be in samples. We have instrumentation to test samples and that's how we determine results."

Norm Gahn drew a tough assignment as Arvizu's cross-examiner, because, theoretically, she was right. Even with the advanced stage of our science and technology, we are not yet able to prove the absence of a chemical substance as an absolute certainty like we can with the fact that one and one equals two. A molecule or two could be lurking in the solution and slip under the detection limit and its presence would remain unknown.

Unable to challenge Arvizu's bottom-line contention, Gahn was left with trying to chip away at the edges of her testimony. Arvizu was well prepared to meet even minor challenges to her most unessential points, so despite the prosecutor's best efforts, she left the stand unscathed.

As with Dr. LeBeau, I did not observe Arvizu's appearance and demeanor. The physical characteristics of a witness should mean very little, but we base much of our assessment of the witness's competence and credibility on his or her appearance and demeanor. Did she appear confident? Was her voice pleasant or harsh? Did she wear too much makeup? And so on.

Still, without observing her, I was not completely confident that Avery's bloodstains in the RAV4 did not contain EDTA. Either the FBI's hastily developed test had some legitimate problems, or Arvizu was very good at making it look that way, and there was no way to tell from the transcripts.

By their guilty verdict the jurors showed which side's expert they believed, but that was not enough to fulfill the aim of my journey because my own conclusion was that I could not conclude. A new procedure quickly developed by the FBI based upon an earlier test that was heavily criticized since it was last used in the O.J. Simpson trial did not prove conclusively that Steven Avery's blood in the RAV4 did not contain EDTA. To be fair I had to throw it away.

On the other hand, the fact that the prosecution could not prove with absolute certainty that the police had not planted Avery's blood in Halbach's car did not prove that they did. The defense had presented no evidence, nothing beyond speculation and implied, but unproven, motivation to back up their claim. The same could be said for the RAV4 itself, the key, and, as we shall soon see, a bullet fragment with Halbach's DNA found in

Avery's garage. The defendant had no obligation to prove his innocence; but using nothing but innuendo to accuse police officers of misconduct—an allegation that, if true, could land them in jail—proved nothing.

Which officers snuck Avery's blood out of the clerk of courts' office and when? Were they the same officers who planted the blood in Halbach's car, or did they hand it off to some co-conspiring cops? Did they know how to avoid contamination and to dilute the proper amount? You'd think it would take more than a few officers to plant so many items and that one of them would eventually talk, if not to the authorities then to someone in a coffee shop or a bar. Was the code of silence really that strong? And what about the prosecutors—knowing the case backward and forward, you'd think they would figure it out. Or were they in on it, too?

At no time did the defense answer these questions. Nor—it occurred to me as I readied myself for the next chapter of my journey—did *Making a Murderer*.

At the same time the frame-up defense would have gone nowhere if it weren't for the glaring abuse of power by the former sheriff and the former district attorney. In fact, if it weren't for the prior officials' misconduct, *Making a Murderer* would have never been made, and I would not be spending all my waking hours trying to determine whether or not the jury got it right.

CHAPTER 12

A REPRIEVE

For three weeks I had immersed myself in court records, news articles, online research, and anything else I could get my hands on concerning the Avery case. Overwhelmed by its details, I decided to take a day off to reflect more broadly about the thirty-year Steven Avery crime saga, and not just the slice of it that occurred between 2005 and 2007.

Until December 2015 or even later, when they either watched for themselves or heard about *Making a Murderer,* the vast majority of Americans would not have even recognized Steven Avery's name, much less that he was allegedly the victim of not just one, but two wrongful convictions—an astonishing set of facts when you stop to think about it. Even the main players in the murder case—Dean Strang, Jerry Buting, and Ken Kratz—knew about Avery's story only in passing until he became a suspect in Teresa Halbach's murder in early November 2005. I wondered how their perspective differed from mine, especially because the 1985 and 2005 cases were so intertwined and I had spent so much time examining the first.

Did any of them really know what Steven and the Avery family were like—the good points and the bad? Did they understand the nuances of the Manitowoc County Sheriff's Department and the District Attorney's Office—its recent history and the complete reshuffling of those at the top? Did they know that both Colborn and Lenk are two of the most honest cops you could find?

Were they aware of the change in leadership in our office in 2002 that ushered in a new way of thinking about the criminal justice system and concern for those who became caught up in its grasp—victims, of course, but offenders, too? Did they realize how Penny Beerntsen's assault on the beach in the summer of 1985 and Avery's wrongful conviction later that year forever changed her life and that of her family? Did the creators of *Making a Murderer,* especially, have any idea that their widely acclaimed series had wreaked havoc upon a community that had been dealing with the Avery case for thirty years and had finally moved on?

Most of all, did they know that they were heaping additional suffering upon the Halbach family, who are having to revisit a nightmare that would have never passed completely, but that they, at least, could have used to honor Teresa's memory and as a sign of their love for her by keeping it more or less to themselves?

I thought back to the day when my own obsession with the Avery case began. It was in the morning on September 5, 2003 when our office received a phone call from Sherry Culhane, an analyst at the Wisconsin State Crime Lab who had just completed DNA testing on evidence associated with Avery's 1985 conviction. After suggesting that DA Mark Rohrer and I sit down, she told us the DNA profile from the last shred of evidence in the Avery case that could be tested, a single pubic hair, matched the DNA of a convicted sex offender by the name of Gregory Allen. Allen was a sociopathic sex predator, with a record a mile long, who made Steven Avery look like a Boy Scout in comparison to his own propensity for sexual violence.

Rohrer and I looked at each other in disbelief. Neither of us had ever heard of Gregory Allen. In fact, we knew very little about the Avery case itself, other than it involved the brutal assault of a prominent local woman along the beach on Lake Michigan. Rohrer was still an undergraduate when Avery was convicted, and by the time my wife and I moved here, Avery had already spent six years in prison. Former DA Jim Fitzgerald hadn't relayed any of the issues or facts involved in the case when he left office and said nothing about a DNA analysis that might soon prove consequential.

The Avery "file" consisted of hundreds of documents that were packed inside expandable file folders in three separate boxes, which were still in Fitzgerald's corner office, the office now occupied by Rohrer. I began skimming through the file while we were still on the phone. Starting with what looked like the most organized part of the file, I came across some police reports and a criminal complaint that didn't belong in the file. What caught my attention was the name of the defendant: Gregory Allen. It was the same name of the person that Sherry Culhane had just told us was the real assailant. *That's kind of strange,* I thought.

I skimmed the criminal complaint. On August 2, 1983—almost two years to the day before Penny Beerntsen was attacked—Allen was charged with exposing himself and lunging at a woman who was walking her dog along the same beach where Beerntsen was assaulted two summers later. I flipped to the signature line on the last page to see who prosecuted the case against Allen. It was Denis Vogel, the former DA who, with the former sheriff, was responsible for Avery's wrongful conviction. A sinking, sickening feeling came over me and would return with varying degrees of intensity over the next several weeks.

After Culhane hung up, Rohrer and I delved further into Gregory Allen's past. CCAP (Consolidated Court Automation Program) revealed that by the time he assaulted Beerntsen in 1985, Allen had already chalked up a considerable record. Worse, because he wasn't charged with assaulting Beerntsen, Allen not only had a past, but he had a future, too. Culhane had alluded to it.

On June 27, 1995, ten years after he avoided prosecution for assaulting Penny Beerntsen, Allen broke into a residence on the north side of Green Bay and assaulted the woman inside, while the woman's daughter lay sleeping in a room nearby. He was convicted of kidnapping, burglary, and second-degree sexual assault "while possessing a bulletproof garment." The presiding judge sent him away for sixty years.

The records also revealed that while Allen was in custody, awaiting trial for the Green Bay assault, authorities in South Carolina issued a Fugitive Complaint asking Wisconsin to return him to South Carolina once the prosecution here was complete. He was wanted on "suspicion of murder" for a crime that occurred in the 1970s. That complaint was later dismissed, but regardless, Allen was one scary guy.

Some of our staff members worked in the office when Denis Vogel prosecuted Steven Avery back in 1985, and one still worked for the county, but in a different capacity. None of them thought Avery was the assailant. Each of them thought Gregory Allen was. Allen had been in and out of court during the preceding six months for stalking, window peeping, and stealing women's underwear—not the types of offenses that go unnoticed by women who work in prosecutors' offices—and they felt certain it was him.

Brenda Petersen, our victim witness coordinator, in particular worked with detectives from the various police agencies in the county. She told us the Manitowoc Police Department was keeping a close eye on Gregory Allen during the summer Beerntsen was attacked, and some of the officers were also convinced that Gregory Allen, not Steven Avery, was Beerntsen's assailant. Brenda also said she watched the entire trial, and she never believed Avery was the assailant. In fact, Brenda and two other staff members were so convinced the attacker was Allen that they went into Vogel's office and told him so. Vogel, however, said it was impossible because Allen was on probation in Door County. The district attorney claimed he called Allen's probation agent and the agent told him that Allen was in Sturgeon Bay at the time of the assault—he had an alibi.

The independent investigation conducted by the DOJ later found out otherwise. Gregory Allen wasn't on probation the day

Penny Beerntsen was attacked, as Denis Vogel had said. The "sand-man," as some of the officers had taken to calling Allen, was free to roam the beach and terrorize his next victim, which is exactly what he did when he grabbed Beerntsen and manhandled her over the dunes.

I thought back to the telephone conversation I had with Denis Vogel a few days after Sherry Culhane from the crime lab had called us with the news. He seemed unconcerned about Avery's wrongful conviction and interested only in covering his tracks.

In the ensuing week we were confronted with a disturbing body of evidence all but proving that Steven Avery's wrongful conviction did not happen by mistake. It was instead a colossal in-justice perpetrated upon Avery and his family by the misconduct of the sheriff, the district attorney, and a handful of others who circled the wagons. After moving too fast to arrest him with the scantest of evidence, they soon found out they had the wrong man. Rather than cut him loose and start over, they knowingly and intentionally sent him to prison for eighteen years. At least that's the way it looked to us and most others who carefully ex-amined into the facts.

The Steven Avery saga did not end with his exoneration, how-ever. I reflected that day upon all that had happened since. Public outcry, private lawsuits, and independent investigations followed his exoneration. He became an instant hero and household name in Wisconsin, even posing for a picture with the governor, who soon regretted the not-so-positive association. Aiming to re-form police interrogation and eyewitness identification techniques, the state assembly passed the "Avery Bill." Having filed a wrongful conviction lawsuit, Steven Avery was poised to reap millions.

Somewhere along the line the wrongly convicted man had turned into a cold-blooded killer. Or had he?

My thoughts increasingly turned back to the turmoil I felt ten

years earlier when my then-solid belief in Avery's guilt collided
with my fear that the frame-up defense might set him free.

It was only two weeks until the start of the murder trial and two
major issues remained unresolved—both of which were bound to
have a major impact on its outcome. The first issue was whether
the court would permit the defense to present an alternate suspect theory, so-called "Denny" evidence, named after a 1984 Wisconsin Court of Appeals decision bearing the same name. Under
Denny and similar cases in other states, the defense is allowed to
introduce evidence that a specific person or persons other than
the accused may have perpetrated the crime. In other words, they
get to name names.

But they can only do so under very strict criteria. They must be
able to show that the alternate suspect had motive, opportunity,
and at least some evidence connecting him to the crime—as the
court in *Denny* put it, "not remote in time, place, or circumstances." The rule is called the "legitimate tendency test," and it
makes sense because without its restrictions, a jury trial with one
or more alternative suspects could rapidly devolve into a glorified
courtroom whodunit—especially in the hands of skilled trial
lawyers like Buting and Strang.

Hoping to prevent that from happening, the prosecution
months earlier had filed a "Motion Concerning Third-Party Lia-
bility." Filing the motion so early was a preemptive strike by Kratz
and the prosecution team, because the defense had not yet
tipped its hand by naming the person or persons they planned to
blame for Teresa Halbach's murder. In fact, they waited until January 10, 2007, less than a month before trial, to file the defendant's "Statement on Third-Party Responsibility."

In it they identified as possible third-party perpetrators "every
customer of the salvage yard, every family friend, and every member of the Avery extended family who was present at the salvage
yard during the hours in question."

The pleading was broad, perhaps impermissibly so, but the

motion carried weight because Steven wasn't the only member of the Avery family to have had trouble with the law.

His older brother, Chuck, had a violent past, most notably an incident six years earlier when his former wife accused him of rape and attempting to strangle her with a telephone cord. Steve's younger brother, Earl, having been convicted of battery and sexual assault charges in 1992, stemming from an attack on his current wife—apparently, wives don't fare well in the Avery family—had potential, too.

Chuck and Earl both worked at the salvage yard and were on the premises the day Teresa Halbach was murdered, so they both had "opportunity" as required by *State* v. *Denny*.

But did they have motive? If the court found in favor of the defense, the floodgates would open wide. Buting and Strang would spend days deflecting the jury's attention away from Steven Avery and toward one or more of his aforementioned siblings—or, for that matter, anyone else with an unsavory past who happened upon the Avery Salvage Yard on the day Halbach was murdered.

They wouldn't have to *prove* that Earl or Chuck or someone else was the perpetrator—the defendant never has to prove anything because it would shift the burden of proof away from the prosecution, where it belongs. All they would have to do would be to convince one or two strong-minded jurors that someone else might have done it and Steven Avery would walk away a free man.

On January 30, 2007, just two weeks before the start of what was expected to be a six-week long trial, the parties gathered in court for the final pretrial conference. Shackled in handcuffs and leg irons, and clumsily clad with a stun belt, Steven Avery was escorted into the courtroom by five deputies standing ready with sidearms and Tasers, just in case. Security outside the courtroom had been ramped up, too. With so much riding on his decision concerning the defendant's third-party responsibility *Denny* Motion, Judge Willis had taken the matter under advisement a few weeks earlier, but now he was ready to announce his decision.

It wasn't good news for the defense. After conceding that the persons identified by the defense had the opportunity to murder Teresa Halbach, the judge said there was nothing to demonstrate that any of them had a motive to kill her. And without evidence of motive, he explained, the evidence failed the legitimate tendency test under the *Denny* case.

Not allowed to blame someone else for Halbach's murder, the defense team would be left with arguing the conspiracy theory and harping on reasonable doubt. The jury would never learn about Chuck or Earl Avery or any other violent miscreant that was roaming the salvage yard that day. It was very good news for the prosecution.

The defense fared much better with the blood vial defense. With each side wanting to shape how the issue would evolve, it had been a long and torturous route. At that same hearing on January 30, Judge Willis sided with the defense and denied the state's motion to exclude the blood vial evidence. The way was cleared for Buting and Strang to accuse the police of secreting some of their client's blood from the vial and planting it inside Halbach's car.

With Judge Willis's decision to permit the frame-up defense, Avery's trial for Halbach's murder would become intertwined with his wrongful conviction case twenty-two years earlier. With the blood vial defense still viable and the allegations that Colborn, Lenk, and a group of unnamed and unnumbered cronies from the sheriff's department planted Halbach's SUV at the salvage yard and its ignition key in the defendant's bedroom, he had a legitimate shot of walking away a free man—especially with Strang and Buting at his side.

The prosecution, I thought, was in trouble. At the time—a decade before researching the matter in full—I was disconcerted by the fact that Colborn and Lenk were the officers who found the key, and only after other searches failed to turn it up. If only Kratz could get Brendan Dassey's confession in front of the jury, I thought, the defense would not stand a chance. But Dassey's Fifth

Amendment right not to incriminate himself meant Kratz and his team could not force him to take the stand.

There was one more option. It strikes some as unseemly, but prosecutors do it all the time. We use little fish to get bigger fish by cutting them a deal. Kratz could offer Brendan Dassey a plea agreement in return for his testimony against his uncle, maybe a reduction in the charges, or, more likely, an agreement to recommend a parole eligibility date that would get him out of prison when he was still relatively young. I heard rumblings of an offer at the time and years later learned that Kratz had, indeed, offered a deal. The state would recommend parole eligibility after fifteen years of confinement—not a bad deal, given the severity of the crime.

Convincing Brendan Dassey to accept a plea agreement wouldn't be easy. The close-knit Avery family is fiercely loyal to each other, and Allan Avery would undoubtedly pressure his grandson not to testify against Steven. Kratz had to be careful. You don't offer much lenience to a cold-blooded killer, even if he's a sixteen-year-old boy with diminished mental capacities whose role model in life is Steven Avery. In the end the parties failed to strike a deal. Without Dassey's confession the outcome of Steven Avery's trial was anyone's guess.

The six-week trial, streaming live on the Internet from Milwaukee to Madison to Green Bay, would begin on February 5, 2007—precisely fifteen months after the SUV was discovered at the edge of the Avery Salvage Yard. Weeks earlier the Green Bay and Milwaukee television stations had decided how they would cover the trial. Key moments, like the opening statements and closing arguments, would be broadcast live and all six stations would cover the lawyer's daily press conferences on their evening news. The astonishing twists and turns of the past fifteen months were about to culminate in a dramatic trial. DEFENSE GEARING UP TO ARGUE BLOOD WAS PLANTED, read one of the headlines in the *Manitowoc Herald Times Reporter.*

* * *

On the eve of trial I thought the chances of a conviction were better than even, but "better than even" isn't good enough for the state. Shouldering the burden of proving guilt beyond a reasonable doubt, the prosecution must present overwhelming evidence. The Manitowoc County Sheriff's Department and the prosecution team were under a great deal of stress—not only because an acquittal would add to the suffering of the Halbach family, but because in a sense they were also on trial.

No one in the public outside law enforcement and the court system knew at the time, but on the night before the trial began, and a few days after the *Herald Times* reported that the defense would be allowed to present evidence of the wrongful conviction lawsuit and the blood vial, former chief inspector Gene Kusche died unexpectedly, sitting in his favorite living-room chair in the comfort of his home. Kusche was a diabetic and the official cause of death was acute myocardial infarction—a heart attack. Although friends said he wasn't a religious man, he had a Bible at his side. Had the stress of the upcoming trial and Judge Willis's recent decision to allow the defense to introduce testimony supporting their evidence-planting claim taken a toll on Kusche's health? There's no way to know if his heart finally succumbed to the stress of knowing that Avery might go free because of his and the sheriff's and DA's conduct in 1985, but there is no question that elevated anxiety is bad for the heart, especially for someone with diabetes. Kusche had obviously been in denial. I ran into him in the courthouse parking lot a few weeks before he died. In the midst of television trucks, with their live feeds and monstrous antennae rising thirty feet high into the sky, we spoke briefly about the Avery case. It was a shame Avery was released from prison, he said with a straight face, because Allen and Avery could have both assaulted Penny Beerntsen on the beach that day. The not-so-subtle inference: *If we hadn't cut him loose, Teresa Halbach would still be alive.*

Kusche had expressed similar doubts at his deposition in the wrongful conviction lawsuit a year earlier. "Yes," he replied to one of the plaintiff's attorneys, "I've heard that DNA evidence supposedly exonerated Mr. Avery, but I don't know that on personal knowledge because I haven't seen the reports. I don't believe everything I read in the newspapers. Who knows," he suggested, "maybe the DNA evidence was fabricated? Or maybe they both did it."

The headline in the local paper the night before he died covered the judge's decision to allow the jury to hear the blood vial and wrongful conviction evidence. Was the bravado Kusche showed during our conversation in the parking lot a few weeks earlier his way of masking his fear that Avery might walk for Halbach's murder, in part because of his role in the wrongful conviction two decades earlier? Maybe this fear was too much stress for Gene Kusche's aging heart to take. Or was his death just another odd coincidence in a case that was chock-full of odd coincidences from the very beginning?

Judge Willis is no Lance Ito—in fact, he's just the opposite. Despite its complexity, he was determined that the trial would be concluded in six weeks or less. But given the amount of pretrial publicity, as well as the strongly held views of some on the panel, it took a full week to select the jury. Nevertheless, by week's end the 144 prospects on the panel had been winnowed down to the chosen sixteen—eight women and eight men, four of whom would serve as alternates.

The first day of trial arrived. Kratz delivered a three-hour opening statement that was compelling, if predictable. Using PowerPoint slides and high-tech schematic drawings, he showed the jury the Avery Salvage Yard, with its cluster of trailer homes and outbuildings. Speaking in a pleasant, low-key, comforting way, he laid out a convincing account of Avery's guilt. "I promise," Kratz assured them, "by the end of this case, you will have no doubt who murdered Teresa Halbach."

Dean Strang hit a home run for the defense. With his sincere and thoughtful tone and demeanor, he asked the jurors not to prejudge his client's guilt. Once they heard all the facts, he told them, they would have serious doubts about the state's evidence, including how the ignition key for Halbach's RAV4 car got into Avery's bedroom and how his blood got into her car. He said the sheriff's department focused almost exclusively on the defendant in the investigation because of their disdain for him, calling their technique "tunnel vision."

"The police didn't kill Teresa Halbach," Strang said, "they have that in common with Steven Avery, but they wanted to believe he did." He told the jurors he was going to ask them at the end of the case "to get it right this time."

Kratz and the rest of the prosecution team started presenting their case the next day. With Tom Fallon from the attorney general's office and Norm Gahn assisting, he began by laying out a timeline leading up to Halbach's death, with phone calls and a paper trail detailing her whereabouts on Halloween Day, 2005.

The prosecution presented a steady stream of physical evidence, starting with the human remains found in Barb Janda's burn barrel and Avery's fire pit behind his garage. The bone fragments included a skull section that remained intact enough for an expert to determine the deceased had been shot twice in the head—just as Brendan Dassey had said.

Sherry Culhane, still a DNA analyst at the Wisconsin Crime Lab, said the chances were one in a billion that the charred tissue from one of the bone fragments found in the fire pit did not belong to Teresa Halbach. She also tested the bloodstains lifted from Halbach's car, and they matched Avery's DNA profile, as did biological evidence left on the vehicle's key.

Jerry Buting turned the state's presentation of the physical evidence on its head by suggesting in one blistering cross-examination after another that the evidence was planted. He relentlessly attacked the investigating officers for what he perceived as their lack of caution in following procedure. He questioned how four police officers failed to find a bullet fragment containing Teresa Halbach's DNA before it was discovered months later in Steven's garage, terming it the "magic bullet."

"Did you see a bullet on November sixth?" he asked one of the officers from Calumet County, who immediately replied that he had not.

"Because if you had, you would have collected it, right?" Buting asked rhetorically, "because it would have been an extremely important piece of evidence, right? There were four of you in that garage, and not one of you found a bullet or a bullet fragment."

"Correct," the officer replied.

Buting pulled no punches when he challenged how the ignition key from the RAV4 ended up in Avery's bedroom, all but indicting Colborn and Lenk on the stand for planting them. Kratz tried to soften the blow by suggesting the key wasn't discovered earlier because the initial searches of the expansive buildings on the property, including Avery's trailer, were cursory sweeps and not detailed examinations. But to many in the courtroom, the explanation rang hollow.

Kratz also called Calumet County deputy Kucharski, who was in the bedroom with Lenk and Colborn, when the key was found. "Based upon your positioning a couple feet away from that key, did you believe that either Lenk or Colborn had an opportunity, out of your eyesight, to place, or what's called 'plant,' that key there?" Kratz asked.

"No, they did not," the officer replied.

But Buting beat up on him on cross-examination and the deputy had to retreat: "My actual observations, I would have to say that it could be possible, as in I was doing other things, I was taking photographs, I was searching the nightstand."

I recalled also the disputed blood evidence—the defense claim that police planted Avery's blood in Halbach's car from the blood vial kept in the clerk of courts' office.

A television reporter interviewed Steven's father, Allan, outside the courthouse a few days into the trial. "We're sick and tired of them saying bones were found on Avery's Auto Salvage," Allan said. "They found nothing. All they found is somebody put a car there.

"Brendan Dassey is innocent and my son is innocent," he continued. "If you start from the beginning, they plugged the highway off and kicked us out of our houses for eight days so they could plant evidence. This is not right. We need to give our justice system a good goin' over."

Kratz called Bobby Dassey, Brendan's older brother, the following day. Bobby testified that he saw a girl walking toward his Uncle Steven's trailer at two forty-five p.m. on Halloween Day. He also said a few days after Teresa Halbach went missing, his uncle jokingly asked him if he wanted to help hide a body, and then he kidded that she probably went to Mexico.

Brendan and Bobby's brother, Blaine, also testified, telling the jury he saw a huge bonfire burning when he returned from trick-or-treating the night Halbach disappeared. He said he saw someone near the fire, but Blaine claimed he couldn't remember who it was.

I remembered going home the night the jury began deliberations confident that they would see through the now-discredited conspiracy theory and swiftly return a guilty verdict the next day, probably in the morning. Now that the prosecution had shown the blood vial defense for what it was, a desperate attempt to shift blame, I couldn't imagine how they could do otherwise.

Other than the happenstance of Lenk and Colborn finding the key, the defense had presented little of substance. In light of all the rest of the evidence, even that seemed fairly harmless now. For more than a year Buting and Strang had shouted "police conspiracy" to anyone with ears, but now I assumed the jurors had heard enough conjecture and were ready to decide.

I should not have been so confident. The jury resumed at nine the next morning. After several more hours of deliberating with-out reaching a verdict, they sent Judge Willis a note—the jury wanted a magnifying glass. That's right, a magnifying glass.

Prosecutors squirm when deliberating jurors make a request or have a question they want answered by the judge because it usually means they're having serious doubts about the state's case. *Why do they want a magnifying glass?* I asked myself. Was it to inspect the photograph of the blood stains in RAV4? Were they buying the defense that the blood was planted and asking for a magnifying glass so they could take a look for themselves?

It was impossible to say, but Judge Willis gathered the parties and brought in the jury. They were not to conduct their own in-vestigation, the judge told them, they were to base their decision on the evidence in the record, and nothing more.

The jury resumed deliberating a few minutes later and retired at six that evening. Still, there was no verdict. They'd sat stone-faced through five weeks of testimony and there was no way of knowing which way they were leaning. It had me on edge. I could only imagine the level of discomfort Kratz and the rest of the prosecution team felt—not to mention the Halbachs.

Not long after the jurors began deliberating the next morn-ing, they sent an even more distressing note to Judge Willis. They wanted to review the testimony from Sherry Culhane—and, worse, they only wanted her cross-examination.

Now I was really worried.

Jerry Buting had established two things during his cross-examination of crime lab analyst Culhane, which I assumed were now on the minds of the jurors. First, Steven Avery's DNA was not found on the trigger of the rifle that he allegedly used to shoot Teresa Halbach. Second, there was no blood on the rifle's barrel.

"The victim in this case was shot at close range, wasn't she?" Buting had asked. "And you would typically find blood spatter on a rifle barrel that was used to shoot someone at close range, wouldn't you? Yet, when you examined the rifle that my client allegedly used to shoot the victim in this case, you didn't observe any blood spatter, isn't that right?"

Buting's assumptions weren't valid. A gunshot at close range doesn't always leave blood spatter, and the absence of the shooter's DNA on the trigger wasn't unusual. But thanks to *CSI* and other popular TV crime shows, jurors often assume there's always physical evidence left at crime scenes, and now they almost insist on proof by DNA. Sherry Culhane had appropriately qualified her answers, but it didn't matter. Buting had sown doubt in the minds of some of the jurors.

Judge Willis called in the lawyers again. After some prodding by the judge, the parties agreed that the fairest way to handle the jury's request was to read all of Culhane's testimony concerning the rifle, not just her cross-examination by Buting. So the clerk called in the jury and Judge Willis read the testimony in its entirety out loud. After deliberating a few more hours, the jury retired for the evening.

Two and a half days, and, still, no verdict.

I fell asleep that night thinking about Teresa Halbach's parents. They'd sat stoically through the entire trial, expressing quiet confidence in the system that they hoped would bring justice to the man who murdered their daughter. No parent of a murdered child expects closure, but a guilty verdict would at least end the drawn-out legal proceedings against Teresa's killer. I thought how an acquittal would devastate them, how it would add insult to an injury that you'd think could be insulted no further. If anyone could handle such pain, it would be the Halbach family with their unshakable faith, but hadn't they already suffered enough?

Just after four-thirty the following afternoon, the bailiff made the announcement. After deliberating for three days, the jury had reached a verdict. The parties and a sizeable crowd assembled. When everyone was in place, the clerk called in the jurors. They filed into the courtroom with their heads down. *Not a good sign for Steven Avery,* I thought.

"Has the jury reached a verdict?" Judge Willis asked in a calm but firm voice.

"Yes, Your Honor," the foreperson replied.

"Please hand the verdict forms to the bailiff."

The bailiff handed over the papers while the courtroom seemed to wait in silence. The judge had previously warned the spectators against outbursts. After carefully, silently reading through the forms, he announced the verdicts.

"'As to the charge of "Party to the Crime of First-Degree Intentional Homicide" as charged in count one of the Information, we the jury find the defendant, Steven A. Avery, guilty.'"

It was finished. Perhaps as a compromise offered by the jurors most convinced of his guilt to those who were not so sure, the jury found Avery not guilty on the "Mutilating a Corpse" charge. But with the homicide conviction, Avery's fate was sealed—he would spend the rest of his life behind bars.

CHAPTER 13

BULLETS AND BONES

Newly discovered evidence, especially game-changing evidence like Brendan Dassey's confession, opens up brand-new avenues for police and prosecutors to explore. An accomplice's confession corroborated by physical evidence is a gold mine for the state. If even half of what Dassey told police was true, there was very likely physical evidence inside Steven Avery's residence backing him up—blood, bullets, tissue, and who knows what else. So it wasn't a surprise that within hours of eliciting Dassey's confession, a new search warrant was obtained for Avery's bedroom and his garage.

The search of the garage bore fruit in the form of two bullets—one partially intact and the other fragmented. The first was lodged inside a crack toward the front of the garage, the second found a day later underneath an air compressor in the rear of the garage. A firearms expert later determined that the second bullet was fired from Avery's gun—and if that wasn't damning enough for Avery, testing on that same bullet yielded Halbach's DNA.

Additional scientific testing further corroborated Dassey's confession that Halbach was shot in the garage. Investigator Gary Steier sprayed luminol liberally on the floor to see if there were signs of blood on the floor where Dassey said Steven Avery shot her in the garage. After closing the garage door and turning off the lights, he observed a faint bluish white glow in the north-east corner of the garage; another larger area contained a light luminescent glow on an area west and north of the garage floor. This second glow aligned with a sketch Dassey made for the police that included his indication of where he and his uncle used Halbach's clothes to clean up her blood on the floor before they burned her clothes. Wisconsin crime lab forensic scientist John Ertl was present when luminol testing was conducted initially on November 8, 2005.

"That wasn't just a spot on the floor," Ertl testified during Avery's trial, "it was more of a smear . . . roughly three- to four-foot diameter area and faintly glowing under the luminol."

That section was the area behind the lawn tractor and the rear of the snowmobile. It reacted to the luminol by glowing faintly, however it did not react when Ertl conducted a more specific test using phenolphthalein.

"Well, there was something that had been spread out in a large area that was reacting, I don't know what," Ertl explained to the jury. "Cleaning chemicals dilute blood and would react, but it may not show up with phenolphthalein if it was diluted enough."

Ertl's testimony squared with evidence that Avery and Dassey had tried to wipe clean any trace of the murder with bleach. Not only were there bullets in the garage, but one of them was intact enough to confirm it was fired from a Marlin Glenfield Model 60 .22-caliber rifle that had been hanging from a gun rack above Avery's bed.

A firearms expert testified, "The patterns, the amount of agreement and correlation that I see, and saw, on this bullet, when I compared it to test fires, was enough for me to be able to conclude that it had been fired from this Marlin rifle, and could have been fired in none other."

The discovery of two bullets in the garage, one fired by Avery's rifle, where Dassey said his uncle shot Halbach multiple times, is powerful evidence of guilt in itself, but there was more. One of the bullets contained Halbach's DNA.

Testing done by crime lab analyst Sherry Culhane matched the biological material on the bullet with Halbach's DNA. Nothing, though, was ever uneventful in the thirty-year Steven Avery crime saga, and Culhane's testing of the bullet for DNA was no exception. Culhane's inadvertent, but nonfatal, error during the testing procedure was played for all its worth in *Making a Murderer*. The analyst's own DNA, probably from her saliva, contaminated the control sample, and Buting ripped her apart on the stand. She had made a mistake, but her mistake did not affect the integrity of the results, since it was the control sample, and not the biological material found on the bullet, that was contaminated.

In a justice system where an attorney's duty is to zealously represent his client, mischaracterizing evidence is rarely an obstacle for the defense. It certainly wasn't in Jerry Buting's words at the nightly press conference after Culhane had testified earlier in the day.

"Jerry, let me get this straight," a reporter asked him. "So you're saying that Halbach's DNA may have wound up on this bullet test because the DNA may have already been in a test tube?"

"The DNA . . . is so sensitive that these contamination logs prove that they get contamination from cases that aren't even in front of 'em," Buting enthusiastically answered. "Cases that are put away, locked up, done with, lo and behold, all of a sudden, bingo . . . they get someone else's profile. Where does that come from? They don't know. Where did her DNA come from in that contaminated control? She doesn't know."

"So, in other words, if you don't know where Culhane's DNA came from, you might not know where Halbach's DNA came from?" the reporter questioned.

"That's right. Remember now, this bullet wasn't even found in November. This bullet was found under suspicious circumstances, to begin with. So she's testing it four months after all the other . . . after she does all these other tests. For some reason she still has the evidence from those other tests."

The implication Buting wanted the jury and the media to draw was convincingly refuted by Sherry Culhane's testimony.

"During the extraction procedure I inadvertently introduced my own DNA into the negative control," she explained.

"Did that have any impact on your interpretation of your results?" the prosecutor asked.

"It did not have any impact as far as the profile from the evidence sample. It's just the fact that I introduced my own DNA into the manipulation control."

Asked to explain how a trace amount of her DNA could have made it into the control sample, Culhane said she believed it happened during the extraction procedure when she was explaining something to two new analysts, who were being trained.

"I felt as if I was far enough away from my workbench not to introduce my DNA," Culhane testified, "but apparently I was incorrect."

The bottom line is that none of Culhane's DNA was on the biological material from the bullet—it was only in the control.

Sherry Culhane—along with Colborn, Lenk, and Manitowoc County law enforcement in general—was one more public servant raked over the coals by Buting and Strang. The defense team had an excuse—they were doing it as part of their job. Not so with the creators of *Making a Murderer,* who through their skilled, but agenda-driven, editing distorted the truth even more than the defense.

It's all but forgotten now, but in one of the many twists of irony in the Steven Avery crime story, it was Sherry Culhane whose work at the crime lab in 2003 exonerated Steven Avery of the 1985 assault of Penny Beerntsen on the beach. Even more ironic is that in the first Steven Avery trial, Culhane took pains to spell out the limits of what could be gleaned from hair analysis before the advent of DNA testing. Trying to dispel the significance of a hair recovered from Avery's shirt that was similar to Beerntsen's, Avery's attorney asked Culhane whether it was possible to prove identification by hair analysis.

"No," Culhane candidly replied.

"Is the hair of many people consistent with each other?" the attorney continued.

"Yes."

"Can you give an opinion as to the probability whether the two hairs are from the same source?"

"No."

"All you can say is that it's not impossible that they're from the same source, isn't that correct?"

"That's right."

It's not the job of the scientists at the crime lab to win convictions for the state. When Sherry Culhane worked on the Avery case in 1985, she did just what she should have: She used the tools of science available at the time to analyze the physical evidence objectively, and then she testified truthfully about the results. When she told the jury that the hair found on Avery's shirt was consistent with the hair of the victim, "consistency" meant something less than 90 percent certain. It isn't surprising that in the years following Avery's wrongful conviction in 1985, hair examination lost whatever meager standing it previously held in the scientific community. Even before the advent of DNA, most courts throughout the nation ruled it inadmissible.

Still working at the crime lab eighteen years later, Culhane remained the analyst assigned to this case, and it was she who isolated the DNA on the pubic hair that set Avery free. But this time the odds weren't one in ten—this time they were 1 in 251 billion, and she made that fact abundantly clear in her report. There is no evidence to suggest that when Avery was accused of murder two years later, she had changed her stripes and willingly joined a conspiracy to distort evidence in a murder trial of a man she had helped to exonerate of an earlier crime. She readily admitted she made a mistake, but then maintained her devotion to objectivity and science by explaining that her error had no effect upon the DNA testing's results.

Even if it succeeded, attacking the reliability of crime lab analyst Culhane's DNA test results would not be enough to blunt the impact of the bullets, because the bullets themselves had to be explained away. The method of doing so took on a number of forms—some offered by the defense in Avery's trial, some by *Making a Murderer,* and others by myriad social media sites in its wake devoted to proving that Avery and Dassey were the victims of diabolical police and prosecutorial corruption.

Dassey had told police that Avery shot Halbach somewhere between five and ten times in the garage, leading some to ask where the rest of the bullets were. A legitimate question to be sure, but one with an obvious answer, since Avery and probably Dassey presumably would have picked up the bullets and could easily have missed the two that police later found.

The bullet underneath the air compressor and the fragment in the crack would have been difficult to find, as shown by the fact that the police missed them in their previous searches of the garage. It's also likely that some of the bullets did not exit Halbach's body, especially the ones Avery shot into her head.

A more credible challenge is why weren't the bullets found during prior searches of Avery's garage? Such damning evidence, how could it have possibly been missed?

But there was nothing nefarious in the way the bullets were found, at least it didn't sound that way from the testimony of Kevin Heimerl, the state investigator who found them.

"I was standing in the garage and I looked down at the floor. In front of me there was a crack in the concrete, and I observed this round, gray object that resembled the head of a roofing nail."

Investigator Heimerl explained how and where he found the second bullet fragment the next day:

"We had been processing this garage, searching this garage. As you look at this photograph, we approached the compressor from its left, and it was a large object," Heimerl testified. "As we reached this area, I had to get onto my hands and my knees in front of the compressor and utilized a flashlight to look under the compressor. . . . I found what appeared to be a bullet."

Despite the impression left by *Making a Murderer,* the bullets were not found by Manitowoc County officers—Colborn and Lenk as they did not participate in the search of the garage. Like every other evidence-planting claim raised by the defense, there was no affirmative evidence that the bullets were planted or an explanation of how the police managed to pull it off.

If considered objectively, it should come as no surprise that the bullets were missed during the earlier searches. Initially the police had little information concerning the exact cause of Teresa Halbach's death, or where she died. On February 28, they received the crime lab's findings with respect to charred pieces of her skull, which had been retrieved from the fire pit behind Avery's garage. Crime lab analyst Kenneth Olson detected traces of lead metal on the "suspected entrance defect" on a piece of the skull—suggesting that she had been shot in the head. Prior to then, the cause of death was unknown.

On March 1, the day after the crime lab results were delivered, in one of the most controversial scenes captured during *Making a Murderer,* Dassey told Investigators Mark Wiegert and Thomas Fassbender that Avery shot Halbach with multiple rounds, in the garage. He answered them after they repeatedly and forcefully asked him, "What happened to her head?"

This scene, a short clip of hours of interrogation footage, resulted in the loudest public outcry by far that Brendan was unfairly treated and coerced until he finally guessed answers that would please the police.

Without solid physical evidence prior to this, police did not know how or where Halbach was murdered; investigators had no more reason to search the garage than anywhere else in Steven Avery's home. But now, armed with specific new information and with a precise mission in mind, they spent hours that very day in

Avery's garage, searching for bullets and blood. The two bullets were in locations easily missed—one underneath the air compressor and another lodged in a crack. Bottom line: it's easy to see how they missed them during the prior searches.

Social media observers have argued that if Steven shot Teresa in the head with a .22 caliber rifle as Brendan says he did, the bullets would not have exited her skull, which is interesting because the same bit of physics might also at least in part explain why only two bullets were found. It's true that a .22 caliber bullet does not possess the kinetic energy necessary to exit a bone as thick as the skull, but if it passes through soft tissue instead, it will exit the body and sometimes carry the victim's DNA with it, as one of the bullets in this case did.

When Brendan Dassey was interrogated—and make no mistake, it was an interrogation in every sense of the word—he was asked to draw a diagram of where Halbach and Avery were in the garage when Avery shot her. When the crime lab analyst conducted the luminol test that evening, the glow appeared in the area where Dassey placed Halbach in the diagram. The bullet found underneath the compressor had apparently exited soft tissue, perhaps her cheek or her shoulder, and not bone.

As in nearly every other stage of my journey, the more thoroughly I examined the "magic bullet" defense, the more I became convinced that it was nothing but smoke and mirrors.

If the search of the garage after Dassey's confession was a bonanza for the police, the search of the bedroom was a bust. Despite the horrific scene depicted by Dassey, they came up empty-handed when they searched Steven Avery's bedroom: not a drop of Halbach's blood, not a strand of her hair, no biological evidence at all that would match her DNA.

Its absence understandably makes people wonder. However, as I looked into it further, I found a few explanations that seemed to make sense. Besides, the lack of Halbach's hair or blood in Avery's bedroom took nothing away from the bullets that killed her being found in the garage—or, for that matter, the mountain of other evidence that pointed to Avery's guilt. Two bullets, one confirmed as fired from the defendant's gun and containing the victim's DNA, discovered in a location where an accomplice said the defendant shot the victim. Evidence like this would typically make for an open-and-shut case for the state.

Nevertheless, despite the mountain of additional evidence arrayed against the defendant, the jury was out for three days. To many, Steven Avery's guilt somehow remained in doubt. His luring of Halbach to the salvage yard, the discovery of her SUV at the edge of the premises with his blood inside and its ignition key in his bedroom, the "other acts" evidence dating back decades and continuing to the night before Halbach was murdered, when he invited his nephew's girlfriend over for rough sex—in addition to the bullets fired from Avery's gun in the garage, where Dassey said he shot her—all of this pointed squarely toward Steven Avery's guilt. I'm not fond of the phrase, but with evidence as compelling as this, if ever there was a "slam-dunk case," the Steven Avery case should have been it.

But for one reason and one reason alone it wasn't—Avery's wrongful conviction in 1985. Without it, the evidence-planting claim would have been laughed out of court, and Jerry Buting and Dean Strang probably run out of town.

And then there were the bones. Within days after the RAV4 was found, investigators found two "burn sites" on the premises containing some of Teresa Halbach's charred remains. In a burn barrel in a field behind Steven's sister Barb's residence, fragments were found from four different types of human bones. In a burn pit area behind Avery's garage, they found more bones, including skull fragments and part of a tibia with enough charred tissue to later be identified by DNA testing as Halbach's. In the same burn pit, they found teeth fragments and metal rivets from her jeans. Later another burn site was found in a nearby quarry, but with the exception of three bones that could potentially be human pelvis bone fragments, the remaining bones discovered there were not human.

The defense claimed Halbach's body was burned somewhere else and then planted at the salvage yard—just like the car, the blood, the key, and the bullets. The list was getting long. Clever on-line commentators later termed it the "traveling bones defense," and it's impossible to disprove it completely.

The majority of Teresa Halbach's bones were found in the burn pit and the grassy area around it twenty yards from Avery's bedroom window. "I would say that virtually every part of the skeleton, at least a fragment or more of almost every bone below the neck, was recovered in that burn pit," Dr. Leslie Eisenberg, a forensic anthropologist and the state's expert on all things bones, explained to the jury.

She said it was "highly unlikely" that the bones in the burn pit were not burned there. If the bones had been moved to the pit from another location, she stated, she would expect to see break-age due to transport, but she didn't.

Cross-examined by Dean Strang, Dr. Eisenberg did, however, con-cede that the condition of Teresa's bones—most were crushed into small pieces—could have resulted from being transported, either from the salvage yard to the crime lab by police or, theoretically, by someone who burned them elsewhere and then placed them where they were found.

The defense expert, Dr. Scott Fairgrieve, who had reviewed the photos and reports concerning the bones, but had not ob-served them in person, testified it was *possible* the bones were transported to the salvage yard from some other location. How-ever, based upon his examination, he would go no further than that, testifying that in his professional opinion it could not be concluded with perfect certainty that the remains had not been moved. A tepid response from an expert retained by the defense.

* * *

Rodney Pevytoe, with the Arson Bureau at the Wisconsin Department of Justice, on the other hand, investigated the burn pit and was almost certain the charred bone fragments had been burned in the pit behind Avery's garage and not moved there from another location. He found wiring from what he believed were more than five steel-belted radial tires in the burn pit and some of the bone fragments were "inside the wire, deeply inside of it in some cases . . . to the point where I actually had to, physically, pull apart the wire in order to get in there."

He told jurors that Halbach's bones could not have been thrown on top of the wires afterward and had to have been burned with the tires the way they were found. The soil in the pit appeared consistent with having been exposed to oils from burning tires, he added, and several objects near the fire had evidence of charring and oxidation. He found a rake with wires from steel-belted tires in its teeth and surmised that it was used to stir the fire, as well as a spade shovel and a screwdriver—perhaps to chop up bones as the fire died down.

Nonscientific evidence also dispelled the defense claim that the bones were planted. Steven's brother Earl told a Calumet County investigator that on Wednesday night, November 2, just two days after Teresa disappeared, Steven asked Brendan to remove the tire rims and wire out of his burn pit and put them on the large pile of tire rims out in the salvage yard. This struck Earl as unusual because the five or six rims and the wire had already been placed outside the burn area for their nephew to pick up. Brendan did not have to take the rims out of the fire pit; they were already set aside.

It's all but inevitable that amid their presentation of evidence and occasional squabbles over the law, the lawyers and even the judge involved in a murder trial lose sight of the humanity of the victim. With testimony and photos as gruesome and grisly as those presented in the Avery case, by the end of the trial even jurors are prone to consider the evidence strictly in a clinical sense—forgetting, for example, in this instance that Teresa Halbach was a twenty-five-year-old life-filled, loving daughter and sister and friend of spectators in the courtroom who dearly missed her. This is to be expected since, if and until the proceedings move on to a sentencing hearing, a trial is not about the victim's life—it's about whether there is sufficient evidence to determine who took it.

I suspect, however, that on an occasion or two during the trial—and perhaps on a less-mindful level of consciousness during its entirety—the lawyers, the judge, and certainly the jurors did not forget about the victim and her family at all. The best we can do is to make certain that we honor the spirit and the soul of the victim. Ken Kratz did just that when he addressed the jury during Steven Avery's trial, and, not surprisingly, so did Dean Strang.

With Teresa Halbach and her gorgeous smile beaming from the PowerPoint screen, Kratz addressed the jurors in his opening statement.

"I'm going to introduce you to somebody, this remarkable young woman was twenty-five years of age, she was single, and she was a freelance photographer. She had her own photography business that, although in its infancy, was doing quite well. This woman—and I will remind you several times in this opening and throughout the trial, I will remind you that we're talking about a real person. We're talking about somebody's daughter, somebody's sister, a lot of people's friend. Teresa Halbach had her whole life in front of her and the evidence is going to show that on Halloween of 2005, that all ended, that ended in the hands of the defendant, Steven Avery."

Given the role they play in a criminal trial, very few defense attorneys could pull this off, but before turning to what he perceived to be the shortcomings of the state's case, Dean Strang sincerely paid tribute to Teresa Halbach as well:

"The second thing you are not going to be able to do—I'm quite certain you are not going to be able to do—is bring Teresa Halbach back through that door, or, better yet, back through the door of her mom's house. We are not going to be able to do that. Convicting a guilty guy, convicting the person who killed her, wouldn't do it. Convicting someone who didn't kill her, certainly won't do it. The life that was before October 31, 2005, never will be lost. It's etched in Mom's heart. It's etched in her brother's, and her two sisters' minds, in their memories, in the people they are. That life is not lost. The life that could have been, going forward beginning November 1, 2005, is forever lost, not forgotten, but lost. This is human tragedy, and if you or I understood why people have been killing each other since we crawled out of caves, we would stop it. But somebody killed this woman and that life going forward is lost. You can't get it back. I can't get it back. The gentleman at this table can't get it back."

CHAPTER 14

WHO IS STEVEN AVERY?

It's almost universal. Despite their initial idealism, most professionals who work in the criminal justice system develop an edge of cynicism after a while. We see too many repeat offenders, I suppose. So it isn't surprising that from the moment Steven Avery walked out of prison, the courthouse crowd started taking bets on when he'd be back. They knew what he was like before he had been sent there, and if they didn't, one of the old-timers filled them in. The cat-burning incident, ramming into the wife of a deputy's car and accosting her at gunpoint—these and some of his other brushes with the law became part of courthouse lore.

Avery had another strike against him, too, one not shared by most former offenders trying to stitch their lives back together after serving their time. Because his conviction and sentence had been vacated, when he walked out of prison, he wasn't on parole. That meant no supervision, no counseling, no weekly meetings with a parole agent to keep tabs on him—no support.

In an interview with a *Milwaukee Journal Sentinel* reporter, he described how he was often depressed and full of frustration and anger.

"Sometimes it'll last all day," he said. "That's when I try to stay away from everybody. Sometimes I cuss them out, sometimes I just go for a ride—it ain't nothing to put on a hundred miles."

156

He confided that he cried sometimes because his twin boys didn't want anything to do with him. "There's probably too much going on inside my head, brain can't put it all in," he told the reporter.

He complained about the state not providing him with counseling or other help in the transition—"They just let you out the door"—but he also admitted that he would have refused to see a psychiatrist even if one had been offered. "I can't tell him my problem. I'll sort it out myself," he said. "What can he do that I can't?"

Avery gave assurances that he didn't really want to return to prison, but when he reflected about how he used to sit on a picnic bench in the prison yard and count the jets that flew by, his words didn't sound very convincing: "Sometimes," he said, "I feel like it's easier in there. Some days, just put me back there, get it all over with."

The joy of freedom faded after a while and Avery's life took a turn for the worse. While he beat the predictions of the most pessimistic courthouse prognosticators, it wasn't long before he had a few run-ins with the law. After one particularly serious incident, perhaps Avery should have been "put back in there" for a while. Better yet, maybe he should have been placed on probation with someone to keep an eye on him, with jail or prison hanging over his head.

He had taken up with a similarly lost soul by the name of Jodi Stachowski not long after he was released from prison. Steven moved in with Jodi, who was living in the trailer next to his sister, owned by Rollie Johnson and it was love at first sight.

The honeymoon didn't last long because a few months after they began seeing each other, Jodi had to call the police. Shortly after Steven moved in with Jodi, one weekend when he was up north, he found out she was out at the races and she hadn't let him know she was going out. This was a major offense in a domestic violence abuser's controlling mind.

When Jodi came home a little after eleven at night, she and Avery got into an argument. She told him "to pack his shit up and move out." He pushed her, causing her to fall into a chair and hit her head. He got on top of her and hit her, telling her he should kill her. He ripped the phone out of the wall when she tried calling 911. Before she reached the dispatcher, he strangled her and she lost consciousness. He dragged her out to the car when she came to and said, "I should get the gun and kill you."

In light of the conflict of interest stemming from Avery's wrongful conviction lawsuit, we sent the case to a local attorney who agreed to serve as a special prosecutor. Due to discrepancies between Jodi's original version and what she told the officer a few days later and her request to drop the charges, the special prosecutor told the police to issue a disorderly conduct citation instead of issuing criminal charges. Somehow the media never got wind of the incident. As far as the public was concerned, Steven Avery was still an innocent lamb.

Interviewed nine years before *Making a Murderer* aired, Jodi had stood steadfast with Avery, holding hands with him and telling the documentarians that the sheriff's department was trying to set him up again. However, she changed her tune in an interview with Nancy Grace a month after the documentary aired.

Making international headlines, she said she was pressured by Steven Avery to come off right on *Making a Murderer* and she wasn't telling the truth. It was all an act, she said. He told her to smile and be happy and threatened her if she didn't obey his demands.

"I didn't know what to do. I didn't want to get hurt. Steven is one person I don't trust. He's like Dr. Jekyll and Mr. Hyde," she said. "A nice person, semi-nice person, and then behind closed doors he's a monster. He told me once—excuse my language—'all bitches owe him' because of the one that sent him to prison the first time. We all owed him—and he could do whatever he wanted."

She said she believed Avery and his nephew raped Halbach while she was tied up on the bed and then murdered her, just as

Brendan Dassey had said. Crying, she told Nancy Grace that she still felt guilty because she was supposed to be with Avery the day Teresa Halbach was murdered and felt she could have stopped him and saved her life. Asked why she believed Steven Avery was guilty, she recounted an incident when he tied her to the bedpost with rope and wanted to videotape having sex with her, only backing down after she repeatedly refused.

"He's not innocent," she said later. "I ate two boxes of rat poison just so I could go to the hospital and get away from him and ask them to get the police to help me."

Avery responded from prison in a three-page handwritten letter sent to WISN TV/Radio in Milwaukee.

How much money Jodi get to talk bad! he wrote. *The state $.*

A typed statement was attached to his letter, reading, *The real killer is still out there. Who is he stalking now? I am really innocent of this case and that is the truth!!! The truth will set me free!!!!!!!*

The documentarians responded, telling a reporter from *TV Guide* that they could not speak to what Jodi was saying now: "But when we filmed nine years ago, this is an accurate portrayal of what she was saying at the time."

Which of Jodi Stachowski's versions was the truth? To find out more, I consulted the Calumet County police reports.

On September 13, 2006, about five months before Steven Avery's trial, Calumet County investigator Mark Wiegert and Division of Criminal Investigation (DCI) special agent Thomas Fassbender interviewed Jodi's mother.

Sandra Stachowski and her husband had legal custody of Jodi's thirteen-year-old daughter. They stopped letting her go to Avery's trailer because she "hated" Steven Avery and cried when she had to go there. Sandra and her husband had to go through Avery before they could speak with Jodi on the phone. In one conversation he threatened to take their granddaughter away from them and put her in a foster home.

Jodi told her mother that Avery beat her in front of her granddaughter and told her on many occasions that he could kill her and nobody would miss her. They locked themselves in the bathroom on one occasion because they thought he was pouring gas around the trailer to light it on fire.

Their granddaughter wrote them a letter not long before Jodi began serving her jail sentence for the drunk-driving offense: *I love you and papa with all my heart and I hope nothing happens to you or papa and I'm sorry that on Mother's Day weekend I went with my mom because all they did was fight, fight, and fight. I didn't really have any fun because Steve made me stay in the trailer for one day because I was really hyper and I was playing cards with (redacted) boys. Goodness I hate Steve Avery. I wish he would go to prison. Oh my goodness.*

Now, with Jodi's mother's and daughter's statements, it was no longer just Jodi's words building the accusation against Steven Avery. Still, just because Avery was violent and sexually abusive with Jodi, that doesn't prove he murdered Teresa Halbach. Taken in total, while not proof in and of themselves, Avery's strangling of Jodi to the point where she lost consciousness, threatening to kill her, and tying her to the bedpost, essentially intending to rape her, are legitimate factors to consider.

Besides, as we will now see from other court documents, Jodi was not the only victim of his propensity for violence and sexual rage.

"Other acts" evidence is evidence of a crime or "other bad act" committed by a defendant other than the crime for which he is on trial—at least as it pertains to the Avery case. The general rule is that other acts evidence is not admissible at trial because jurors might think, *If he did that one, he probably did this one, too.* If the prosecution wants to use the "other act" not to prove that the defendant "acted in conformity therewith," but for one or more of a traditional set of criteria instead, the court may allow it to be admitted.

There's an entire body of law interpreting this evidentiary rule that would fill another book. But for our purposes it is enough to know that the general criteria include "proof of motive, opportunity, intent, preparation, plan, knowledge, identity, or absence of mistake or accident" and that a judge can admit the evidence, but only if "its probative value is not substantially outweighed by the risk or danger of unfair prejudice."

The prosecution had so much ammunition in Steven Avery's case that they had to file a first and then a second supplemental motion to their initial motion to admit evidence of "other acts." All of it, they said, should be admitted because it was relevant to his "motive, intent, and plan."

With her uncle safely behind bars, awaiting trial for Teresa Halbach's murder, on January 23, 2006, Steven's niece sat down with Calumet County officer Wendy Baldwin and told her about her relationship with her uncle. She was seventeen when Avery was released from prison in 2003 and she often hung around with him, going "ice fishing and stuff," as she explained it.

He started asking her to meet him at Walmart and other stores because he didn't know what to get for his house. He always bragged about his money and got angry if she refused.

She began to feel uncomfortable when he started kissing her good-bye. "I'm like, 'What are you doing? I don't kiss nobody good-bye except for my ma and dad,'" she said. "And then he would say, well, he would tell me how, like, my mom and dad hated me."

"You know that's not true, right?" the officer interjected.

"Ah, now I do," Avery's niece replied. "But before, I would believe him, because, I don't know why, I think it was because I was around him so much."

She was describing classic "grooming" behavior, and the details rang true.

"Your mom loves you a lot," the officer interjected again, before asking her to describe what happened later.

The niece cried as she described how her then-forty-two-year-old uncle raped her on her cousin's bunk bed.

She told him to stop, because he was just in prison for a rape that he did not commit. "So why would he try doing something dumb like that?"

Her uncle laughed and told her that it was meant to be, and "I'm gonna marry you someday when I get all my money, you'll see."

His niece became upset when she described what she did to try to make him stop: "I kept on telling him no, and . . . when I would try to get up and pull away, he would spread my legs with his elbows. And—and then he, like, held my hands back down and he just . . . I don't know, it's—it's sick, I don't . . ." At this point the officer's report said the niece started crying.

During this and other encounters Steven Avery threatened not just his niece but her family, too, saying he would set her house on fire if she didn't do what he wanted.

"He said he would hurt my dad, or he would hurt my mom," she told the officer, "and I didn't want them to get hurt."

When she heard Avery might be released on bail, she told her dad she wasn't going anywhere by herself, and "I even told my managers that I won't work alone if I knew he was out."

Like many victims of sexual violence, she blamed herself.

"I hated all the stuff he did to me," she said. "So I would just be upstairs, writing journals saying that 'I hate myself, I hate myself,' and I have one of these planners, and I wrote all the bad stuff. I blacked it all out now 'cause then he started forcing me against my mom and dad saying that they're bad. And I believed him, 'cause, I don't know, I used to hang out with him a lot, thinking he wasn't a bad guy."

Concerned about its inflammatory nature and the risk of poisoning the jury pool if the information was released, Judge Willis ordered that the parties' briefs and his written decision concerning the "other acts" evidence and be kept under seal. But shortly after the trial it was unsealed, and thanks to the crowd-sourcing efforts of a group of concerned citizens, it is now available online for anyone with access to the Internet.

I knew Steven Avery was far from a Boy Scout, both before and after his wrongful conviction in 1985. Still, as I continued reviewing the prosecution's motions to admit "other acts" evidence, I was surprised how much I did not know about him. Some of it dated back nearly a quarter century and was extremely disturbing.

In an interview in January 2006, forty-two-year-old Amy Harris (pseudonym) told a Calumet County officer that Avery had sexually assaulted her when she was seventeen or eighteen years old—she couldn't remember which. It happened while she was staying at his and his ex-wife's house a few years before his wrongful conviction in 1985 while he was still married to Lori. She was lying on the couch when Avery came over and began fondling her. She told him to stop, but he put his hand over her mouth and then forced her to have sex. He told her during the assault "there would be trouble" if she yelled or screamed.

The next allegation against Steven Avery concerned a more recent event. Seventeen-year-old Melissa Hansen (pseudonym) told Wisconsin DCI special agent Steven Lewis that Avery had called her on her cell phone the day before Teresa Halbach disappeared. He asked if she wanted to join him in his trailer and "have a little fun" and that they could "have the bed hit the wall, real hard." Melissa told Avery he was wasting her cell minutes and hung up the phone.

The other acts motion continued with Avery's history of physical violence against women—starting with the abuse he heaped upon his ex-wife, Lori, before his wrongful conviction in 1985.

Lori stayed at the domestic violence shelter several times after he beat her during their marriage. She said the abuse was so extreme that she thinks her husband would have killed her if he hadn't been sent to prison in 1985. Typical among perpetrators of domestic violence, he threatened to kill her if she ever left.

Avery continued to abuse Lori and their children from inside the prison walls by sending them threatening letters. *I hate mom; she will pay; I will kill you,* he wrote in one of the letters. *I will get you when I'm out; Daddy will git mom when daddy gits out,* he wrote in another.

The Findings of Facts from their divorce case are instructive: *Mr. Avery is impulsive; had threatened to kill and mutilate his wife; and refused to participate in programming while in prison.*

Citing what they termed an "escalating pattern of abuse," the prosecutors turned next to the violence Avery's girlfriend Jodi Stachowski suffered at his hands. With her boyfriend safely behind bars, on January 19, 2006, Jodi told Calumet County officer John Dedering that Avery frequently abused her during the eighteen months they lived together. He struck her hard enough on three or four occasions to leave bruising, including a big one on her right cheekbone after one of the beatings.

Recounting an incident that made international headlines after her interview with Nancy Grace a full ten years later, Jodi told Officer Dedering more about the night Avery strangled her. She remembered falling to her knees and blacking out. When she regained consciousness, he was trying to drag her out the front door of the trailer. She was able to get to her feet, but he grabbed her by her sweatshirt and dragged her over to his truck and forced her to get in. It was the only time she stood up for herself, Jodi said, and "look what happened."

There was corroborating evidence for Jodi's claim of abuse, including a recorded jail telephone conversation between them on January 27, 2006. Steven asked her to deny he ever abused her, and said "if she cared about him," she should "tell the police that she just fell down while she was drunk and that's how she got the bruises."

It's amazing how many inmates ignore the notice above the phone in the jail warning that calls to and from the jail are recorded.

* * *

In their next bid for "other acts" evidence, the prosecution sought to admit the circumstances surrounding the now-infamous cat-burning incident. When it occurred, nearly a quarter century earlier, Avery was twenty years old.

"The jury must be allowed to consider the vicious and cold-hearted torture and death of Avery's cat," the prosecution argued, because of its "striking similarity" to the "object of Avery's torture on a bonfire." In this last phrase they were presumably referring to Halbach's body. His "sadistic personality . . . is highly relevant to whether he killed Teresa and mutilated her body after she died."

Righteous indignation is one of the occupational hazards prosecutors should strive to avoid, but the prosecution team's zeal concerning the cat-burning incident, as illustrated in the following words, shows that we don't always succeed:

> *"The state argues that facts at trial will include after stabbing Teresa Halbach, the defendant took a rifle and shot her several times, including in the head while in his garage. Importantly, the cat, which Avery threw on the fire (alive), jumped off the fire, while burning, and the defendant was forced to reapply flammable liquid to the cat, and, once again, throw the cat on the fire until it burned to death. The state argues that to ensure a similar episode would not occur with the victim, Teresa Halbach, the defendant 'made sure' the victim was dead by shooting her with a rifle (for up to ten times). Without knowledge of the burning-cat story, the jury may be left to speculate as to why the defendant would shoot Ms. Halbach so many times after having possibly caused life-ending injuries to her minutes before by stabbing. The state agrees that burning a live cat is disgusting and sensational behavior. However, it is behavior the defendant alone engaged in, and its relevance cannot be ignored due to what is sure to be a graphic description of the animal's killing."*

No doubt, Avery's lighting a cat afire twenty-four years earlier was reprehensible, but the prosecutors were stretching the argument well past its breaking point. If the cat-burning incident was relevant at all, "its probative value," as the law puts it, "is substantially outweighed by the danger of unfair prejudice."

While also remote in time, the prosecution's next request had teeth. Referring to Avery's ramming his pickup truck into Sandra Morris's car, and then holding her at gunpoint, the state argued that the issue "of whether this defendant 'seized' Ms. Halbach should include consideration by the jury of this defendant's 'seizure' of Sandra Morris at gunpoint in 1985."

Regardless of the merits of the motion to admit it as evidence in Avery's murder trial, the details of the Sandra Morris incident were revealing—especially in light of *Making a Murderer*'s portrayal of the event as little more than Avery not handling his emotions in an appropriate way.

Sandra, a second cousin of Avery's, and her husband, Bill, a reserve deputy at the sheriff's department, lived just up the road from Steven and Lori. Avery had been watching her with a pair of binoculars, off and on for months, as she got into her car before leaving for work at five-thirty in the morning. Standing at the edge of the road, he would expose himself and occasionally masturbate as she drove by.

She spoke with Avery's father, Allan, to get Steven to stop—a fact omitted by *Making a Murderer*—but when the problems continued, an anonymous neighbor went to the police and told them about some of what he had been doing in the neighborhood. At approximately five-thirty a.m. on September 20, and again on November 27, 1984, he jumped into the middle of the road without any clothing on as Sandra drove past. She almost ran into him once, because it was raining and visibility was poor.

On January 3, 1985, again at approximately five-thirty a.m., Sandra drove past Steven and Lori's house and then noticed

Steven's vehicle coming up behind her at a rapid pace. He started passing her, but then rammed into the side of her car, forcing her off the roadway. He confronted her, pointing a rifle at her, and ordered her to get into his vehicle. She pleaded with him to let her go because her baby would freeze to death if he didn't allow her to take the child to her parents' home. Steven looked into her vehicle, saw the child in the front seat, and let her get back into her car. He followed her for a while. When she arrived at her parents' residence, she called 911. Police later searched Steven and Lori's house and underneath a child's bed they found a 30-06 rifle with a live round in the chamber.

The relevance of the Morris incident to Teresa Halbach's murder was a stretch, but the state stretched it nonetheless. They compared the "fixation" Avery developed with Sandra Morris to what he had with Teresa Halbach. "He began by exposing himself to both Ms. Morris and Ms. Halbach," argued the prosecution— again stretching the facts unless they had undisclosed evidence that he had exposed himself to Halbach on a prior occasion. "After these contacts failed to generate the desired result," they continued, "Steven Avery used a firearm in an effort to force the unwilling victims to submit to sexual intercourse."

Judge Willis had his work cut out for him. The law required him to apply a three-step analysis for every item of "other acts" evidence offered by the state: Was the evidence "material to proof of Steven's motive, opportunity, intent, preparation, plan, knowledge, identity, or absence of mistake or accident"? Was it relevant? And was its "probative value substantially outweighed by the danger of unfair prejudice"?

As I reviewed the court's lengthy written decision, it forced me to carefully consider whether and how much Steven Avery's history of physical and sexual abuse had to do with whether he was guilty of Teresa Halbach's murder. I thought the judge would side with the prosecutors on two of the "other acts": Avery's sexual assault of his seventeen-year-old niece in 2004 and his telephone call to Melissa Hansen the day before Teresa Halbach was murdered when he asked her to come over and "have a little fun." But in the end the court decided not to allow *any* of the "other acts" into evidence, which I'm sure was a none-too-popular decision in the prosecution camp.

Judge Willis ruled that Steven Avery's sexual assault of his niece had no relationship to the charges he currently faced and that its only "probative value" was to show that Avery had a "propensity to commit sexual assaults," which is exactly what is forbidden by the law. He pointed out that the niece was not only an "acquaintance, but a relative of the defendant"; while Teresa Halbach was a business acquaintance and her sexual assault ended in murder.

Whatever probative value such evidence may have would be far outweighed by the prejudice which attended the introduction of such evidence, the judge concluded. *The evidence is not admissible.*

The prosecution fared no better with the telephone call to Melissa Hansen asking her if she'd "like to come over and have a little fun," and his suggestion that they could "have the bed hit the wall, real hard." I found the prosecution's argument convincing. It occurred only one day before Halbach's disappearance, and, as the prosecutors put it in their motion: *The defendant's failed attempt to lure [Melissa Hansen] to his trailer for a stated sexual purpose less than 24 hours before Ms. Halbach's arrival is highly relevant to the murder and sex assault charges—so highly probative that its admissibility again appears obvious.*

But it wasn't so obvious to Judge Willis. *Since the state does not assert that Mr. Avery had any thoughts of killing Melissa Hansen,* he wrote, *it has not clearly articulated any reason for admission of the Melissa Hansen evidence (on the murder charge). Nor,* the judge wrote, *[do I] perceive any meaningful relationship between the offered other acts evidence and the first-degree sexual assault charge.*

As I read further and considered Judge Willis's reasoning, I thought he was right. *The offered evidence would show that the defendant attempted to induce Melissa Hansen to come to his residence to have sexual relations with him,* he explained. *However, it also shows that he asked her to do so voluntarily and when she spurned his advances, he did not pursue the matter any further. That is a far cry from kidnapping a business acquaintance, sexually assaulting her, and then murdering her. . . . The evidence is clearly inadmissible.*

I thought Avery's strangulation of Jodi Stachowski, occurring months, not years before Teresa's murder, stood a better chance. But again, after reviewing Judge Willis's decision, I thought he was right. *The defendant's alleged behavior against Jodi Stachowski is significantly different (than the murder of Teresa),* he explained, *both in terms of the nature of the acts involved and Avery's relationship to her. Domestic violence is unfortunately an all-too-common occurrence in today's world.*

The prosecution also wanted the jury to hear about Avery and Jodi's sexual habits—information I would have omitted from these pages if they did not have some bearing on his state of mind around the time Halbach was murdered.

Jodi told investigators that Avery kept pornographic magazines and movies all over the house. They had sex every day, sometimes as many as five times a day, she said, and several times they experimented with bondage and had sex after he tied her up.

The prosecution also seized upon statements from a few of Avery's former fellow inmates—unaffectionately known as "jailhouse snitches"—that he planned to build a "torture chamber" when he got out. Avery shared with them details of how he would rape, torture, and murder young women. From the prosecutors' perspective, all of this evidence was highly relevant to Halbach's murder and the horrific manner in which she died.

Again, despite our natural reluctance to consider these things, I thought the prosecutors had a point. However, that's not how Judge Willis saw it.

The Court fails to find any meaningful relationship between the other acts evidence and the charged offense. There is not a significant relationship between men who are unusually sexually active with their girlfriends and those who commit forcible assaults against some other victim, the judge wrote. *The evidence has virtually zero probative value and would be highly prejudicial. It is clearly not admissible.*

One of the deciding factors for determining whether "other acts" evidence should be admitted at trial is its nearness or remoteness in time—how long ago did the event occur? Most of the rest of the evidence offered by the prosecution was two decades old, which was a major factor in the judge's decision to exclude it.

The court was especially unimpressed with the state's argument that the jury should be allowed to consider Avery's throwing the cat in the fire nearly a quarter century earlier. In unusually blunt language—particularly from him—Judge Willis could find "no serious argument" to the state's contention that Avery's "placing the object of his torture," as the prosecution had referred to the cat, bore a "striking similarity" to the burning of Halbach's body after the murder.

As I wrapped up this stage of my journey, I wondered if the court made the right call. Judge Willis's rejection of *all* the "other acts" evidence the state wanted to present to the jury was, I'm sure, met with dismay by the prosecution team. They undoubtedly thought it was inordinately favorable to the defense.

Like so many other standards in the law, whether the "probative value" of evidence is "substantially outweighed by the danger of unfair prejudice" is in the eye of the beholder. The eyes of a cautious judge, like Judge Willis, rarely behold "other acts" evidence worthy of admission. I'm sure he was guided by what he believed the law required, and there is no doubt that erring on the side of the defense is the better part of valor when it comes to having a conviction upheld on appeal. Steven Avery certainly received a fair trial.

On the other hand, the jury had returned a verdict of not guilty, the consternation concerning the court's decision not to admit all that damning evidence against Avery would have rivaled the level of discord throughout the state of Wisconsin after a Green Bay Packer loss.

CHAPTER 15

A MOUNTAIN OF EVIDENCE AND A MOLEHILL OF DOUBT

Rummaging around in Steven Avery's past had not been a pleasant task—at least examining his history of violence and sexual deviancy hadn't been—but it provided a context with which I could approach his actions leading up to and through the day Teresa Halbach disappeared. Not bound by the "other acts" evidence rules of evidence—a man's liberty, after all, was not in my hands—I was free to consider his prior criminal conduct in my pursuit of the truth. There was no escaping the fact that Avery posed a grave risk to women he was close to, as well as to those who had the misfortune of crossing his path.

There are more than enough sexually aggressive and violent men to fill the nation's prisons and jails, but not many of them have the capacity to commit a murder as horrific as the one Avery is alleged to have done. When coupled with the fact that he was the last person known to have seen Teresa Halbach alive, Avery was a likely suspect, perhaps the main suspect.

I had to be careful not to give Steven Avery's propensity for violence more weight than it deserved. His prior crimes of physical and sexual violence did not prove, in the words of the "other acts" evidence statute, that he had acted "in conformity therewith" on this particular occasion. As the stockbrokers are fond of saying, past performance does not guarantee future results.

For this final leg of my journey, I had to examine Avery's conduct, both his actions and his words, before, during, and after Halbach disappeared—hour by hour, minute by minute, if I could.

In fact, it turned out I had to begin my journey ten months before she disappeared.

Alison Lang, Teresa Halbach's predecessor at *Auto Trader* magazine, was in charge of Manitowoc County and the surrounding area until Halbach took over in spring 2005. On January 25, 2005, she was assigned to take a photo of a vehicle at Avery's residence. She knocked on his door and he said he'd be right out, so she took the photos of the vehicle and then asked what text he wanted to use for the ad. Avery said he forgot to write one up and went into his trailer.

After taking much longer than normal to draft a few lines, Avery ducked out and asked Lang, who had been waiting on the porch, if she wanted to come in. She told Avery it was against *Auto Trader* policy to go inside a customer's residence, so she went to wait in her car. He "creeped me out," she told police because of the way he was staring at her.

Teresa Halbach had a similar experience on one of her prior dealings with Avery.

On October 10, three weeks to the day before she disappeared, Halbach did a "hustle shot" for Avery, which is an assignment taken at the customer's request and not through the photographer's employer. In other words, Avery had contacted her directly and asked her to come out to the salvage yard. When she arrived, the silver 1984 Pontiac Grand Prix that he was putting up for sale was parked right in front of his garage, closer to his trailer than the cars were in most of the other appointments she had with him, when the cars were parked either up front outside the office or closer to his sister Barb's residence.

The receptionist at *Auto Trader* told police that Halbach confided in her that on one prior occasion, probably the October 10 appointment, Avery had come out wearing nothing but a towel. Halbach was concerned by the incident.

On November 4, Halbach's colleague in her freelance business, Thomas Pearce, told police that Halbach had received repeated calls on her cell phone recently from an unknown number. She told him she had received similar calls from early to midsummer, but they'd stopped until right around the time of her October 10 appointment with Avery. The caller would never leave a message; and as far as Pearce knew, she never answered the calls. She also told him one of her male customers had invited her into his residence and made some comments that made her uncomfortable enough that she decided to leave. Pearce had warned her to be careful when she was alone in rural areas.

Avery had purchased leg irons on October 9, the day before he called Halbach and then met her wearing only a towel. Jodi Stachowski, his girlfriend who told police about their daily sex life, was in jail at the time, serving a sentence on her drunk-driving conviction. Had Avery, deprived of his daily sexual relations with Stachowski, planned to assault Halbach, but lost his nerve? When police searched his residence after the murder, they found a picture of an erect penis on his computer desk with an indication it was taken on October 10, the day he had called Halbach.

It was time to examine the events of October 31. Was there more I could learn about that day that might bring me closer to the truth?

One thing I learned was that Avery didn't own the van he called *Auto Trader* to take a photo of that day. It was his sister Barb's, and she didn't even want the vehicle sold. Two weeks after Halbach disappeared, Barb told two state investigators that she got into an argument with her brother about selling the van. She did not want a picture of it in *Auto Trader* because she was going to keep it for one of her sons, who was getting his driver's license. Barb said her brother was very demanding and told her she was doing a bad job raising her kids.

By having Barb sell her vehicle, Avery could use her name to set up the appointment—and that's exactly what he did. Barb lived with her sons, Bryan, Bobby, Blaine, and Brendan, at the salvage yard right next to Steven Avery's trailer.

The receptionist stated that when she took the call for *Auto Trader* on October 31, at eight-twelve a.m., it was from "somebody who identified himself/herself as 'B. Janda'" (Barb's married name is Janda), and was "difficult to understand." The caller gave her Barb's home phone number and address and also asked her to send the same photographer "who had been out there before."

The receptionist told the caller that they typically needed more than twenty-four-hour notice, but she'd see what she could do and someone would get back to him as soon as possible.

Why did Avery give Barb's telephone number? Not only did she not want to sell her van, she would be at work all day and not home to meet with the photographer. If he gave the receptionist his cell phone number instead, he could be reached when they called him back. And why did he use "B. Janda" and not give his sister's full name? *B* could be the first initial of a male or female name—maybe that had something to do with it. Was Avery trying to hide his identity from Halbach? He knew he made her feel uncomfortable at the last appointment and she would probably not want to come back.

This scenario seemed likely, and as I investigated further, I found out that it worked—Teresa Halbach had no idea she was meeting with Steven Avery that day.

At nine forty-six a.m., the receptionist left Halbach a voice mail asking if she could fit in an appointment that day for "B. Janda," adding that she couldn't find a record for him, but the caller said she had been out there before. The receptionist gave Halbach the name and number Avery had given her and asked Halbach to call her back and let her know if she should schedule the appointment for that day or for the following Monday instead.

What would Teresa Halbach have thought? The receptionist had told her that she could not find a "B. Janda" in their system because they go by phone numbers, not names. Halbach would have recognized the address as the Avery Salvage Yard, but with the information she was given, she would assume she was meeting with "B. Janda," not Steven Avery.

As I thought back to my late-night binge on *Making a Murderer* two months earlier, I was struck by the series' portrayal of how Halbach's appointment with Avery came about that day. His eight-twelve a.m. phone call requesting a photo shoot from "that same girl they sent out last time" was omitted; as was any hint that if she knew it was Avery who had called for the appointment that day, she probably would have never gone to the salvage yard. There was no mention that Avery's sister, Barb, owned the van, or that Barb didn't even want to sell it, or that he used the name "B. Janda" when he set up the appointment and gave Barb's home phone number instead of his own.

I remembered hearing the message that Halbach left for someone that viewers could only assume was Steven. In reality it was left on his sister Barb's answering machine. By withholding that fact the series gave the clear impression that she was willing to meet Avery that day—something that could not be any further from the truth. She even asked to be called back as she did not yet have the address.

"Hello. This is Teresa with *Auto Trader Magazine*. I'm the photographer, and just giving you a call to let you know that I could come out there today, in the afternoon. It would probably be around two o'clock or even longer, but if you could, please give me a call back and let me know if that will work for you, because I don't have your address or anything, so I can't stop by without getting a call back from you. And my cell phone is 920-737-****. Again, it's Teresa 920-737-****. Thank you."

Halbach had just unknowingly told the man who would murder her later that day—I was having fewer doubts by the minute—that she would meet him at the salvage yard in just a few hours.

As I looked closer at the timing of events, it was obvious that Steven Avery had planned his day around Teresa Halbach's expected appearance at the salvage yard. Steven told his brother Earl before lunch that he had to go home because someone was meeting him from the magazine. The receptionist told him that morning he would get a call at the number he left—his sister Barb's home number—to let him know if "the same girl they sent last time" could fit him in that day. Earl later told police that Steven had to go home to meet someone for an appointment—somebody from the *Auto Trader*, Earl thought.

Steven admitted the same to a detective at the family's cabin up north where he and some of the other family members, including Brendan Dassey, had gone on the weekend following Halbach's disappearance. He told the detective that he had worked at the garage at the salvage yard until eleven that morning; then he went up to his trailer to wait for the photographer.

"On Monday, after Teresa left, you didn't go back to work," the detective asked him. "Why not?"

"Well, I made some, couple phone calls," Avery replied.

"Okay. But you didn't go back to the shop."

"No, no."

"You stayed in your house. Did they know that? Did Chuck and Earl know that you're not coming back after lunch, or whatever?"

"No, no, they didn't know that."

The detective pressed further: "Is it unusual—I mean, did they care?"

"Oh, yeah, they care," Avery assured him.

"Okay, but I mean, can you just kind of come and go like that, as you please?"

"No, I mostly . . ."

"Is it common?"

"This is the first time that I stayed home."

Interviewed months later by Calumet County investigator Wiegert, Jodi Stachowski said the same thing.

"Would he ever come home from work during the day?"

"Never," replied Jodi, though she later qualified her answer by saying, "Once, maybe twice he came home."

"Otherwise he'd stay at work all day?"

"Uh-huh. He'd eat up at his mom's and stay there."

When questioned by the detective at the family cabin up north about what he did after leaving work that morning, Steven Avery said he spoke with Bobby Dassey, Barb's son and Brendan's brother, who lived next door to his trailer.

But that's not what Bobby said. Interviewed by Investigator Wiegert back in Manitowoc on the same day, Bobby said he worked third shift and was home sleeping that afternoon. No, he said, he had not spoken with his uncle Steven at all that day.

Did Avery go to Barb's house after leaving work that morning to see if *Auto Trader* had called? If so, he would have heard Halbach's eleven forty-three a.m. voice mail on Barb's answering machine, saying she would be able to make it later that day. Only Steven Avery knows and he isn't talking, but it sure looked that way to me.

The pace of events picked up as the lives of a victim and her assailant were about to intersect. Halbach arrived at George and JoEllen Zipperer's residence on Highway B, outside of Manitowoc, to take a picture of a '77 Firebird they had up for sale, around two-fifteen that afternoon. JoEllen later told police that Halbach was smiling ten minutes later as she walked back to her car, but JoEllen was in the backyard and did not see which direction the photographer went as she left the property.

Cell phone records indicate that Avery called Halbach's cell phone at two twenty-five p.m., about the same time she left the Zipperer residence. He used the *67 function again, making it an anonymous call.

Two minutes later, at two twenty-seven p.m., Halbach received a return call from the receptionist at *Auto Trader*, Teresa told her she'd be able to go get that photo at the salvage yard, and said she was on her way there right now.

Avery called Halbach a second time, at two thirty-five p.m., again using *67 to block his identity. The call lasted zero seconds, which meant Halbach didn't answer that call. But as far as Avery was concerned she did even better—she arrived at his residence approximately ten minutes later.

Out of curiosity, a detail-oriented Avery-obsessed Redditor friend of mine checked Avery's other fourteen calls that day, and learned that in not one of them besides those two to Halbach, did he use *67. His other calls included four to family members, one unblocked call to Halbach after she died, one to *Auto Trader*, and the eight remaining to various businesses and government agencies.

Whether or not Avery planned ahead of time to murder Theresa at the salvage yard that day, there was little doubt that he lured her there with the intent to rape her. Why else would he leave the name "B. Janda" with her employer and give them his sister's home phone number to call back? What made him decide to take off work that afternoon, something he almost never did? Why did he keep changing stories with police about his interaction with Halbach that day?

Steven Avery had arranged, if not a murder, an assault. There was no doubt in my mind.

I had learned everything I could about the hours leading up to Teresa Halbach's arrival at the salvage yard. Now it was time to examine what happened after she got there.

Bobby Dassey told police he saw her drive up; he witnessed this from his window as he got up at approximately two-fifty p.m. After that, things get sketchy until four thirty-five p.m., when records indicate that Avery placed a call to Halbach's cell phone. Although by that point it either was powered down or destroyed, for there was no cell site communicating with the phone. Avery later told police that he was hoping to catch her so she could come back for a hustle shot before she drove too far, but if he had already killed her, it would be a good way to cover his tracks. There was no reason for him to think she was still in the area, because he placed the call nearly two hours after, by his own account, Halbach had left.

If Avery killed Halbach, as all the physical evidence and Brendan Dassey's confession suggested, what did he do with her body after he murdered her?

Earl Avery and his brother-in-law Robert Fabian provided information to Calumet County investigators that might give us a clue. They had been rabbit hunting and drove up in the family's golf cart—the Averys use it to get around the salvage yard—to Steven's trailer home, at about five that night. They noticed Steven unloading his snowmobile off a trailer, which they both found rather odd.

Earl thought something was wrong with Steven. He was in a daze, standing straight up, stiff as a board, and staring at the snowmobile or looking down at the ground. Steven was clean and had showered, but he did not at all look relaxed.

Steven was planning to sell the snowmobile or trade it in to TA Motorsports in Manitowoc, so it didn't make sense to Earl that he was unloading it off the trailer and storing it in his garage. He'd have to reload it later and take it to town.

Robert Fabian spoke with investigators on November 10. He said he could see smoke coming from the burn barrel in front of Steven's residence when he and Earl drove up in the golf cart. It smelled like plastic, he said. Also, Steven's garage door was closed and his pickup truck had been parked so that it blocked the view of the inside of the garage.

Robert told the officer he saw Steven walk outside toward his pickup truck with his snowmobile already on the trailer. It looked like he had cleaned up, as Robert put it, and he had changed into a white short-sleeved T-shirt and blue jean shorts from what he was wearing when Robert first arrived. Robert and Earl drove up in the golf cart and tried to chat with Steven for a while, but he was quieter than usual. Steven was very quiet, Robert continued, and didn't even chuckle when Robert asked him if wanted to buy a Polaris instead of the Ski-Doo on the trailer, though it was some kind of standing joke between the two of them.

Calumet County investigator Wendy Baldwin and Special Agent Kim Skorlinski from DCI (the state police division) interviewed Barb Janda. Barb said three of her sons—Blaine, Bobby, and Brendan—were all inside the house when she came home from work at five o'clock. When her boyfriend, Scott Tadych, dropped her off between seven forty-five and eight p.m. after visiting his mother, who had back surgery that day, she saw a fire in the pit behind her brother's garage. According to Barb, it was about three feet high, though other witnesses would tell police it was higher.

Barb saw two people standing near the fire. She couldn't tell who they were, but she mentioned that her son Brendan had been spending a lot of time with his uncle Steven lately. Brendan didn't have a lot of friends and he helped his uncle with stuff around his house.

Later, Barb told investigators that Brendan had helped her brother Steven clean up his garage the evening Halbach disappeared and his jeans had been stained with bleach.

Police interviewed Steven Avery several times. He was cooperative and answered their questions at first.

After a confession the next best thing for a prosecutor is a series of conflicting statements from a suspect who thought he could talk his way out of being in trouble. Inconsistent statements can be put to good use by suggesting at trial that the defendant was lying.

A more savvy offender will exercise his right to remain silent—"Sorry, Officer, I'd rather not talk today, but I'll call my lawyer to tell him you stopped by." It's one of the things that every criminal defense attorney worth his salt reminds his clients for next time they get in trouble. The right to remain silent applies not only on the streets, but also in the courtroom. If an officer or a prosecutor comments on a defendant's silence, it's grounds for mistrial because it violates a defendant's Fifth Amendment right not to be compelled to incriminate himself.

Avery could have said nothing, but instead he spoke freely with the police and gave them inconsistent details about his contact with Teresa Halbach. He also spoke with family members and anyone else who would listen to him. It would all come back to haunt him at trial.

When Robert Fabian first arrived to meet Earl around four-thirty, he overheard Chuck ask Steven if the photographer from *Auto Trader* had arrived yet. Steven replied that no, she hadn't shown up yet.

When Jodi Stachowski called collect that night at eight fifty-seven p.m. from the jail, Avery didn't say anything about a photographer. Although he did tell her Brendan Dassey was over and that he had been doing some cleaning.

Three days after Halbach was murdered, on November 3, Avery called *Auto Trader* and told them that the photographer had not made the scheduled appointment at the salvage yard on October 31. He said Halbach notified him by phone that she wouldn't be able to make it after all.

Later that same evening Avery told Andy Colborn, who had driven out to the salvage yard between six-thirty and seven-thirty, that Teresa Halbach was there on October 31 and took pictures of the van, but he only saw her from his window and never spoke to her. She had only been there for a few minutes and then she left. Colborn recounted his conversation with Steven Avery from the witness stand at Avery's trial, with Ken Kratz doing the questioning.

"Did you inquire of Mr. Avery whether or not he had personal contact with this woman on the date she was out there?"

"I asked Mr. Avery if she had said where she was going. And he said, 'I never talked to her. She was only here five or ten minutes and she left.'"

"But he never talked to her?"

"That's what he told me, he never talked to her."

"Did he describe that further, how he knew she was there?"

"He said he saw her out the window taking the pictures."

Avery's memory changed when he was interviewed by the police again the following day.

It was November 4, now four days after Teresa disappeared. After Calumet County investigator Mark Wiegert requested their assistance, Detective Dave Remiker and Jim Lenk drove out to the salvage yard and spoke with him from ten-twenty until ten thirty-five a.m. This time Avery said he had engaged in small talk with Teresa Halbach and that she had been in his trailer, where he paid her for the job.

"All right," Kratz asked Remiker during the trial, "at that time, Detective Remiker, did you have any reason to believe that Mr. Avery had been involved in this missing person's case? In other words, other than information that you'd received from Calumet County?"

"No," Remiker replied. "He said he had contact with her. He said that she had been in his residence, where he paid her for the services, and said, 'Hi, how are you doing?' Some small talk."

During the two years since his exoneration, Steven Avery had become a hero of sorts—an improbable, yet compelling icon of innocence. A legendary survivor of an imperfect court system, he was accustomed to wearing the mantle of victimhood with ease. Holed up at the family cabin up north, Steven called in live to the Nancy Grace show shortly before being charged with Halbach's murder. He shared his troubles with America and accused the sheriff's department of framing him in revenge for his thirty-six-million-dollar wrongful conviction lawsuit.

"Mr. Avery," Nancy Grace asked, "why do you feel that you're being framed?"

"Because every time I turn around, the county's always doing something to me."

When asked about the tooth fragments and bones that were found in his fire pit, Avery explained that the salvage yard was rarely locked and anyone could just drive right in.

"I worry about it every minute," he said. "I look out the window. Is a squad car here? Are they going to pick me up? When are they going to pick me up? When I'm sleeping, are they going to come in? I always have that fear.

"I think Manitowoc County is trying to set me up real good because they're taking everything," he said, "but they don't seem like they found anything because there ain't nothing there. They've been watching us. They've been sitting up by the end of the driveway. But I'm done talking to them."

On November 9, 2005, Avery was charged with being a felon in possession of a firearm—the sexual assault and murder charges would be added later. Two days later, the governor was scheduled to appear in the Manitowoc courtroom where Avery was wrongfully convicted twenty years earlier to sign into law a criminal justice reform bill that was to bear Avery's name. With news of the legislation's namesake's arrest, the ceremony was promptly called off. The "Avery Bill" was rather blandly renamed the "Criminal Justice Reforms Package."

CHAPTER 16

MOTIVE AND INTENT

I once heard from a speaker at a prosecutors' conference that jurors in a criminal case are in a constant state of conflict—they're afraid to send an innocent person to prison, but they don't want to let a guilty one go free. With the exception of an occasional juror who takes a kind of perverse joy in passing judgment on another, I have found the speaker's observation to be true—jurors have an exceedingly difficult job. The prosecutor's job, the speaker continued, is to "ease their pain" by presenting evidence so clearly and forcefully that the defendant's guilt is unmistakable.

One way a prosecutor can do that is by giving jurors a credible explanation for why the defendant committed the crime—his motive, if one can be found, which is closely related to his intent. It helps them put the pieces together and allows them to leave the courtroom with their heads held high, comfortable in the knowledge that they reached a just and true verdict.

After examining one piece of physical evidence after another in the Avery case—the RAV4, Avery's blood inside it and his DNA on its hood latch, its ignition key in his bedroom, a bullet from his gun in the garage, and Halbach's bones in a burn pit behind his garage—I was increasingly convinced that Steven Avery, and probably Brendan Dassey, too, were guilty as charged. The "other acts" evidence proffered by the prosecution and the circumstances in which Avery called for and met Teresa Halbach at the salvage yard the day she disappeared added to my confidence. I had arrived well beyond the point of reasonable doubt. In addition to direct evidence, investigators look for opportunity and motive. There's no question that Avery had the opportunity to rape and murder Halbach. He was the last person known to have seen her alive, and after first denying it, he reluctantly admitted to police that he had spoken with her at the salvage yard on the afternoon she disappeared.

But where, you ask, is the proof of his motive? There is, of course, only one place where things like motive and intent reside—in a person's minds. It's a dark and dreary trip—one that should only be taken with care and from which one is immensely grateful to return, but if I were to complete my overall journey, it was a trip I had to take. I had to try to get inside Steven Avery's mind on the day Teresa Halbach was murdered. While motive and intent are rarely apparent from physical evidence alone—and with Steven's denial, his own words were of no help either—we can, as the courts encourage in regard to so many issues that arise in the law, infer their existence by considering the "totality of the facts and circumstances" surrounding the case.

My examination of Steven Avery's motive began where most viewers of *Making a Murderer* ended theirs: Why would someone poised to reap millions of dollars in a wrongful conviction lawsuit run the risk of being sent back to prison? Having been led by the film makers to conclude that the police planted evidence to set up Avery for the murder, viewers naturally answered the question posed above by simply stating that, he wouldn't. In effect, they finished their analysis of what may have motivated Avery to murder Halbach before they even began.

But if the evidence-planting claim was nonsense, and by this time I was confident it was, then the question was worth pursuing. Why did Avery risk being sent back to prison when he was on the cusp of receiving millions of dollars? Like most questions about human motivation, the answers are best found by looking well into the person's past, which in Avery's case meant going back twenty years.

Anger and frustration had settled into Avery's heart during his years of confinement after the 1985 wrongful conviction, as evidenced by the threatening letters he sent to his soon-to-be-ex-wife Lori from prison. Add his propensity for violence and inability to control his runaway sexual desires, both of which were a deeply disturbing part of his psychological makeup long before he was wrongly convicted in 1985, and you have the makings for an unmitigated disaster when he was released.

Prison records corroborate the fact that Avery was and would continue to be a danger to society upon his release. Eight years into his sentence, in 1993 he described himself succinctly to his caseworker at the prison in an "ORDER TERMINATING RESPONDENT'S PERIODS OF PHYSICAL PLACEMENT AND RETAINING MONITORED CONTACT BY TELEPHONE AND CORRESPONDENCE." The caseworker's notes read: *He describes himself as an impulsive man, a person who acts out of anger, an individual who possibly would be better off if he thought before he acted.*

The caseworker believed that Avery was in need of serious help but pointed out that he wasn't willing to assist in his rehabilitation.

> *Mr. Avery is an individual who has significant needs, and perhaps of most concern to me is that fact that he is not involved in any programming as a result of his own choice.*
> *Programs that would provide him with insights into parenting skills; hopefully tools to deal with the type of anger flashes that flare up in a [sic] domestic violence; anger management programs; sexual treatment; sexual behavior programs. They are all available as well as academic programming, in the institution.*

Avery's risk factors multiplied when he got out. No longer residing under the structure of a carefully regimented prison system where behavior is strictly monitored and opportunities to offend are minimized, he faced a whole new set of challenges upon his release. Not least among them was his choice of where to live. His decision to move into an ice shanty when winter arrived is a case in point. After living eighteen years in an eight-by-twelve prison cell, perhaps he felt the need for confinement. Its close quarters made it feel just like home: "I wanted somethin' small," he told a reporter, "everything was, I don't know, just too big. It didn't feel right."

Continuing to explore what may have motivated Avery to commit such a heinous crime, I moved forward to the last time he made an appointment with Teresa prior to the day she disappeared. What was he thinking with regard to Halbach when she snapped a picture of a Grand Prix that he was selling just weeks before she died?

It had been less than two months since his fiancée, Jodi, who later informed police that they were accustomed to having sex every day, and sometimes multiple times per day, was incarcerated. On his desk Avery had copies of a picture of his erect penis, along with a note (*back to patio door*) and another with Teresa Halbach's personal cell phone number. He came out to do business with her while he was dressed "just in a towel," which concerned her enough to at least mention it to a coworker shortly after it occurred. Driven perhaps by the same kind of madness that led to his drawing of a torture chamber in prison and comments he made to other inmates, he bought handcuffs and leg irons the day before her visit, just a short time before she was murdered. Jodi would not be released from jail for months, and Barb Janda told police she didn't think the handcuffs and leg irons were intended for Jodi—begging the question, then whom were they for?

Fast-forward to the night before Halbach disappeared. Avery called his nephew's ex-girlfriend and invited her over so they could "have some fun," suggesting that they could have sex and "have the bed hit the wall real hard." Presumably, he was referring to the same bed upon which he tortured, raped, and murdered Teresa Halbach less than twenty-four hours later. If this isn't proof of motive and intent, I don't know what is.

The next morning, at eight-twelve a.m., Avery concealed his identity when he called *Auto Trader* magazine and asked for "the same girl they sent last time." The receptionist wasn't sure if the caller was a male or a female, as the voice was too hard to understand. He left a name with an ambiguous gender, "B. Janda," and gave Barb's telephone number instead of his own, even though he was the one planning to meet the photographer.

Why didn't he call Halbach directly, as he had done on the prior occasion when he called her for a hustle shot? He obviously had her phone number. Why go through the *Auto Trader* receptionist unless he didn't want Halbach, who he'd upset on the previous appointment, to know he was calling?

After I considered all these facts, it seemed clear to me that the overriding motive behind Avery's actions was to act upon his perverse satisfaction from engaging in physical violence and unwanted sexual aggression, without a whit of remorse or concern for the harm he inflicted upon his victims.

Would Avery have been capable of committing such a horrific murder if he not spent eighteen angry years in prison after suffering his own injustice at the hands of the former sheriff and district attorney? Would his heart and soul have been sufficiently depraved?

It's impossible to know. His wrongful conviction certainly didn't help, but given the violent and sexually deviant conduct he engaged in from his young adulthood to the very night before he murdered Teresa Halbach as set forth in the state's "other acts" motion, it's hard to conclude with any level of confidence that he wouldn't. His sexual deviancy knew no bounds and never lay dormant, not even in prison, where he told fellow inmates of his violent plans regarding women when he was released.

On March 9, 2006, police interviewed a former cellmate of Steven Avery. He was no longer incarcerated and therefore had no expectation of a reduced sentence if he provided information. Ex-con Ronald Rieckhoff spoke with Investigator Gary Steier from Calumet County in a telephone interview that was summarized as follows:

> RIECKHOFF *indicated he had seen the news in which inmates had been telling the police that AVERY had shown them a torture chamber on a piece of paper. RIECKHOFF indicated he was in prison with STEVEN AVERY in STANLEY PRISON in the Wausau area and had spoken to STEVEN approximately 20 times. RIECKHOFF indicated he was in Unit 3 and AVERY was in Unit 2, but he would talk to STEVEN AVERY in the recreation field and in the prison library. RIECKHOFF indicated STEVEN hated all women and would resort to the saying about women, find them, feel them, fuck them, forget them.*

> *At approximately 3:30 p.m., I (Inv. STEIER) again had telephonic contact with RONALD RIECKHOFF. RONALD stated he had been in prison with STEVEN AVERY since 2001 and had spoken with STEVEN approximately 20 times while he was in prison. RIECKHOFF stated he was a paralegal and from time to time AVERY would ask him questions. RIECKHOFF stated STEVEN AVERY had told him he wanted to kill that young bitch that had set him up for the rape when he got out. RIECKHOFF again stated he would talk to STEVEN AVERY in the recreation field or in the prison library. RIECKHOFF again indicated in RIECKHOFF's words, he hated all bitches, he hated all women. RIECKHOFF again reiterated STEVEN's comment to him, I'll find them, feel them, fuck them, forget them.*

Years later, long after Avery was convicted of Halbach's murder, Jodi Stachowski's words to Nancy Grace concerning Avery's attitude toward women revealed that he was true to his word after his release: "We all owed him," Jodi explained, "and he could do whatever he wanted."

Unlike intent, the prosecution need not prove motive at trial. But if motive can be divined, as it can in the Avery case, it adds context and meaning to the crime. My journey into Avery's mind had done just that, though I was glad to leave it behind. His obsession with aggressive and violent sex doesn't prove he raped Halbach, any more than his fascination with fire and history of threatening to burn people and burning a live animal prove that he burned her body. It does, however, provide context and meaning and shows what was likely on his mind that afternoon as he awaited Halbach's arrival. Nothing comes within a thousand miles of excusing his crime, but it had proven worthwhile to explore what was going on in his mind—if for nothing else than to dispel or confirm my increasingly solid belief that he murdered her.

It wasn't only Avery's motive I had to explore. Out of fairness to the defense and to *Making a Murderer*, and for my own peace of mind, I also had to consider the motives of Colborn, Lenk, and the sheriff's department as a whole. What drove their conduct while they investigated the crime? Was there any evidence that they were driven by a desire to frame Avery for Halbach's murder?

Who could forget the moment in *Making a Murderer* when the camera zoomed in on a group of lawyers huddled around a blood vial with a puncture the size of a hypodermic needle in the rubber stopper on its top? It was the cornerstone, the lynchpin for the defense, and its powerful imagery was skillfully put to use by the documentarians in subsequent episodes when it was suggested that police had planted other evidence as well. The image of the key to Halbach's SUV lying on the floor in Avery's bedroom had a similar effect.

Exposed to this convincing but disingenuous clip of video, viewers were like putty in the hands of the documentarians. Avery's blood in Halbach's vehicle? *Planted.* The SUV's ignition key found by Colborn and Lenk in Avery's bedroom? *Planted.* The bullets in Avery's garage? *Planted.* Halbach's bones, including portions of her skull, found in the burn pit in Avery's backyard? *Planted again.*

Once you accept as fact that the police planted the evidence, it's easy to conjure up the motive that drove them to do so—or as the defense and *Making a Murderer* suggested, several. Revenge, anger, an effort to avoid embarrassment or financial ruin because of Avery's wrongful conviction lawsuit. Each of these separate but related motives were at work in the actions of the police, at least as the defense and *Making a Murderer* would have it.

Given the close-knit nature of law enforcement agencies, where little remains a secret for long, if Colborn and Lenk were trying to frame Avery, others in the department would presumably be aware of it too. So I would need to consider their possible motivation too. What would make these individual police officers and the department as a whole so hell-bent on framing Steven Avery? What did they have to gain, and why would they risk getting caught? It had been ten years and counting since the alleged frame-up occurred. The case had been in the sights of conspiracy theorists worldwide since December 2015, and at the mercy of tireless, self-styled vigilante justice groups, threatening to blow the lid off the conspiracy. Yet there was still no evidence of a cover-up. Could even the police code of silence keep something this big under the lid for this long?

Rather than assuming that the lack of evidence that the cops were dirty meant they weren't, I dug into the facts and circumstances surrounding the evidence-planting claims.

The first thing I discovered was that this was no easy conspiracy to pull off. For it to work, somebody else had to have murdered Teresa Halbach. The defense made it abundantly clear they were not suggesting the police had anything to do with her death. "In this, the police had something in common with Steven" was how Dean Strang put it in his opening statement.

If the killer was someone other than the police, how did he know evidence pointing to the real killer would not arise, like his own DNA in the RAV4? What if someone saw suspicious activity and called it in? How did the police know the real killer would not get liquored up and brag to his buddies that he killed Halbach? Or that his wife, tired of being abused and with the hope that he would be put away for a long time, would not call the police and tell them what he had confided to her in a momentary lapse of judgment when a few honest words came out of his mouth?

Careers were at stake; and in many instances, including those of Colborn and Lenk, these were long, distinguished careers, with retirement not far off on the horizon. Would smart, accomplished, and well-respected officers like Colborn and Lenk risk all that? If they were found guilty of planting any evidence—their DNA in the RAV4 or fingerprints on the blood vial as examples of tangible proof—losing their jobs would be the least of their worries. They'd be put away in prison, and that is the last place a police officer wants to end up.

And for what? Getting back at Steven Avery because they were embarrassed by a lawsuit in which they stood to lose not a dime? To regain respect for their department, which had been given a pass by the attorney general in her independent review of the conduct of a sheriff and district attorney who had long since moved on? The more I considered their possible motivation for planting evidence, the less it made sense. The pros were badly outweighed by the cons. In fact, they stood to gain nothing and lose everything.

While it's true that individuals occasionally act against their self-interest, it would be rare for dozens to do so in concert. Those knowing of, but not participating in, an alleged frame-up would be in trouble, too. It's hard to imagine that dozens of officers and staff would not hear about a conspiracy as grand as that alleged by Buting and Strang. If deemed part of the conspiracy or its cover-up, the additional officers would run the risk, too, of getting caught and losing their jobs.

Even for police familiar with physical evidence and traces of DNA and fingerprints left behind at crime scenes, the logistics of framing Avery for Halbach's murder would be a nightmare. It wasn't just one piece of evidence that police are alleged to have planted—it was seven—the bone fragments and teeth, the RAV4 and its license plates found in another vehicle closer to Avery's trailer, the blood, the DNA on the hood latch, the key, and the bullets. Another piece that would have had to be part of the planting, and didn't make the cut for *Making a Murderer,* was Halbach's electronics that were found in a burn barrel in front of Avery's trailer.

They weren't all planted at the same time. Avery's blood first had to be placed in the RAV4 or added with others present while it was being guarded, possibly by sneaking under the tarp the day the vehicle was found on the property on November 5. The key would have to have been placed in Avery's bedroom a few days later, then the bones, which may or may not have been planted on the same day. And finally the bullet fragment found months later with Halbach's DNA on it, fired from Avery's gun after Dassey confessed. How many cops were involved? How many crime lab analysts? How did they communicate? Who was the leader? Who planted what and when?

What role did the real killer have? Did he simultaneously plant evidence without being caught? Or was he just the recipient of good fortune who became ecstatic when he learned that Steven Avery was being charged with the murder instead of himself?

Why, during the intense search for Teresa Halbach, did nobody notice—not a motorist, a bicyclist, or a pedestrian—Andy Colborn driving Halbach's oft-reported and well-described SUV as he made his way to the salvage yard? One man did come forward stating that he recalled seeing a "green SUV" while he was in the vicinity of the salvage yard between three-thirty and four p.m. on October 31. He testified in court: "It was possible that it was hers, but it was also possible that it wasn't." That's certainly not very damning evidence, especially when he also never saw who was driving.

None of the Averys saw anything, either, other than headlights a few days later, but not where the RAV4 was hidden. Not Steven Avery, his parents, his sister, Barb, and her sons, who resided in a separate residence on the property, or neither of Steven's two brothers, one of which resided on the property and both working there daily. Depending upon which item of evidence they were planting, the officers would have to remain undetected by all of them and a very protective, loud-barking dog named Bear, which had held them at bay away from the burn pit on the first few days, while they searched other places on the massive property.

Someone also had to place Teresa Halbach's cell phone, PDA, and camera in a burn barrel on the other side of the driveway in front of Steven Avery's trailer to make it look as if they were burned inside the barrel—the same barrel that had emitted the smell of burning plastic, on the evening Teresa disappeared and in to which Avery was observed throwing a bag. Before planting the items there, the malefactor would have had to smash them to pieces and then place them into the barrel. Why would the officers destroy them first and lug along a large tire rim to place on top of the barrel? They could have achieved the same result by tossing the phone, PDA, and camera in the barrel, each intact.

Did police know that Avery would build a large fire in the burn pit behind his garage on the night Halbach disappeared and deem it a suitable site to plant her bones? Foresight like that is reserved for tea leaves and crystal balls.

For argument's sake, let's say they didn't actually plant bone fragments belonging to Teresa Halbach, and instead dug up her grandmother's bones for mitochondrial DNA. This ridiculous claim was made by an excessively imaginative conspiracy theorist.

Police spoke with Teresa's mother and were told that Teresa's grandmother was very much alive, albeit in poor health. That put an end to that line of speculation. But perhaps they were able to plant the bones of another girl who died around the same time that Teresa Halbach did, as suggested by a slew of online commentators after *Making a Murderer.*

In either scenario, how did police get a tibia, a bone fragment with a small amount of charred tissue, the only one that DNA testing could be done on? Although only a partial profile could be created, due to the extent of the damage, Sherry Culhane testified that it matched Halbach's DNA profile and that only one person out of every billion would meet that same criteria. Did police find Teresa Halbach deceased inside the RAV4, burn her, and plant her bones? Or did they find her already burned by the real killer, and decide to move her bone fragments, more than twenty teeth fragments, and five rivets from her Daisy Fuentes jeans, which she was wearing, to Avery's burn pit? And did they, for good measure, put four of the larger bone fragments next door in his sister Barb's burn barrel? It doesn't make sense. And then there's the blood. Halbach's blood was found in the back of her SUV and so was Avery's. His blood was identified in six different places confirmed by DNA testing. One of those stains was located right next to the ignition and Avery had a substantial cut on his finger, on his right hand—presumably, the finger he would have used in turning the ignition key.

Nick Stahlke, the forensic scientist called as a blood spatter expert from the crime lab, testified that along with other stains, the ignition stain was consistent with being left by a person who was actively bleeding. Are we to believe that when Colborn, and whoever else was helping to plant the blood, opened both the driver door and the rear passenger door. And carefully left the active bleeding type of bloodstain? Even discounting the bloodstain on the ignition, which conspiracy theorists demonstrated on the Internet could be duplicated with a simple Q-tip, the remaining five stains could not have been placed there in the same manner.

Taking the license plates off the RAV4 and then tossing them in a salvaged station wagon in a much more populated area of the property seems like another unnecessary risk to take. Why not leave them on? Or, for that matter, why fold them in half if you are trying to frame somebody?

Testing on three of Avery's bloodstains in the RAV4 proved negative for EDTA. Are we to believe the defense's contention that police planted his blood, which was extracted from a blood vial drawn years ago and kept in the clerk's office, in Teresa Halbach's vehicle? In Avery's favor a defense expert testified that minuscule traces of EDTA preservative would not be able to be detected under any test devised. But it was well argued then, and in the aftermath, that the FBI EDTA test was the best test in existence at this point in time. The blood in the vial was tested and proved positive for EDTA. That container with the alleged planted blood came from tested positive for EDTA, but the blood in the RAV4 did not goes a long way to negate the theory that it was the same blood.

Let's look at the defense's accusation that Manitowoc County detectives Jim Lenk and Andy Colborn planted the ignition key in Avery's bedroom. The key was found by Lieutenant Lenk when he, Sergeant Colborn, and Calumet County deputy Kucharsky were searching Avery's bedroom. How could Lenk handle the key and toss it without getting his own DNA on it while the other officer was two feet from him? Why not plant it during one of the earlier searches? Most of all, why would a trained and experienced lieutenant haphazardly drop the key when a Calumet County officer was sitting on the bed two feet away? Wouldn't it work better if he put it somewhere else? He'd know where investigators had searched previously.

Unlike the documentarians, I had gone well beyond the visual impact of a blood vial with a syringe hole or a key lying in plain view on the floor to investigate the evidence-planting claims, and after peeling back the layers, the defense accusations had evaporated into thin air. The experience reminded me of a U.S. presidential candidate's television advertisement a quarter century ago when he chided his opponent for a policy proposal's lack of substance: "Where's the beef?" There was simply nothing there. Neither Buting nor Strang nor the documentarians themselves had produced a shred of affirmative evidence that Lenk, Colborn, or anyone else associated with the Manitowoc County sheriff's department had conspired to set up Avery for Halbach's murder. It was nothing but innuendo. I was convinced more than ever that Avery had murdered Halbach, probably just as Dassey had described.

There are social media commentators even more obsessed than I am with Steven Avery's case and with *Making a Murderer,* and I am certain they will find fault with my analysis of his motive and that of the police. But I had seen enough. The contrast between the clearness of his motive to rape and murder Halbach with the sheriff's department's lack of motive to frame him could not have been clearer. Steven Avery had lost yet another round in my mind.

Whoever said jury instructions are boring is wrong. It's one of the shortest on the books, but after the instruction that explains the meaning of "beyond a reasonable doubt," it's my favorite by far. The statute's unassuming title is "Juror's Knowledge," and its purpose is to advise jurors that when they walk into the courtroom they don't have to leave their common sense at the door:

> *WI JI 195: Juror's Knowledge:*
> *In weighing the evidence, you may take into account matters of your common knowledge and your observations and experience in the affairs of life.*

The instruction is especially applicable to circumstantial evidence, and once I carefully examined the common sense implications of the circumstantial evidence in the Avery case, I was surprised how convincing it was as further proof of his guilt.

First, it's easy to overlook the significance of the fact that he was the last person to see Teresa Halbach alive, especially because he denied ever seeing her that day when he spoke with Robert Fabian and his brothers, Chuck and Earl. At four-thirty in the afternoon, probably within an hour of murdering Teresa, he told them the photographer had not shown up. He was obviously covering his tracks.

He gave conflicting statements to the police, another sign that he had something to hide. First, he told them he saw the photographer through the window, but never talked to her; she took the picture of Barb's van and drove away. The next day, he told them that he spoke with her briefly, paid her, and then she drove off. His inconsistent statements, especially when considered in light of his calling *Auto Trader* and using *67 on his phone is convincing evidence that Avery lured Teresa to the salvage yard that day with the intent to assault her.

Further, both Dassey and Avery admitted they were together on October 31. In fact, they said they happened to be cleaning the very same garage where Dassey told investigators Avery shot Halbach. Dassey's mother even told police that he had bleach on his jeans when she saw him later that day.

What are the odds that two men accused of killing a woman in a garage would be cleaning that very same garage on the very same day that they are accused of killing her and using bleach to clean the floor?

One of the most common, and understandable, questions of those who have watched *Making a Murderer* is that with a murder as violent as that which befell Teresa Halbach according to the account of Brendan Dassey, why was there no blood or hair found in Avery's residence? There are a few plausible explanations. A plastic covering on the mattress would be easy to remove and destroy. Avery may have had everything—mattress, carpeting, and furniture—encased in plastic wrap.

Those of us in the business sometimes refer to the *CSI* effect. Because of it and similar television crime shows, most people assume that almost every crime, especially one as violent as that depicted by Dassey in his confession, leaves a wealth of physical evidence in its wake. The facts are otherwise. Blood spatter on walls, for instance, even in a stabbing case, is not as common as one may think.

Moreover, Dassey's description of Halbach's wounds before she was shot by Avery may not have resulted in a great deal of blood spatter. He stated that Avery stabbed her once in the stomach, not numerous times, and his description of how he cut her throat when his uncle told him is suggestive of a superficial wound, considering that by Dassey's account, Halbach was still breathing when Avery started to choke her. We will never know exactly what happened in the trailer that afternoon, but it would be inaccurate to assume that Halbach was not murdered there as Dassey said she was solely because of the lack of physical evidence that some of us might expect.

There are other explanations for the lack of evidence in the bedroom and the rest of the trailer home. Avery and Dassey had from October 31 to November 5 to clean up evidence of the murder. A great deal of cleaning can be accomplished in five days..

Second, *Making a Murderer* portrayed Avery as someone who did not go out of his way to clean or declutter. It implied that he was not capable of cleaning up thoroughly enough to hide every ounce of DNA from a crime scene. I was surprised to read that there were contradictions to that assumption. Jodi Stachowski told police that she and Avery were both "clean freaks." And on February 23, 2016, a retired Calumet County officer told Fox 6 News in Milwaukee that she was inside Avery's home early in the investigation and it was extremely clean. She was surprised when she heard Dean Strang tell a news reporter, "Steven Avery can be accused of being a lot of things, but a really good housekeeper doesn't make the list."

"Just the bleach containers on his kitchen cupboard and how immaculate his house was, he cleaned that house. I believe he spent all of his time cleaning that house and trying to get rid of the remains, and that's why he didn't have time to crush the car. It's just my opinion," the Calumet County officer said.

"All I can remember is his house was so clean. And when his attorney, this kind of struck me, a couple weeks ago, his attorney and Ken Kratz [the prosecutor] were on one of the news shows and I can't quote him, but his attorney said, 'One thing I can say about Steven Avery is that he's not a very good housekeeper,' and my jaw dropped when he said that, because when I was in there, it was so clean. It was so clean. Not just uncluttered, but clean, clean," the deputy said.

Given he had five days between the murder and the discovery of the RAV4, and based upon the Calumet County deputy's observations that the trailer home was extremely clean, the lack of physical evidence like blood or hair is not as unbelievable as was implied.

More convincing evidence comes from the blog entry of a reporter who interviewed Steven's father, Allan, during the time of the trial:

> Then, Allan Avery told me about how Earl and Chuck said, "They lost the best janitor they ever had." Steve was "clean." Allan said that was all Steve did in prison, was clean. He said he could sweep up a floor in 15 minutes flat. He said that Steve's trailer was clean and that he didn't like a dirty house.

Another item of interest on this point is that Avery moved the furniture in his bedroom after Halbach was killed. I located this information in the court transcripts for Brendan Dassey's trial. Jodi Stachowski was shown a depiction of how the bedroom was found by police on their first entry and asked if that's the way the furniture was positioned before she went to jail in August 2005:

> Q.: Now, before you went into jail, looking at Exhibit
>   No. 73, was the room set up or configured that way?
> A.: No, it wasn't.

Jodi was then asked to explain how the bedroom was different:

> Q.: Could you tell the jurors, please, how it was differ-
>   ent? What . . . First of all, where was the bed when—
>   when you went into jail? How was it situated?
> A.: In the corner underneath the two windows. When
>   you first walk in the door, you'd walk straight into
>   the bed.
> Q.: Which, uh, side, or which wall was the headboard on?
> A.: The headboard was on the farthest wall, the small
>   window.

Jodi's description of where the bed was situated matched a sketch (Exhibit 208) that Brendan Dassey drew on March 1, 2006, and what he told police per Detective Mark Wiegert's testimony in Dassey's trial:

> Q.: Okay. What is 208?
> A.: Two-oh-eight is Brendan's drawing.
> Q.: Okay.
> A.: And that's how he claims the bedroom was on
>   October 31, right?
> Q.: Yes.

Without any further explanation, the defense claim that there should have been physical evidence of Halbach's gruesome murder in the trailer home is quite convincing. Add the selective edit-ing of *Making a Murderer*, and it's easy to see why so many viewers were convinced that the murder did not occur there. But if you spend the time to investigate why the police may not have found physical evidence other than the key in the trailer home, you come away with an entirely different picture—especially if you keep all the rest of the evidence in mind.

Stepping back to consider the evidence-planting claim in its entirety, as opposed to the lack of evidence found in the trailer home, led me to a similar conclusion. The police were not accused in this case of planting a single item like a gun or a knife at the crime scene, as is typical in such cases. They were accused of planting hundreds of partial bones, bullets, a vehicle, blood, a key, electronics and DNA material on a hood latch. Such a feat would require the involvement of more than a few revenge-minded officers.

It isn't just the evidence planters who would have to be involved. There isn't a police officer or a prosecutor in the country who will tell you that a dozen, or even a few bad cops could hide their misdeeds from at least some of the other participants in a criminal investigation. Prosecutors, especially, by the time the case goes to trial are acutely aware of every detail of the investigation, including how the pieces fit together and the timing and manner of their discovery. Not only that, the code of silence would have to continue for more than ten years and counting, for no one in law enforcement or anywhere else has come forward to report the misdeeds of their colleagues.

So who would likely have been "in on it, too," as my former Facebook friend accused me of being, so many months ago? Police from four jurisdictions, including the state police under the governance of the Wisconsin Department of Justice, the Wisconsin Crime Lab, also under DOJ's governance, and three prosecutors, one of them from DOJ and none of them from Manitowoc County.

If that weren't enough, the conspiracy would have to be hatched soon after Colborn fortuitously came upon Halbach's SUV on November 3, 2005, and lasted all the way until March 1,

202

2006, the day police allegedly planted the bullets from Avery's gun in his garage. As the defense and *Making a Murderer* would have us believe, this was the opportunity police had been patiently waiting for: a multi-month, multi-agency, multi-disciplinary, multi-jurisdiction conspiracy and a master plan to get Steven Avery once and for all!

CHAPTER 17

Colborn and Lenk

Whatever one thinks of *Making a Murderer*, there is no question that it has caused a great deal of suffering to a number of people, harmed some on a minor level, but others on a grander scale.

Take Ryan Hillegas, Teresa Halbach's ex-boyfriend for example. After *Making a Murderer* aired, Ryan was the number one alternate suspect, at least in the eyes of one viewer, who believed so strongly that Hillegas was the killer that he got on a plane and flew across the country to meet with the Avery family. He showed up and knocked on their door on Christmas Day. He sat down with them, telling them he agreed that Steven and Brendan were innocent, and that Hillegas was the killer. Even the Averys tired of his theory, and they called the police to come to the salvage yard and escort him off the property.

Bobby Dassey, Steven's nephew and Brendan's brother, and his future stepfather, Scott Tadych, who later married Steven's sister, Barb, didn't escape public scrutiny either. At around three-ten on the afternoon of Halbach's death, Dassey and Tadych passed each other on the road, each on their way to hunt for a few hours before it got dark but in the opposite direction. But neither of them could give police an account of their whereabouts other than that provided by the other. They had opportunity and no alibi, except for each other, and that was enough reason for vigilante viewers of *Making a Murderer* all over the land to accuse them of murder. Neither Dassey nor Tadych had anything to do with Halbach's murder, but by carefully editing court testimony, the makers of *Making a Murderer* had made them into murderers.

Jodi Stachowski, Avery's ex-fiancée who stood by him in *Making a Murderer,* was, according to Avery in a letter he wrote to a Milwaukee television station, a backstabbing alcoholic after she dared to set the record straight in an interview with Nancy Grace. She told Grace what life was like with Steven Avery, how he choked her for not telling him she went out and where on one particular evening, how she tried to poison herself just to get away from him.

But it was too late. Netflix watchers had already formed their opinion that Avery was innocent, and the internet was abuzz with insults that any money Jodi made from the interview probably just went to booze. Perhaps her reputation could be restored if readers took the time to review the police reports, which are available online. What they will find is that Jodi gave similar statements about being abused by Avery both before and after the murder, long before *Making a Murderer* aired. Much of what she said to Nancy Grace is substantiated by those reports.

Steven's niece—Candy Avery's daughter and the adopted daughter of Earl—was only seventeen when she was victimized by Steven Avery. Had anyone read her statement before *Making a Murderer,* he or she would have seen that she was a young girl, who was taken advantage of by her deviant uncle. When Avery didn't get his way, he threatened to kill himself and harm her family.

Not surprisingly, the incident did not make the cut in *Making a Murderer,* and the victim is left knowing that millions of Netflix viewers consider the monster who assaulted her to be a harmless man down on his luck because of a justice system out to get him. One viewer from the United Kingdom saw fit to mention online that having sex with a minor of Avery's niece's age is not considered a crime in European nations.

The "Truthers" are visitors on the Reddit website who believe Avery is innocent. The "Guilters" believe the opposite. And then there's another group who have not yet come up with a suitable name. Most of them believe that Avery is guilty or lean toward his guilt, but they feel strongly that he did not receive a fair trial. Without knowing what part of the trial they specifically feel was unjust, it's hard to comment on their concerns, but presumably, they are mostly upset by Colborn and Lenk and what they consider irrefutable proof that the two of them planted evidence. And again, who wouldn't if all you know about these two officers and about the Avery case was what you learned from *Making a Murderer*?

I believe I was successful in my effort to not allow my impression of Colborn and Lenk to color my thinking along this journey as we near its end. But having satisfied myself, and perhaps some of you as well, that they did not plant evidence, it is appropriate to share a bit of their character as I have come to know it over the years. Certainly there were others—Detective Dave Remiker, Detective Mark Wiegert, and Special Agent Thomas Fassbender come to mind—but Colborn and Lenk bore the brunt of the accusations from both the defense and the documentary, so it seems fitting to set the record straight.

Neither of these men will be destroyed by *Making a Murderer*. Their strength of character will not allow it. I have witnessed how their lives were upended by the series, and I thought they deserved more than just my giving readers my opinion of them. I wanted to back it up with facts.

I reviewed county records—the personnel files of Andy Colborn and Jim Lenk. In truth, I was not looking to redeem them.

Rather, I was putting them under a microscope. I was not only searching for supporting documentation of the flattering adjectives I frequently used to describe them, but I was also looking for any bit of corruption, or unsavory act, committed by them.

It was unlikely I would find anything. If they had blackmarks on their records they would have been found by Strang and Buting and used to Avery's advantage in court.

As I sifted through their files, I saw a trend. The two qualities that stood out most were professionalism and integrity. I wasn't surprised. I've known both Colborn and Lenk for decades and their personnel files only confirmed my impression.

I've shared examples throughout the book to show that they aren't the villains they were made out to be. They were cast in that role without an audition because someone had to play that part. In the interest of full disclosure, I did find one mark on Colborn's record. He caused some minor damage to his squad car on one occasion. Aside from that, I really couldn't find any other negative information. Allow me to introduce you to the real Andrew Colborn.

After graduating from high school, Andy Colborn served for twelve years in the United States Air Force. When he was honorably discharged in 1988, his final rank was that of staff sergeant E5. He won awards and medals for meritorious service, and his dedication, along with relentless and unselfish devotion, are cited repeated by his superiors.

"Exceptional performance and leadership" and "outstanding daily performance and contributions" led to his status as a noncommissioned officer in March 1982.

In February 1992, Colborn was hired as a corrections officer at the Manitowoc County Jail. This was the time frame when he took a phone call and transferred it to another party in the Detective Unit to investigate. Although he had no authority to do anything other than transfer the call, he was accused of hiding evidence that would have exonerated Steven Avery a decade earlier than he was.

Colborn held that position until March 23, 1996, when he was hired on as a sworn law enforcement officer with the county sheriff's department. Over the years he received awards and recognition, promotions, and took on many tasks and roles: evidence technician and photographer, grants management and field-training program leader are just a few. In 2013, he received the Officer of the Year Award for his work with domestic violence victims and was nominated three other times.

> *Lieutenant Colborn quickly earns and maintains the highest level of trust by being sincere and honest with others. His integrity and standards of business ethics are unquestionably high. He is especially respectful and shows a great deal of consideration in dealing with people. I have observed Lieutenant Colborn communicate and develop information from very hesitant and unwilling victims in several sexual assault cases. Lieutenant Colborn's demeanor and attitude makes for a comfortable presence during these contacts. He is a strong supporter of organizational values and actively upholds them through all aspects of his work. He can always be trusted to honor his commitments.*

Jim Lenk's records show the same glowing reports of professionalism and integrity, not one involving discipline. Lenk is retired now, with his wife to Arizona, where it's warm. The last few years he's been battling a medical condition. His wife told me she thinks *Making a Murderer* has been bad for his heart.

For months now, I've seen my share of Andy Colborn and Jim Lenk memes. Their key-finding skills have been the brunt of Internet jokes.

A friend of mine spoke to Colborn about *Making a Murderer*

and how he felt about it. He responded that he hadn't watched it, but had heard about it. When asked what he'd say to defend himself, his response spoke volumes about who he is.

"Thank you, that's very kind of you, but this isn't about me. It's about Teresa."

CHAPTER 18

THE CONFESSION

The most damning piece of evidence against Steven Avery, at first glance, appears to be the confession of his nephew and accomplice, Brendan Dassey. Ken Kratz shocked all who watched his March 2, 2006, press conference when he described Dassey's statement in excruciating detail:

> "I know that there are some news outlets that are carrying this live, and perhaps there may be some children that are watching this. I'm gonna ask that if you're under the age of fifteen, that you discontinue watching this press conference. We have now determined what occurred sometime between three forty-five p.m. and ten or eleven p.m., on the thirty-first of October. Sixteen-year-old Brendan Dassey, who lives next door to Steven Avery in a trailer, returned home on the bus from school about three forty-five p.m. He retrieved the mail and noticed one of the letters was for his uncle, Steven Avery.
>
> "As Brendan approaches the trailer, as he actually gets several hundred feet away from the trailer, a long, long way from the trailer, Brendan already starts to hear the screams. As Brendan approaches the trailer, he hears louder screams for help, recognizes it to be of a female individual, and he knocks on Steven Avery's trailer door. Brendan says that he knocks at

least three times and has to wait until the person he knows as
his uncle, who is partially dressed, who is full of sweat . . .
opens the door and greets his sixteen-year-old nephew.

"Brendan accompanies his sweaty forty-three-year-old uncle
down the hallway to Steven Avery's bedroom. And there they
find Teresa Halbach completely naked and shackled to the bed.
Teresa Halbach is begging Brendan for her life. The evidence
that we've uncovered . . . establishes that Steven Avery at this
point invites his sixteen-year-old nephew to sexually assault
this woman that he has had bound to the bed. During the rape
Teresa's begging for help, begging sixteen-year-old Brendan to
stop, that "you can stop this." Sixteen-year-old Brendan, under
the instruction of Steven Avery . . . cuts Teresa Halbach's
throat . . . but she still doesn't die."

For all who heard this press conference, and believed that it
was true, Dassey's confession was the last straw for Steven Avery.
Here was a potential alibi witness, a person whom Avery had told
Jodi he was with on the night of Halbach's murder. Yet, instead of
coming forward and saying that he was with his uncle that night,
and there was no way that his uncle could have murdered Halbach, Dassey came forward with details about how he and Avery
brutally sexually assaulted and murdered Halbach. It left all, including myself at the time, shocked and convinced that Steven
Avery was guilty. But like all things with the Avery case, Dassey's
confession is not necessarily what it appears to be on first sight.

Confessions are odd things. Prosecutors love them, and defense attorneys hate them. In the end they are nothing more
than statements, but juries often give a confession more weight
than hard scientific evidence. They readily dismiss the drunk at
the bar who brags about bringing his car up to 150 miles per
hour, but they have a difficult time grasping the possibility that a
defendant who confessed might not have been telling the truth.
To be fair, false confessions are counterintuitive. Why would someone confess to a crime, especially a murder, and face going to

prison for the rest of his life if he did not in fact commit the crime. On the surface, it makes no sense, but the truth is that it happens more often than you think.

Dassey's confession was never admitted into Avery's trial because a deal had not been cut, hence the prosecution could not call Dassey to the stand, and a police rendition of the confession would be inadmissible hearsay. As such, the jurors, most of whom knew all about the confession were instructed to put it out of their minds. Leaving aside whether that's even possible and how hard the jurors may have tried the confession is still worthy of our attention because if true, it is the most solid evidence that Avery is guilty. It's also worth exploring because the methods of interrogation that elicited it understandably upset a great many viewers of *Making a Murderer*. As with many other things, my own opinion about Dassey's confession drastically changed after I watched *Making a Murderer*.

As the trial unfolded in 2007, everything I knew about Dassey's confession came from Kratz's press conference. From his secondhand account, there was little reason to doubt its truthfulness, or for that matter, its voluntariness. *Making a Murderer*, in the eyes of many of the viewers, showed otherwise.

The documentary showed a quiet, troubled, sixteen-year-old boy. He sat in a bleak room on a small sofa with two middle-aged investigators appearing sympathetic and concerned, but not very convincingly. The two officers were displaying more than a fair amount of anxiousness, in their all-too-eager desire to get the goods on Steven Avery. Dassey leaned back into the sofa, almost never looking up, occasionally gnawing on a fingernail or two. He took his time responding to questions, and when he did respond, it was often nearly inaudible. It took all of thirty seconds for a theme to emerge from the investigators' questions:

"We know there were some things you left out. And we know there were some things that maybe weren't totally correct that you told us. We've been investigating this a long time now. We

pretty much know everything. If, in fact, you did some things,
and we believe some things may have happened that you didn't
want to tell us about, it's okay. . . . As long as you are honest
with us, it is okay."

Dassey's most common response to a question was silence. He never lifted his head.

Things took a turn for the worse when the investigators used leading questions in order to get some very important information that Dassey appeared not to know:

Wiegert: Come on. Something with the head.
   Brendan? What else did you guys do? Come on.
   What he made you do, Brendan. We know he made
   you do something else. What was it? What was it? We
   have the evidence, Brendan. We just need you to . . .
   to be honest with us.
Brendan: That he cut off her hair.
Wiegert: He cut off her hair? Okay. What else? What
   else was done to her head?
Brendan: That he punched her.
Wiegert: What else? It's okay. What did he make you do?
Brendan: Cut her.
Wiegert: Cut her where?
Brendan: On her throat.
Wiegert: You cut her throat? What else happens to
   her? In her head? Extremely, extremely important
   you tell us this . . . for us to believe you. Come on,
   Brendan. What else? We know. We just need you to
   tell us.
Brendan: That's all I can remember.
Wiegert: All right, I'm just gonna come out and ask
   you. Who shot her in the head?
Brendan: He did.

* * *

213

I was stunned. If I had known the circumstances of Brendan Dassey's confession in 2006, when Kratz held his press conference, I would not have been so easily convinced of his and Avery's guilt. In court, when questioning one's own witness, an attorney is prohibited from using leading questions, and for good reason. Leading questions suggest an answer. The concern is—and it is a legitimate concern—that an attorney will shape the witness's testimony if he is allowed to ask leading questions. The attorney might as well just take the stand and tell the jury what he wants it to hear. The same problems are at work when police use leading questions to interrogate a suspect; the suspect's responses are not only used by the police to shape their investigation, they are admissible in court.

After watching *Making a Murderer,* I was convinced that Dassey's confession at a minimum, wasn't reliable—which is a slightly different issue than whether it is true. So, in keeping with my overall plan to journey through the Avery case, I dug deeper into its details.

When it comes to confessions, there are two questions. One, is it true? And second, is it reliable? The voluntariness of a confession, which is what the law is traditionally most concerned with, has more to do with whether a confession is reliable than it does with whether it is true. If the defendant was coerced into making the confession, the law prohibits its use at trial because its reliability is in question, and people should not be imprisoned based upon unreliable evidence. The confession may very well be true, but it also might not be.

When determining whether a confession is admissible, the courts only look at whether the confession was voluntary. By considering the circumstances surrounding the confession, the judge is supposed to determine whether a confession was voluntarily made. Was there police misconduct? Did the police physically coerce the defendant? Did they place undue mental or emotional pressure upon the defendant? For how long was the defendant interrogated? What is the defendant like? How old is he? Is he intelligent? Was he fed? What is his education level? Is he easily manipulated? All of this should enter into the judge's analysis. If the defendant voluntarily made the confession, it is admissible; if not, it is not admissible. The courts are not supposed to let the truthfulness of a confession influence their analysis of whether it is voluntary. They are two separate questions. An involuntary confession is inadmissible even if it can be shown to be true.

Before Brendan Dassey's trial, Judge Jerome Fox ruled that his confession was voluntary and allowed the state to admit it at trial. Dassey's attorneys raised the issue on appeal, but the Court of Appeals affirmed the lower court's ruling. Dassey has now raised this issue in federal court, and the parties anxiously await its decision.

The task of deciding whether a defendant voluntarily made a confession is not an easy one. It requires one to view police conduct from the perspective of the defendant. Only the circumstances surrounding the confession and the defendant's personal characteristics can be considered. Readers need to decide for themselves whether Dassey's confession was voluntary, but there are some things to consider that were not presented in the documentary.

After watching *Making a Murderer*, I viewed the entire four-hours March 1, 2006, video taped interrogation of Brendan Dassey. It was painful to say the least. Here are my observations, which I'll state in an overview first and then in detail:

Brendan was not physically hurt. He was not physically threatened. In fact, his interrogators never raised their voices. In a nutshell, Investigator Mark Wiegert and Special Agent Thomas Fassbender, sometimes unfairly dubbed "Liegert" and "Factbender" by critics, did not force, threaten, hurt, or yell at Brendan. They offered him breaks, snacks, and drinks to keep him comfortable.

None of this means that Dassey voluntarily confessed. The days of false confessions caused by overt police intimidation and brutality are thankfully, for the most part, in the past. Today most police departments use a method of questioning called the Reid Technique. It is very effective in obtaining confessions, which is great if the police have the correct suspect. However, it is also prone more than some would like to admit to obtain false confessions. This is especially true in the case of young, poorly educated, and easily manipulated individuals, who are already at a higher risk of falsely confessing, like Brendan Dassey.

The Reid Technique has two stages. First the interrogator asks simple questions to lower the suspect's guard and get a feel for when he is telling the truth. Then the interrogator begins asking substantive questions about the crime. Interrogators are trained in the "skill" of detecting when suspects are lying or being evasive. Once the interrogator determines the suspect is lying and is involved in the crime in some way, he moves on to the next stage, which is to elicit a confession.

The biggest problem with the Reid Technique is that an interrogator cannot accurately determine whether a suspect is lying. In fact, studies have shown that officers trained to detect lies are slightly worse at doing so than others, most likely because they deal with criminals on a regular basis and are more likely to assume deception. That bias poses a problem because the officer may proceed with the interrogation with an unfounded confidence in the suspect's guilt, aiming for a confession instead of the truth.

The second stage of the Reid Technique is eliciting the actual confession. The interrogator will control the discussion and go off on long monologues. He may act as if he knows everything and is simply trying to help the suspect get off as easily as possible "if he only tells the truth." Sometimes the interrogator will try to get the suspect to admit guilt in some mitigated manner. He will try to provide the suspect with an "out," even though it will really be an admission of guilt. If done effectively and for a long-enough period of time, such techniques can be emotionally taxing upon a suspect to the point that he falsely confesses. It has happened before, and many believe that it happened to Brendan Dassey.

Independent of whether Dassey's confession was voluntary is the question of whether the details he gave in his statement were true. From some of the segments of his interrogation that were played in *Making a Murderer*, it seemed as if he did not know details about the murder that he should have known if he and his uncle Steven had killed Halbach in the manner he confessed. Why couldn't he remember that Avery shot her in the head? Why did the police have to suggest this fact in their questioning before he could answer it?

I went back and looked at the reason that police were speaking to Dassey in the first place. After all, *Making a Murderer* insinuated that police "targeted" him in order to build a more solid case against Avery. But this seems unlikely because there was plenty of evidence against Steven Avery by the time Brendan Dassey confessed. Avery was already in jail on high cash bail, having been arrested four months earlier.

I learned that Dassey's confession on March 1, 2006, shown in *Making a Murderer*, was not only an extremely small clip of the entire interview, but it also contained spliced footage. Furthermore, it was not the first time they had spoken to Brendan Dassey. It was the fourth.

The first time police interviewed him was at the same time as the rest of the family in November 2005. Law enforcement was unaware of much of the evidence leading to Steven Avery at the time. They were just trying to ascertain what occurred by speaking to potential witnesses, and hoping to get a few leads to look into. When Dassey was interviewed, he told them minor details of that day, none of which implicated himself. Police didn't consider his involvement again, until months later, but not without good reason.

The subsequent two interviews were on February 27, when Dassey admitted that he was invited over to a bonfire by his uncle Steven and saw a few of Halbach's body parts, notably her toes. Since these were the interviews that ultimately led to Dassey's conviction, I wanted to know why the officers called him out of class at Mishicot High School that day.

After hours of reading statements from the 1,116-page Calumet County Investigation report, I eventually found what I was looking for. On February 20, 2006, Investigator Wiegert and Investigator Baldwin met with Kayla Avery and her mother, Candy, at her home. The reason for the meeting, as noted in the activity report, was to speak to Kayla about allegations made by Jodi Stachowski that Avery had beat Jodi up. The entire interview, up until the last paragraph, consisted of Kayla giving examples of abuse she witnessed that substantiated what Jodi told police, in addition to a few comments concerning Kayla's own dealings with Steven: *Kayla did state that on several occasions, STEVEN would grab her arms and pull them up over her head and pin her to the wall and then he would let her go.* Kayla also told police that she would become very scared and would tell him to stop.

The next paragraph told me everything I needed to know. It was buried on page 435 in a paragraph unlikely to elicit consideration beyond that of it being a simple side note someone made when referring to an unrelated portion of the dialogue. An "oh, by the way" remark, but for me, it was exactly what I was looking for. The paragraph read:

> *As I was talking with Kayla, she stated to me that her cousin, Brendan who had been burning things with Steven on Halloween night had been acting up lately. I asked Kayla what she meant by him acting up to which she stated Brendan would just sit there and stare into space and start crying. Kayla also told me that Brendan had lost approximately 40 lbs. since this all started a couple of months ago. Kayla and her mother CANDY, both told me at that time they both remember seeing the bonfire by STEVEN's house on Halloween night. Kayla and CANDY had stopped by Kayla's grandmother's, Delores, on Halloween night and they remember seeing the fire down by Steven's trailer.*

*That was the end of my conversation with Kayla, Candy and
Earl Avery.*
Investigation continues
Inv. Mark Wiegert
Calumet Co. Sheriff's Dept.

Police spoke to Brendan Dassey a week later. During that interview it quickly became clear to the officers that he knew something about Teresa Halbach's murder. They knew that he was helping his uncle burn garbage in a fire that night, and they thought that he might have seen something in the fire. As in the later interrogation shown in *Making a Murderer*, Dassey did not readily respond to questions with much detail. As investigators expressed their concern and willingness to listen, it resulted in some leading questions. Eventually Dassey admitted that he saw a body in the fire, first the toes and then the rest. Dassey said that his uncle told him to keep his mouth shut and threatened him when he noticed he had seen the body. Dassey said Avery told him he stabbed her in her RAV4 and hid the vehicle under some branches planning to crush it later.

Dassey had offered this information after a great deal of probing and leading questions. At one point, when asked if Steven Avery was injured, Dassey said he cut his finger on glass near the garage. Later, when the interrogators asked leading questions, Dassey said that Avery cut his finger with a knife when he was stabbing Halbach.

It became very apparent, just from this statement, that the investigators should not have been asking Dassey so many leading questions if they wanted to rely upon what he told them. For at least some of his responses, he simply told them what they wanted to hear. It was obvious that even the investigators picked up on this during the interview.

Dassey was allowed to go to his final class of the day after speaking with Wiegert and Fassbender for just under two hours. He wrote two statements and signed both of them. Police contacted his mother, Barb, who met them at the high school, and was updated on the situation. Once he was done with class, Barb and her son agreed to go to the Two Rivers police station with the officers to participate in a second videotaped interview.

At three twenty-one p.m., in an interview room at the police station, the officers began the second interview that day, of course starting off with the *Miranda* warnings. Dassey's demeanor was different during this interview. He talked more freely, responding to questions in a narrative form. He stated that he got home from school around three forty-five, ate dinner around eight, and then received a phone call from his uncle Steven asking him to come over to the bonfire. Dassey said that he saw Teresa Halbach's car when he got home from school, and that later he saw toes, hands, a person's belly, and forehead in the fire, all buried underneath some tires and branches. When his uncle Steven noticed that he had seen the body, he threatened to stab his nephew if he told anyone. This time Dassey said that Avery said he stabbed Halbach in the stomach and that he received a scratch on his finger from her fingernails when she struggled to get away from him.

By this time the repetitive leading questions and internal contradictions in Dassey's statements were obvious. In the third interrogation, on March 1, it didn't get much better. During this questioning he provided a different story—this time where he sexually assaulted Halbach and played an active role in her murder. In addition to the details Kratz provided in his press conference the next day, Dassey stated that Avery stabbed Halbach and directed his nephew to slit her throat. Avery then shot her in the garage. They backed her RAV4 into the garage and she was placed in the back of the SUV. Avery originally thought of putting her body in the pond, but decided it was too shallow.

As hard as it is to believe Dassey's confession, after the many times he changed it, often at the prompting of the investigators' leading questions, clearly some of these new details line up with the physical evidence. The bullet with Halbach's DNA was found in the garage after a more thorough search. Before this time the police did not know where she was shot, but knew that she was shot, due to the bullet hole in her skull.

Dassey also told police that Halbach was shot twice in the head, and this information was provided before the police knew it. They were first informed that Halbach was shot in the head in a phone call that Investigator Wiegert received from Kenneth Olson at the Wisconsin State Crime Lab regarding laboratory findings on February 28. Olson told him that one piece of charred skull had a suspected entrance defect and that there were traces of lead. That is what ultimately prompted the infamous "what happened to her head" question from one of the investigators. Dassey answered the question, "Who shot her in the head?" with the simple statement, "He did."

FASSBENDER (F.): Then why didn't you tell us that?

DASSEY (D.): 'Cause I couldn't think of it.

F.: Now you remember it? (Dassey nods "yes.") Tell us about that then.

D.: That he shot her with his .22.

WIEGERT (W.): You were there, though?

D.: Yeah.

W.: Where did this happen?

D.: Outside.

W.: Outside? Before? Tell me when it happened?

D.: When we brung her outside to throw her in the fire.

W.: Okay. So let's back up, okay? So I wanna go through this, okay? So he stabs her (Dassey nods "yes") and chokes her?

D.: Mm-huh.

W.: And then you do what?

D.: I help tie her up.

W.: Okay. And then what?

D.: Then we . . .

W.: You cut her throat somewhere in there?

D.: Yeah.

W.: Yes?

D.: Yeah.

W.: And then what?

D.: Cut off, er, some of her hair.

W.: Okay.

D.: Then we brung her outside and shot her.

W.: Was she alive when you shot her?

D.: I don't know.

W.: Where did you shoot her?

D.: In the head.

W.: Who shot her?

D.: He did.

F.: How many times?

D.: Twice.

Making a Murderer spliced the video so that viewers didn't see the rest of Brendan Dassey's responses showing he knew what kind of gun Avery used, and how many times he shot Halbach in the head, which was not public knowledge and even the police didn't know that then. Investigators did not find out until later that there were two confirmed entrance defects on two different pieces of Halbach's skull. How could they have fed him details that even they didn't know at the time? Discounting for the moment the theory that police planted the bullets in the garage, this detail corroborates part of Dassey's confession. These additional details provided by Dassey were not the result of leading questions.

Dassey's statement that they placed Halbach's body in the RAV4 also explains why splotches of her blood were found in the back of the vehicle, which was consistent with the scenario of her body being placed in the back of the vehicle with blood in her hair. Also, Avery's DNA on the hood latch was not found until Dassey told the police that Avery had opened the hood, although Dassey could not say why.

It seems, then, that at least some portions of Dassey's confession are true.

I started my investigation into Dassey's confession in the hope of forming a solid opinion of his role in the murder. But that didn't happen. In the end I was left, as many viewers were, with more questions than answers.

The events leading to Dassey's confession had a domino effect. Had police never spoken to Kayla Avery on February 20, when they were simply following up on Jodi's statements of Steven's abuse, they most likely would not have met with Dassey a week later. Had Kayla not told police that he had lost weight and was crying a lot, police would not have asked Dassey questions that ultimately led to his self-incrimination in saying he had witnessed Halbach's body in a fire. Had Kenneth Olson not contacted Wiegert the next day, to inform him that one of Halbach's charred cranial fragments had a suspected entrance defect with trace evidence of lead, the March 1 "What happened to her head?" interrogation, which shifted Dassey's role from a witness to a potential accomplice, may not have occurred. Additionally, it's more than likely that they would have never followed up with Kayla Avery after February 20, had her school counselor not contacted police after hearing of Brendan Dassey's arrest.

Kayla Avery was just fourteen when Dassey told her at a birthday party in December 2005, less than two months after Halbach's death, that he had seen Teresa Halbach "pinned up" in Steven Avery's trailer. She told police that her cousin "had gotten very shook up" after telling her that he had seen this and then observing the bones in the fire.

Kayla was concerned enough about this information that she

approached her school counselor in January 2006. A teacher's aid, who was at that meeting with Kayla later testified in Brendan Dassey's trial:

Q.: Tell us what happened?

A.: Kayla came into the office, and she was asked by Ms. Baumgartner if she minded that I was there, and Kayla said, no. And she said she was there because she was feeling scared.

Q.: All right. Let me stop you there, first, and ask who else, if anyone, was present for this conversation?

A.: No one else.

Q.: All right. So there's just the three of you?

A.: Correct.

Q.: All right. And did Kayla reveal to the two of you why she was feeling scared and why she wanted to talk?

A.: Yes.

Q.: And what did she tell you?

A.: She told us that she was scared because her uncle, Steven Avery, had asked one of her cousins to help move a body.

Q.: All right. What else, if anything, did she tell you about that?

A.: She also said she was scared about going to the shop, and she, specifically, asked if blood can come up through concrete.

Q.: All right. Now, was—did she identify which of her cousins may have been asked by her uncle, Steven Avery, to move this body?

A.: No.

Q.: All right. Describe for us, if you will, Kayla's demeanor, her affect, during these revelations?

A.: She—she was scared.

Q.: All right. Did she seem at all confused?

A.: No.

Q.: Was this the first time you ever had contact with Kayla?

A.: Yes.

Q.: All right. Your best estimate, approximately how long did this conversation take?

A.: My best guess would be 15 or 20 minutes.

Q.: All right. How was Kayla's demeanor at the conclusion of this discussion?

A.: I think she still felt scared, but maybe a little bit more relieved.

Q.: All right. Did she, at the end of the conversation, seem confused by anything that she was telling you?

A.: No.

After Brendan Dassey's confession on March 1 and his subsequent arrest, Kayla's counselor came forward to speak with the police. Investigators returned to interview Kayla on March 7 based on the counselor's statement.

Investigator Wiegert and Special Agent Fassbender met with Kayla Avery and her mother, Candy, at three thirty-six p.m. at their residence in Whitelaw, Wisconsin. Kayla provided details concerning her own experiences with Avery and described several attempts he made to grab her, pull her toward him, and kiss her, telling her that she had "big boobies."

When investigators spoke to Kayla about specific statements she made to her counselor, she initially stated that she could not remember and broke down, crying. She later admitted that Brendan told her he saw Halbach "pinned up" when he dropped off the mail and later saw body parts in the fire. According to Kayla, her cousin told her that Steven had threatened that if he told anyone, the same thing would happen to him.

Kayla also stated that her cousin told her that he left Steven's home after seeing Halbach pinned up, but he didn't want to say any more, and Kayla didn't want to know anyhow. The last thing he told her, Kayla said, was that he had heard Teresa Halbach screaming when he walked out of the trailer home. She stated that her cousin had gotten very shaken up while telling her all of this.

Kayla also admitted that she told the counselors at school about this and also provided investigators with a written statement as to what Brendan told her. A transcript of Exhibit 163, with editing for clarity and ease of reading, from Brendan Dassey's trial, reads as follows:

> STATEMENT OF Kayla Avery
> Date: 3/7/06
> Brendan told me that he saw the body parts of Teresa in the fire pit behind Steven's grown. (Editor's note: garage?) Brendan got the mail and brought it to him and he sat in a chair in Steven's bedroom. Then Brendan walked out of the house and he heard skremins (Editor's note: screams?) in Steven's house. When I tried to talk to him at Ashle's B-day party and I asked him to talk to me and he did not want to talk to me about it. I think that Steven should stay in Jail or Prison. I do NOT like him at all I really think that Brendan did something and he got forst. (Editor's note: forced?)
> I HATE STEVEN A LOT
> P.S. Teresa was pind [sic] up
> P.P.S I hope he rots in hell. . . .
> Love
> Kayla Avery

Kayla later testified in Dassey's trial and claimed that none of the statements she made to police were true. She said she made up the story about her cousin seeing body parts. When asked why, she lied to the police, she stated that she was confused and didn't know what to do. When asked what she was confused about, she responded, "I don't know. Everything."

* * *

As a result, Kayla's role in the Dassey trial has been controvercial. It's easy to believe that she was telling the truth when she spoke to her counselors. Why would she go to them unless she was troubled? Others have suggested that her intent was to get Steven in trouble, but then realized she implicated Brendan in the process. Or that it was simply a bid for attention.

Insinuations and assumptions bounced around in one heated online discussion after another. Here is a typical example posted on a Facebook group:

> *Maybe Kayla got in trouble at school and made up the story about Brendan to take the focus off of her. I raised my husband's daughter, and teenage girls lie a LOT. Especially when they get busted doing something wrong. So maybe she lies, and then her parents tell her she is GOING to retract her statement. So she does. Just a theory, could be wrong.*

But a recorded telephone conversation between Dassey and his mother while he was in jail is cited by others in support of the truthfulness of his confession. During this conversation, when there were no police officers present to pressure him or ask leading questions, he told his mother that he and his uncle committed the murder. He explained that the investigators told him that he might only get twenty years if he told the truth. He also told his mother that he did not know how he would face his uncle in court.

The phone call recording offered a stark contrast to the hours of interrogation footage. Brendan Dassey clearly seemed to be telling the truth.

CHAPTER 19

PARTING THOUGHTS

I first became obsessed with the Avery case—and, unfortunately for my wife and our children, "obsession" is the right word—in 2003, twelve years before *Making a Murderer* aired. For more than a decade I have believed this stranger-than-fiction true-crime drama has the potential to engage a broad audience with its implications for today's pressing issues concerning the criminal justice system and its need for reform. It's not every day, after all, that a folk hero celebrity exoneree, who is slated to become the namesake of a state's most meaningful criminal justice reform bill in years, commits an exceptionally brutal murder and then tries to get away with it by accusing the police of setting him up again.

When *Making a Murderer* was released a week before Christmas, 2015—exceptionally good timing for the series' success, it turned out—I was less surprised by the widespread interest the documentary generated than I was with the extent to which the Avery story had previously been ignored. Except for a few summary accounts, as well as a lengthier piece that appeared in the *New York Times*, the national media largely ignored the story even after Steven Avery was arrested for Teresa Halbach's murder. But then, a lot of interesting and tragic things happen in the Midwest that go largely ignored on the East and West Coasts.

I thought the 1985 wrongful conviction, even without the subsequent murder, warranted more attention than it received at the time. Most wrongful convictions happen by mistake or, at worst, because of overzealousness on the part of the police and prosecutors hung up on the notion of winning at all costs. Rarely are they the result of the degree of police and prosecutor misconduct that led to Avery's wrongful conviction when—despite the contrary opinion of Wisconsin's attorney general at the time—the former sheriff and district attorney appear to have sent an innocent man to prison and knowingly allowed the real assailant to go free.

Wrongful convictions more commonly stem from mistaken eyewitness identifications, unreliable forensic evidence, false confessions, the use of incriminating statements provided by jailhouse snitches with something to gain, a Brady violation made by the prosecution for suppressing evidence favorable to the defendant, and other instances of overzealousness on the part of police and prosecutors—all of these are serious problems in their own right. The shortcomings of the police and prosecutors in these cases fall far short of the corruption at work in those exceedingly rare cases when police and prosecutors knowingly convict an innocent man, a category to which most lawyers and non-lawyers alike who have carefully examined the Avery wrongful conviction case believe it belongs.

The creators of *Making a Murderer* devoted much less attention to the 1985 wrongful conviction case than I thought was warranted, which is ironic since that case contains powerful lessons of what can go wrong when police and prosecutors lose sight of their calling to uphold the law justly. Perhaps they glossed over it because video of the 1985 wrongful conviction trial was not available and reconstructing a thirty-year-old case would be difficult at best.

I should not have been surprised that it took Hollywood to give the Steven Avery story the attention it deserved. Who wants to read a book when you can watch a riveting documentary? Released at the end of a year when a seemingly endless series of police shootings of unarmed suspects produced a growing distrust of law enforcement, and combined with the resurgence of true crime in the popular media and a rapidly expanding effort of Internet giants, such as Netflix, to produce original programming, *Making a Murderer* rode a perfect storm to the screens of tens of millions of viewers across the globe.

For months it was the most common fodder for watercooler and coffee break discussions across the land. It made it onto the front page of the *Beijing News,* and Al Jazeera devoted a piece on its website to a topic close to its heart—coercive interrogation techniques of U.S. law enforcement agencies—although it's hard to imagine a wider chasm than that which exists between county sheriff's department detectives in rural Wisconsin and the CIA.

By its skillful use of film and sound techniques and omission of facts that belied its conclusion, *Making a Murderer* has all but convicted two intelligent, honest, and well-respected police officers of planting evidence to frame Avery a second time. This is a narrative now widely accepted by legions of Netflix viewers whose only familiarity with the Avery case is the documentary itself.

Transformed into would-be jurors, who are cleverly manipulated by an all-knowing judge in the form of the documentarians, viewers are shown only one side of the evidence. The prosecution's refutation of evidence-planting claims during cross-examination and rebuttal—the "truth-seeking machinery" of jury trials, as one legal scholar put it—is minimal. Avery's criminal history is deconstructed beyond credulity. His lighting a cat afire after dousing it with gasoline when he was twenty years old is passed off as an accident while horsing around with friends. He didn't intend to cause any harm to his neighbor after he ran her off the road and held her at gunpoint. As *Making a Murderer* would have it, he did so because the woman was spreading rumors about him. Never mind that he had been using a pair of binoculars to watch her for weeks, sexually gratifying himself as she drove by. I had to admit, though, I was impressed. The skill with which the documentarians made light of Avery's criminal history rivaled that of seasoned criminal defense attorneys whom I have seen turn sinners into saints countless times at sentencing.

Nor are viewers informed of the handcuffs and leg irons found by police in Avery's trailer home after the murder. There was no evidence he used the items on the day Teresa Halbach disappeared, but they were in keeping with what appears to have been on his mind in the days leading up to her murder. Left out, too, was his sketch of a "torture chamber" and his fantasizing to fellow inmates about using it to sexually assault and murder young women when he got out, foretelling the atmosphere surrounding his real victim's final hour.

Clinging to claims of objectivity, the documentarians have pointed out that truth is elusive in the Steven Avery case, which is true enough. However, by excluding facts that don't fit their aim and manipulating others, they have distorted the truth beyond recognition and have decided for the rest of us what we are to believe. "High-brow vigilante justice" is how columnist Kathryn Schulz put it in her column about the documentary in *The New Yorker* ("Dead Certainty"). To which I respond, "Right on."

Aiming to draw attention to the shortcomings of a criminal justice system badly in need of reform, the producers set out with a laudable goal, and the fruits of their labor are already contributing mightily to the ongoing discussion concerning criminal justice reform. The unwarranted certainty that some police and prosecutors have in their interpretation of equivocal facts, along with the overzealousness of some in our ranks and our tendency toward a self-righteous belief that we are always in the right, when combined with our awesome and often unchecked authority, has too often led to the abuse of power. The system's inability or unwillingness to treat with dignity and respect those on the bottom rung of the economic and social ladder has caused unnecessary suffering for many who faced long odds of making it even before they drew the attention of the police and the courts by engaging in crime.

The documentary raises other issues, too, including the role of class bias in criminal proceedings, and the disparity in the quality of representation between those with money and those without. The cozy relationship between the media and the prosecution in high-profile murder cases is also worthy of exploration and thoughtful debate, in both legal and media circles.

The success of *Making a Murderer* has brought massive attention to these and other shortcomings of the criminal justice system, and therein lays its opportunity for redemption. But there are other issues at play in the *Making a Murderer* phenomenon that pose perhaps even a greater threat to the criminal justice system than the ones the documentarians identified.

In a world where the line between reality and entertainment is fading fast, where the impact of raw emotion routinely trumps the more reliable conclusions of reason, *Making a Murderer* is part of a troubling trend—the courting of public opinion in support of a cause by the production of a propaganda piece disguised as an objective documentary. Efforts like these have been around a long time, but their application to court cases is new.

In court issues of guilt or innocence are decided based on a full presentation of evidence in a process designed over centuries to ensure that both sides receive a fair trial. Rules developed over centuries are in place to make sure the finder of fact receives only reliable evidence. The documentarians in this case succeeded in transforming in the court of public opinion a disturbed and dangerous man, who murdered a young woman, into a sacrificial lamb at the altar of police and prosecutorial power.

Steven Avery's future will not be decided in the court of public opinion. It will be decided in a court of justice, where the decision belongs. He will get his chance to argue, through his attorneys, why he should be entitled to a new trial. The burden has shifted and he will need more than speculation that police planted evidence. The authorities got it right this time, and barring the revelation of new evidence pointing squarely to his innocence, the nation's most famous exoneree is now "rightfully" where he belongs—in a state prison for life without the possibility of parole.

These are difficult days for law enforcement in Manitowoc County. That an injustice perpetrated by a local sheriff and district attorney three decades ago persists to this very day is one of the many profound lessons of the Steven Avery story. A deplorable injustice perpetrated on Avery thirty years ago has come full circle, and now we are paying for the sins of our forefathers. Nobody who works in the justice system is perfect—far from it. But as a court instruction reminds jurors before they begin deliberations, we have been "called upon to act in the most important affairs of life," so we must try our hardest to do what's right. If we don't, an injustice can fester for years.

Readers may wonder what happened to my concern in the opening chapters of this book with respect to Wolfgang Braun and his possible involvement in Teresa Halbach's murder. In addition to all the evidence clearly pointing to Avery's guilt, there are other reasons I am satisfied Wolfgang was not involved. His wife, Sophie, resumed living with him in Oregon after he left Wisconsin and apparently no longer believes he was involved. Sophie was either exaggerating the facts or making them up out of fear, or perhaps even spite. I also confirmed that the memo I asked our victim witness specialist to draft concerning her suspicions that Wolfgang was involved was forwarded to Ken Kratz, who in turn forwarded them to Buting and Strang. They too apparently discounted Sophie's statements, as Wolfgang was not included in their list of potential alternate suspects before the start of the trial.

ACKNOWLEDGMENTS

I knew I had to write a second book about the Steven Avery case at about the midpoint of watching *Making a Murderer*. The documentary had taken the story to a new level and had raised additional issues that I wanted to explore. A two-month sabbatical from work helped get the manuscript off the ground, but completing it in a relatively short period of time while still working as a prosecutor was not an easy task. To do so, I needed the help and support of many individuals, some of whom are listed below.

A person could spend a lifetime researching the Avery and Dassey cases, and with a limited time to complete the manuscript I did not have a lifetime to give. Fortunately there were others who were willing to share their research.

Special thanks in this regard go to Mandy H, creator of the Facebook Group "Avery/Dassey Case Discussion Group," and two of her tenacious admins, Diana and Emma, for their diligence in researching all sides without bias and encouraging logical and factual debates. Your online discussions helped me understand and see details I may have otherwise missed.

Thanks to my editor, Michaela Hamilton, who kept me on track through the completion of this project. Michaela has been in the book business for a long time and knows what it takes to produce a successful book. She was firm because she had to be, but not once was she unkind.

I owe a special debt of gratitude to my agent, Washington DC attorney and author Ronald Goldfarb, who recognized early on the singular nature of the Avery story and the multitude of lessons it offers for the criminal justice system. Ron is an accomplished lawyer, author, agent, media commentator, and a whole lot more. I can't think of anyone from whom I've learned more about the writing and publishing world than Ron, during our conversations and email exchanges over the past eight years.

I also appreciate my colleagues at work, especially Bob and Jill, for covering my court appearances during my absence, and attorney Joseph Thuermer who filled in as a special prosecutor while I was away.

A special thanks to Brenda Schuler, whose webpage outline *"Wrong-Righting Writing, a comprehensive resource for events leading up to and beyond the murder of Teresa Halbach"* is far and away the most thorough and accurate compilation of all things having to do with the Avery trial. Brenda is as smart as a whip. Her fierce commitment to fairness and setting things right is inspiring. Brenda, I can't thank you enough.

Thanks also to a particularly astute Redditor who wishes to remain anonymous. You know who you are.

A warm thanks to then Green Bay, now Cincinnati television reporter Angenette Levy who covered the Avery and Dassey cases from beginning to end when she worked in Green Bay. Angenette figured prominently in *Making a Murderer*, probing the strengths and weaknesses of each side's case by questioning the attorneys at nightly press conferences during the trials. She generously shared with me her perspective on the trials.

My wife and I are blessed with four of the most wonderful children you could imagine—except of course, your own. Each of them helped in their own way and not once did they complain when I exhibited the self-centered orneriness that can overcome an author or anyone else working under the gun of a deadline.

Our son Joseph provided invaluable computer technical assistance whenever I was in a fix, and all four of them reviewed the manuscript and enjoyed giving their dad feedback, which I enjoyed even more. Tom, in his second year of law school, grasped the new issues that were injected into the Avery case by *Making a*

ACKNOWLEDGMENTS

Murderer more quickly than I did and was especially helpful on the issues of false confessions and coercive interrogation techniques.

Finally, but formost forever, I am forever grateful to my wife, Jody. She contributed mightily to this book, sharing ideas on our nightly walks and pitching in when the manuscript needed some shaping up. She is by far the most wonderful blessing of my life.